Clockmaking

18 Antique Designs
for the Woodworker

Clockmaking

18 Antique Designs for the Woodworker

John A. Nelson

STACKPOLE
BOOKS

Published by
STACKPOLE BOOKS
5067 Ritter Road
Mechanicsburg, PA 17055

Printed in the United States of America

10 9 8 7 6 5 4 3 2 1

Second edition

Originally published by Tab Books, Inc., in 1989

Library of Congress Cataloging-in-Publication Data

Nelson, John A., 1935–
    Clockmaking : 18 antique designs for the woodworker / John A.
Nelson.
        p.   cm.
    Reprint. Originally pub.: Blue Ridge Summit, PA : TAB Books,
1989.
    Includes index.
    ISBN (invalid) 0-8117-2546-X
    1. Clock and watch making. 2. Woodwork. I. Title.
TS545.N45   1994
681.1'13—dc20
                                                              93-48735
                                                                  CIP

To my granddaughter, Hilary Frances O'Rourke,
who was born the same week I finished this book

Contents

_____SECTION III_____
FINISHING AND FINAL DETAILS

SECTION IV
APPENDICES

Introduction

THE EIGHTEEN CLOCKS IN THIS BOOK REFLECT AN ERA WHEN TIME PASSED WITH little urgency. To early Americans, owning a clock was an indication of prosperity, rather than a commitment to punctuality. Today it is a necessity.

I have written this book with two purposes in mind: first, I wanted to make available a complete set of scaled drawings for craftspeople of today and, second, I wanted to present a condensed history of American clockmaking from 1820 to 1910.

On the outset, I would like to make it clear that I am not a clock expert, yet I have always enjoyed, and continue to enjoy, antique clocks. I am a member of Chapter No. 8 of the National Association of Watch and Clock Collectors in New England. If you are interested in clocks, you might wish to consider joining this excellent organization—the address is noted in Appendix C.

Only clocks that are either particularly popular or significant to the history of American clockmaking are included in this book. There should be a clock or two here for people of all tastes and levels of skill, from the inexperienced woodworker just getting started to the master craftsperson looking for something different. All kinds are represented: shelf clocks, wall clocks, and the granddaddy of them all, the tall-case clock. In selecting clocks for this book, I tried to choose a few clocks that are a little different than those usually found in other books, magazines, clock kits, and plans. The banjo clock is a later design with wooden side brackets, instead of the usual brass side brackets. To represent the steeple clock, I choose a very different, very small version. Also included is a column and splat clock and early column clock, because they are usually not found in books and magazines and are milestones in the evolution of clocks in this country.

Everyone includes the beautiful pillar and scroll clock; it is in just about every clock book and appears frequently in magazines on clockmaking. This book is no exception. Also included is an unusual and often forgotten clock, the Victorian black clock. The last clock in the book, the tambour clock, was first made at the beginning of this century. It is not a true antique, but it will soon become one.

All attempts have been made in the instructions given to reproduce the clocks exactly as the craftsmen of yesteryear made them. The joinery shown is exactly as it appears on the originals—if the original clock lasted for one hundred years, your reproduction should, too. I recommend that you use the same construction techniques that were used on the original clocks; this will give you a sense of how early craftsmen worked.

In this book you will also learn a little history of how each clock model originated and about who first developed it, along with information on the maker or company that actually manufactured the particular model. This way you will be able to give a brief history of your clock to family and friends. You will find Seth Thomas made many of the clocks in this book. His wonderful clocks are in production even today.

This book is written in honor of those early craftsmen, known and unknown, who developed the many clocks of America. Considering the crude equipment with which they had to work, it is doubly amazing what they accomplished.

In constructing your clock, you are building a potential heirloom to be enjoyed by you and your family for years to come. I sincerely hope you will enjoy making, displaying, and living with your clock. Any comments and criticisms of this book are most welcome.

JOHN A. NELSON
Peterborough, NH

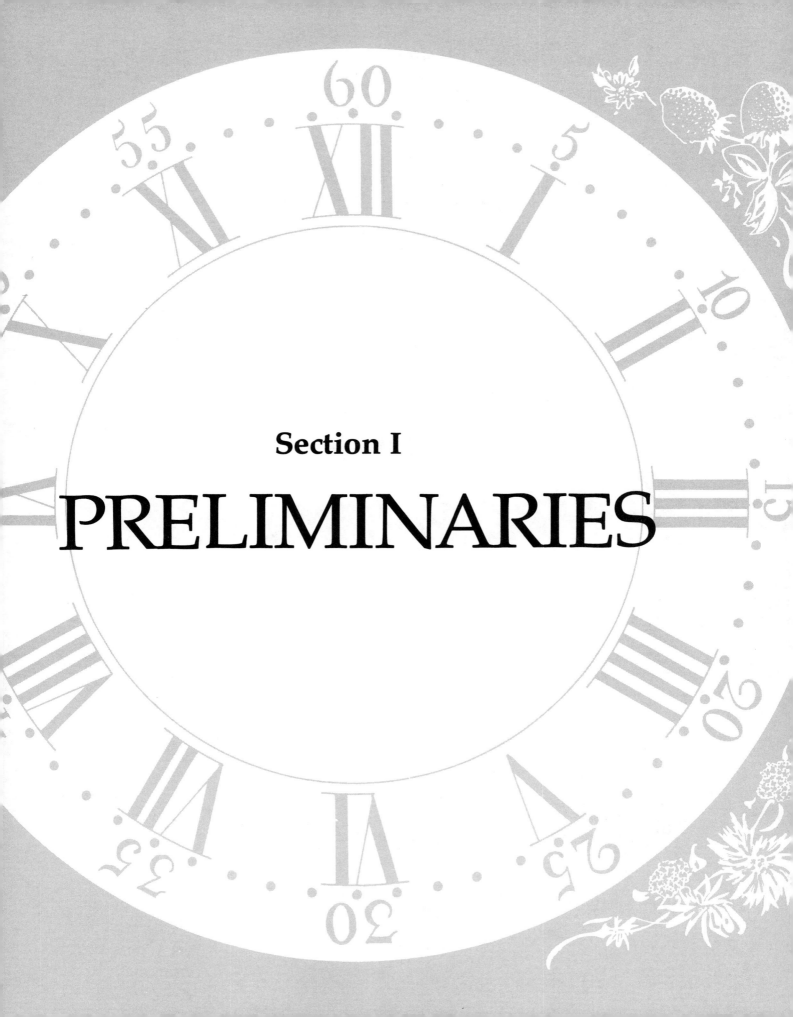

Section I
PRELIMINARIES

A Brief History

I N 1580 OR SO, THE ASTRONOMER GALILEO OBSERVED A SWINGING LAMP SUSPENDED by a long chain from a cathedral ceiling. He studied its swing and discovered that each swing was equal and had a natural rate of motion. He later found this rate of motion depended upon the length of the chain or pendulum. Many years later in 1640 he designed a clock mechanism incorporating the swing of a pendulum, but he died before building his clock design. Later in 1656 Christiaan Huygens added a pendulum to a clock mechanism of his own design and found it kept excellent time. Regulating the speed of the movement was done, as it is today, by simply raising or lowering the pendulum bob—*up* to speed-up the clock, *down* to slow-down the clock—thus the terms "speed-up," "slow-down." *Note:* the *length* of a pendulum is usually considered to be the length from the center of the shaft that holds the hands to the center of the pendulum bob (sometimes it is from the center of the shaft that holds the hands to the bottom tip of the pendulum bob).

Man has always recognized the passing of time and has tried to measure and record that passing. At first, it was the passing of each day, then cycles of the moon, and of course, the passings of the seasons. Time was important in early days, so that people could keep track of plantings and harvesting. In those days, the actual hour of the day was not particularly important.

Sun dials were first used to keep track of time, followed by other simple devices such as the hourglass, indexed candles that burned at a fixed rate, and water power.

Early Mechanical Clocks

The very first early mechanical clocks, which didn't have pendulums, were developed in the last half of the thirteenth century, probably by monks from central Europe, and were placed within the church. They did not have dials or hands and only struck bells on the hour. These mechanical devices were probably placed in the church belfry in order to make use of the existing church bell. It was over 100 years before visible dials and hands were added. These early clocks were very large and were made of heavy iron frames and gears forged by the local blacksmiths.

By the first part of the fifteenth century, small domestic clocks started to appear. They were probably made by the local gunsmiths or locksmiths. After 1630, a weight-driven lantern clock became popular for the home use of the very wealthy. When the swinging pendulum was added in 1656, clocks became more accurate. Very early clock movements were mounted high above the floor because they required long pendulums and large cast-iron descending weights. In reality, they were nothing more than simple mechanical works with a face and hands. They were referred to as "wags-on-the-wall." The long-case, or grandfather clock actually evolved from these early wags-on-the-wall prototypes. Wooden cases were used only to hide the unsightly weights and cast-iron pendulum.

Clocks in the Colonies

Clocks were first brought to the American colonies in the early 1600s by wealthy colonists. To the early colonist, owning a clock was a status symbol. A clock was found in the finest of homes and always displayed in a prominent place for all to view. Most people of that time could not afford a clock of their own and had to rely on the church clock on the town common for the time of day.

Most early clockmakers were not skilled in wood techniques and turned to jointers for their woodworking abilities. These early jointers used the exact same jointing techniques and styles they used on furniture. It was not until 1683 that the first immigrant, William Davis, claimed to be a clockmaker. By 1799, the great number of clocks attracted horological artisans to the New World. Most of these early artisans settled in populous centers such as Boston and Philadelphia. Later, others came to New York, Charlestown, Baltimore, and New Haven.

The handcrafting of clocks grew in all areas of the eastern part of the colonies. At the beginning of the eighteenth century, there were many makes of long-case clocks in the Quaker colony of Pennsylvania. The earliest clockmakers from Philadelphia were Samuel Bispam, Abel Cottey, and Peter Stretch. The most famous clockmaker of Philadelphia was David Rittenhouse. David succeeded Benjamin Franklin as president of the American Philosophical Society and later became Director of the United States Mint.

Nineteenth-Century Grandfather Clocks

After 1800, inexpensive tall-case clocks were made in quantity and were affordable to more and more people. The clockmaking industry spread to Massachusetts, Connecticut, New Hampshire, Rhode Island, and Vermont. In Massachusetts, Benjamin and Ephram Willard became very famous for their exceptionally beautiful long-case clocks. In Connecticut, the first successful, domestic, mass-produced long-case clocks were developed by Eli Terry. In those days, most clock cases were made by local cabinetmakers. The works, either brass or wood, were made by a firm that specialized in clock works. The cabinetmaker engraved or painted his name on the dial, thereby taking claim for the completed clock.

When the Industrial Revolution came about, along with regular factory working hours and the introduction of train schedules, the necessity for standardized timekeeping really brought clockmaking to the fore.

After 1840, wooden movements were abandoned and the 30-hour brass movement became popular—mainly because of its low price. Soon after, the spring-powered movement came into being and really paved the way for a variety of totally new and smaller clock cases.

Nineteenth-Century Manufacturers

Before 1840, manufacturers were mostly individual clockmakers of family-owned companies. In 1840 however, Chauncy Jerome built the largest clock factory and started shipping clocks all over the world. It is said that Jerome Clock Company motivated the organization of the Ansonia Clock Company and the Waterbury Clock Company. These three companies, along with Seth Thomas Company, E. N. Welch Company, Ingraham Clock Company, and Gilbert Clock Company, became the major producers of clocks. By 1851, there were over 30 clock factories in this country. From 1840 up to 1890, millions of clocks were produced, but unfortunately very few actually survived.

Clockmaking in the Twentieth Century

In 1929, during the stock market crash, many of these giants failed. The Ansonia Clock Company moved to Russia, Seth Thomas Clock Company became a part of General Time Instrument Company.

From 1940 to the present, the Sessions Clock Company and New Haven Clock Company were founded. Of the original giants of the clock industry only three exist today. They are all currently divisions of larger companies. Seth Thomas is now a division of Talley Industries, the Ingraham Clock Company is now a division of McGraw-Edison, and Gilbert Clock Company has been replaced by the Sparta Corporation.

No spring-powered clocks are currently being mass-produced in the country.

Clock Classifications

Clocks, as well as many antiques, are classified by their overall style. There are five overall kinds of styles of clocks: Colonial, Empire Victorian, Modern, and Contemporary.

Colonial—up to 1800; tall-case and wags-on-the-wall clocks.

Empire—1800-1840; mostly wooden work movements, shelf clocks, and tall-case clocks. Movements were either 30-hour or 8-day.

Victorian—1840 to 1890; the period of greatest production of clocks and the greatest variety of models.

Modern—1890 to 1940; a period of change from mechanical movements to clocks with synchronous electric motors.

Contemporary—World War II to present; great changes occurred, from the development of electric motors to clocks with very accurate electronic (quartz) movements.

There are three primary kinds of clocks: tall-case clocks, wall clocks, and shelf clocks.

TALL CLOCKS.

Tall clocks are usually called a grandfather clock due to a song of the same name that was popular in 1875. The term "grandfather" clock is now in general use, replacing the old terms, "tall," "hall," "floor," and "long-case" clock. When tall clocks were popular they were referred to as a "new clock." In those days a "new clock" was anything with a pendulum and a clock house, or case.

WALL CLOCKS.

Although the tall clock was the first timekeeper built in the colonies, the wall clock was the first truly American clock. The original and most popular wall clock was the small-case, elegant hanging timepiece called the "patent timepiece"—later called the banjo clock. It was made by Simon Willard of Massachusetts. In its day, it satisfied the American fantasies of luxury and refinement.

Later innovations were added to the wall clock. Craftsman from Connecticut and New Hampshire added a looking glass, thereby adding an additional function. Aaron Willard and Joseph Ives were the first to produce wall mirrored clocks.

SHELF CLOCKS.

By 1850, even the most fashionable wall clocks were replaced by cheaper shelf clocks. The Willards of Massachusetts designed and built the first Massachusetts shelf clock. It was very expensive and usually made-to-order. Affordable shelf clocks came into existence when, in 1807, Eli Terry received an order to build 4,000 wooden geared movements. It took him over 2 years to complete the order, but his experiments building them helped him develop the first true mass-production factory in the country. This made shelf clocks available to everyone.

In 1814, Eli Terry developed the most beautiful shelf clock ever built and manufactured in the United States. It was the very popular pillar and scroll shelf clock. Today originals of these clocks are *very* expensive. This model was made in large quantities for many years and was copied by many other companies of the day.

It is said Chauncy Jerome, a carpenter working for Eli Terry at the time, is the person who actually made the first pillar and scroll clock case, although Eli Terry has always been credited with the clock.

Parts and
Assembly

BEFORE YOU BEGIN BUILDING YOUR CLOCK, YOU SHOULD HAVE A BASIC UNDER-
standing of the parts and interworkings of the clock. If you can visualize how
a clock is assembled, you will be better able to follow the instructions for constructing the many clock designs presented in Section II of this book. An important consideration in clock construction is selecting the appropriate premade
movement for your clock.

Movements

The movement is the heart of the clock. Be sure to purchase a high-quality movement for your clock so you will have years of trouble-free service (Fig. 2-1). In the
long run the extra spent for the movement will enhance the clock (don't forget,
the original lasted for well over 100 years).

   If you want to be as authentic as possible, you should purchase a new movement with the exact same specifications as the original. On the other hand, if you
want a movement that is very accurate and very functional, purchase a simple
quartz movement. When installed, they are not seen, and no one will know it is
not as the original clock was (Fig. 2-2).

Early Movements

In early days of America, inexpensive clock movements were made of hardwood.
The gears, pinions, and plates were usually made of apple wood (Fig. 2-3). More
expensive wood movements were made with brass or ivory bushings pressed
into the wooden plates where the pinions wore against the plates. In later years,
when brass was machined in quantities and came in rolled strips, the clockmaking industry expanded rapidly.

   Hand-crafted brass clock movements were very expensive around 1800. In
those days only the wealthy could afford a clock with a brass movement. Early
brass plates were individually cast, hammered to harden them, and then filed by
hand to smooth them out.

Fig. 2-1. Standard time-only, spring-driven brass movement with a key and a 21-inch-long pendulum.

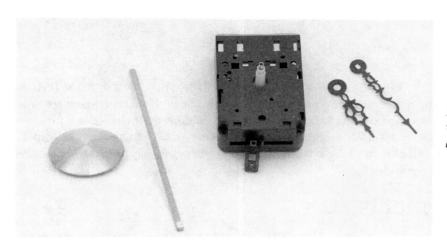

Fig. 2-2. Quartz movements, shown here with pendulum, are very accurate and easily adapted to most any clock case.

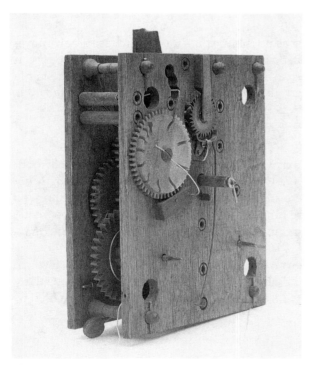

Fig. 2-3. Antique, 30-hour, weight-driven, all-hardwood movements were used in early pillar and scroll, column, and ogee clocks.

A Few Basic Facts

There are a few basic facts you should know about a clock movement before beginning:

- There are 30-hour, 8-day, and 31-day movements available. The 30-hour movement is designed to run one full day, the 8-day for 7 days, and the 31-day for one full month, all with a *little* extra time in the event you forget to rewind it.
- Movements come with or without an hour-counting mechanism. Some strike on gongs, or brass or iron bells, and others play melodies each hour. Some count the hours on a gong and ring a bell on the half hours.
- Movements with a strike mechanism are actually *two* mechanisms built into one movement. On one side is the totally independent time mechanism, the other side, a totally independent strike mechanism.
- The gears (or wheels) are held in place between two plates.
- The gears are powered by either a heavy weight or weights, or by one or more springs.
- The gears are supported on a shaft called an arbor.
- The gears would run uncontrollably if not for the escapement wheel. The escapement wheel allows the final gear to turn one-tooth-at-a-time. A U-shaped part, called a *verge* is the part that allows the escapement gear to move in this manner (see Fig. 2-4). The verge gives the clock its "tick-tock" sound.
- Attached to the verge is a thin stiff wire called a *crutch*. The crutch gives the pendulum its "kick," which, in turn, keeps an even and perfect beat. The crouch must be bent one way or the other in order to make the clock run (or beat) evenly (this will be explained in greater detail later).
- The length of the pendulum is what determines how fast or slow the movement will run. The pendulum is raised to make the clock run faster, and it is lowered to make the clock run slower.
- Except for the tall-case clock, movements are mounted in the clock on arms that extend from either the front of the plate or from the back of the plate. They are referred to as either front-mount or rear-mount movements. Tall clocks simply mounted the movements on a horizontal board that was supported by the sides of the clock case.

Tall-Case Movements

Early clocks required long pendulums and large heavy weights to work properly. A case was made to house the movement, pendulum, and weights. They were made of either wood or brass and came as:

- 30-hour (one day) one weight powered, key or pull wound
- 8-day (one week) two weight powered, key or pull wound
- 8-day (one week) spring powered, key wound (*rare*)

Most early tall-case clocks did not have chimes and struck a large 4-inch-diameter cast-iron bell mounted on top of the movement.

Shelf and Wall Clock Movements

As pendulum lengths became shorter, shelf clocks, like the pillar and scrolls, were developed. Early shelf clocks (up to 1820) had wooden movements. These

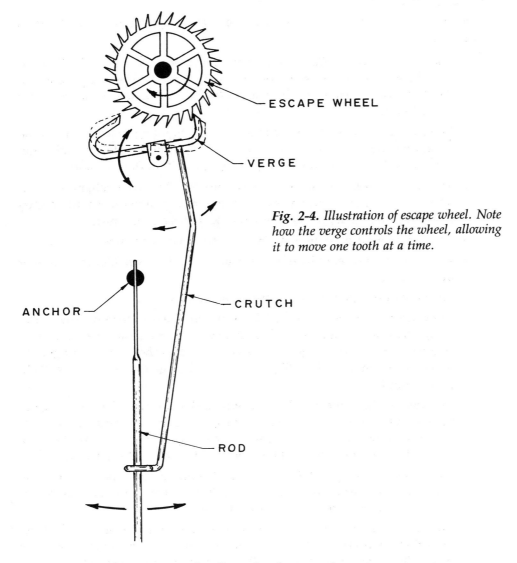

ESCAPE WHEEL

VERGE

Fig. 2-4. Illustration of escape wheel. Note how the verge controls the wheel, allowing it to move one tooth at a time.

ANCHOR

CRUTCH

ROD

shorter movements were made of wood or brass and came as:

- ◆ 30-hour (one day) weight powered, key wound
- ◆ 30-hour (one day) spring powered, key wound
- ◆ 8-day (one week) weight powered, key wound
- ◆ 8-day (one week) spring powered, key wound
- ◆ 31-day (one month) spring powered, key wound

Before the revolution, early Americans wanted the latest in sophisticated mechanisms such as long running movements, second hands, alarms, calendars, and moon phases.

Movements are either front-mounted or rear-mounted. Figure 2-5 illustrates a front-mounted movement and Fig. 2-6 illustrates a rear-mounted movement. The rear-mounted movements are usually the oldest and are harder to find today. Make certain you choose the correct type when ordering.

If you want to be really authentic, visit a clock repair shop and tell them what model of clock you are building and ask if they have an exact or similar movement in their spare parts. Most clock shops have many old movements in stock for parts—even wooden gear movements.

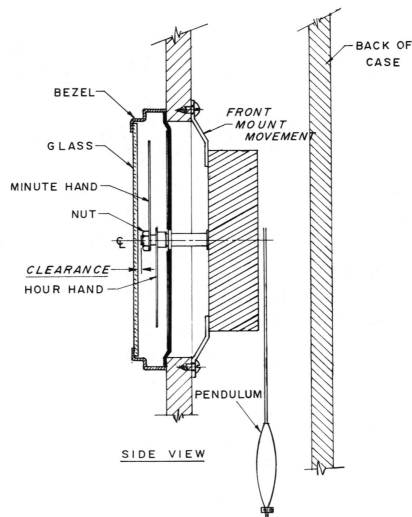

BACK OF CASE

BEZEL

GLASS

MINUTE HAND

NUT

CLEARANCE

HOUR HAND

FRONT MOUNT MOVEMENT

PENDULUM

SIDE VIEW

Fig. 2-5. Front-mounted movements are usually found on newer clocks.

Quartz Movements

Today, quartz movements come in all shapes and sizes. They can easily be adapted to replace any original movement. Although they are not authentic, they keep excellent time, do not require weekly winding, and run very quietly. Quartz movements can be ordered with or without pendulums. They come with bells, chimes, and bim-bam chimes.

Quartz movements are usually held in place by the center shaft. Instructions are usually provided with all quartz movements. Be sure to order a quartz movement with the correct center shaft length. The length should be slightly longer than the thickness of the dial face.

Important: Be sure to order the movement *before* beginning work on the clock so you recheck for fit as you make the case. The movements listed in the parts list are only suggestions. These were the ones I could find with the catalogs I had at the time. Because I have not purchased many of them it is important that you recheck before starting. You may find movements that are actually closer or better than the ones listed. Remember: the new movements are generally not exact copies of the original movements; they are only close replacements. Early cases were very thin, therefore, new movements may not fit correctly unless you widen the case slightly to accommodate the thicker movement. You should stay with the correct pendulum length and use the correct hand style if possible.

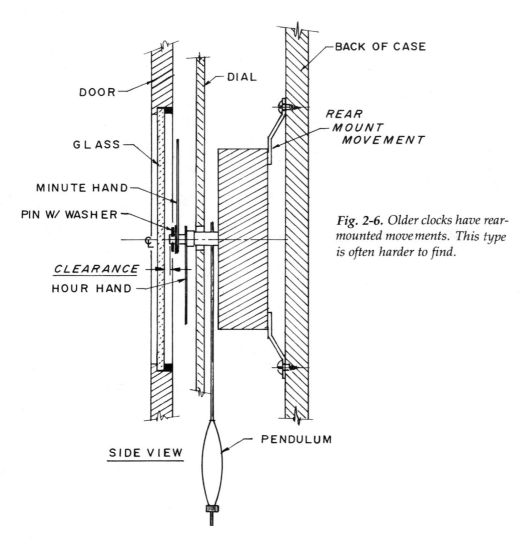

DOOR

GLASS

MINUTE HAND

PIN W/ WASHER

CLEARANCE

HOUR HAND

DIAL

BACK OF CASE

REAR
MOUNT
MOVEMENT

SIDE VIEW

PENDULUM

Fig. 2-6. *Older clocks have rear-mounted movements. This type is often harder to find.*

Dials, Hands and Bezels

The dial face is very important. It is the part of the clock you first notice, and of course the part you look at to tell the time.

Dials

Original dials were made of paper, wood, zinc, brass, and iron. Today there are people who make exact copies of original dials. Very good dial copies can be purchased from the companies listed in Appendix B. *Note:* a dial's size is considered as the diameter of the minute track.

If you purchase a dial, you have a large choice of options:

- ✦ Style—Arabic or Roman
- ✦ Diameter of the minute track
- ✦ Ornamentation of the corners
- ✦ Type of material, paper, wood, zinc, etc.
- ✦ Approximate size of the numbers
- ✦ Color—white or off white, gloss or dull finish
- ✦ Specific shape and size (for example, the steeple clock shape)

Note: Those with a little art ability and a few drafting tools may wish to make their own dial faces (see Chapter 11).

When choosing a dial face, be sure to choose a style that matches the style of clock you are making. This is very important to your clock's appearance.

Clock Hands

Clock hands come in a great variety of styles and sizes. Order hand sizes that match the minute track. The minute hand should be the same size or slightly smaller than the radius of the minute track of the dial. The style of the hands should match the original clock's hands or the clock will not look right. A Terry clock should have Terry-style clock hands, a banjo clock should have banjo style hands, and so forth (see Fig. 2-7).

Fig. 2-7. Be sure that your choice of dial hands is consistent with the style of clock you are constructing.

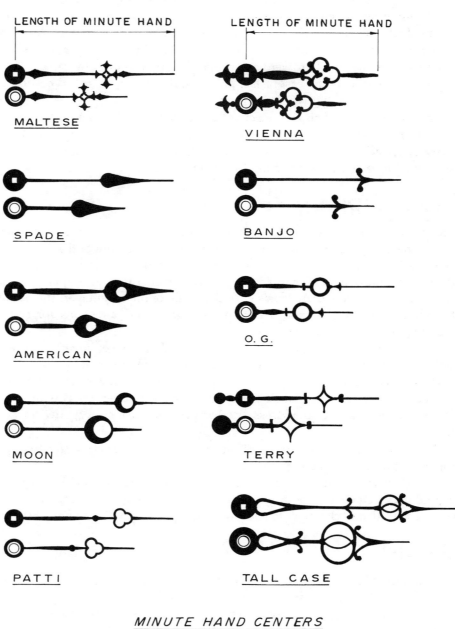

On most movements, the hour hand is simply pushed on the outer center shaft and the minute hand attached to the inner center shaft and held in place by a nut. You can carefully slip the hour hand around on the shaft to any position on the dial you wish, but you must loosen the nut holding the minute hand before the minute hand can be replaced correctly on the dial. Carefully turn the minute hand until the movement strikes *before* attaching the nut. Count the strikes, move the small hour hand to the hour the movement struck, and then attach the longer minute hand pointing toward 12 o'clock. Care should be taken in setting the hands. Never turn the hands backwards.

Bezel

The brass frame that holds the clock dial glass in place is called the *bezel*. Generally, the glass is held in place by small brass tabs that must be soldered in place. If you must add the glass with tabs, use only enough heat to melt the solder so you will not cause discoloring of the metal. As you did with the movement and dial, be sure to purchase the hardware before starting any work on the case. You may have to fit the bezel *to* the case. Also, purchase the dial, hands, and bezel at the same time, so everything will fit correctly.

On some clocks, such as the schoolhouse clock, the bezel and dial are one unit. These are sometimes easier to work with because the glass comes with the assembly already mounted ready for the clock case. Always be sure to order the same style of bezel as was used on the original clock.

Clock Papers

Early clocks were sold with a plain piece of paper attached inside to the backboard. These original plain papers were used to keep dust out of the movement. Some ingenious person (no one knows exactly who) came up with the idea to advertise on these papers, and soon every clockmaker used this space for their advertisements. These early labels gave the name of the casemaker; the address of the company; information about the warranty; and directions for setting, adjusting, and regulating the clock.

Not all labels were accurate. Sometimes the cabinetmaker advertised that he made the movement, when in reality he did not. Sometimes the person selling the clock put his name on the label, but did not have anything to do with making the clock. I have also seen labels pasted over original paper labels with a completely different name and address—perhaps the first use of deceptive advertising.

Today, the condition of the paper on an original antique clock is very important as it governs the value of the clock.

Clocks in this book requiring a label are noted. Excellent-quality copies of original paper labels can be ordered from TEC Specialties (see Appendix B). A clock paper will add character to your new-old clock and make it more authentic.

Decals

Clock decals come in all shapes and sizes. Most are exact copies of original old clock designs. They were put on the glass areas of the clock. Of course, many old clocks had hand-painted reversed paintings on the glass. Today you still can get reverse hand-painted glass (see Appendix B).

You can get a very close effect at a much lower cost by using decals and painting from the back in various areas with various colors. Many decals require that you paint everything in the background black so that just the decal and a small area in the center is left clear. The center area is left open so the swing of the pendulum can be seen.

If you use a decal that covers the entire glass, be sure to paint over the decal from the back with black or brown paint, so that the decal cannot easily be scratched. Visit a clock museum and study how clock glasses were painted.

Assembly of Early Clocks

Nails were used to hold most early clocks together. Glue probably would not have been used, as it was hard to obtain. The nails were hand-forged from pure iron. This gave them a rust-resistant quality; they bent easily but seldom broke. These nails were probably either the rose-head type or completely headless. Because these early nails were hand-forged one at a time, no two nails were exactly the same. By today's standards, using nails may look crude, but it *is* authentic.

Screws were used as early as 1700; therefore, there probably would have been some screws used in the construction of many of the clocks in this book. The first screws were made by hand and were much more expensive to make than nails, so they were not used very frequently. Most early screws were only a half an inch in length or shorter. Their threads were made by hand and were very uneven and wide with rounded edges. The tips of these early screws were always blunt and usually off center.

You will be advised in the directions of each clock whether to use nails or screws. If you do use nails, be sure to purchase square-cut nails from Tremont Nail Company (see Appendix A).

The "black clock" models (1880 to 1920) were screwed together—I assume so that the parts could be painted and finished while they were still flat pieces. On these clocks, very few parts were glued together.

General Instructions

As with any project, carefully study the drawings before starting anything so you know exactly how the clock is assembled and how each part is made. Try to go through each process, step-by-step, in your mind so you will know how to make each part with the tools and equipment you have. As you proceed, keep everything square and all edges sharp.

Ordering Parts

It is important that you order the hardware and movement before going too far, so you can make minor adjustments for slight differences in available purchased parts. You should especially check that the movement's dimensions are correct. Check that the pendulum length is correct, that the pendulum will swing properly in the given space, and that the length of the center hand shaft is long enough or not too long. The tip of the center hand shaft must not touch the dial-face glass.

If you use a quartz movement you should not have any problem at all, except for the length of the center shaft. The pendulum on a quartz movement has no effect on the operation of the movement like a spring-powered movement does, so it can be cut any shorter length if necessary.

The brass dial bezels have the tendency to vary slightly, so you should check these also before going too far. If possible, try to get dial face bezels with the glass and dial already in place. All you have to do is locate and drill the winding holes.

Tools

The clocks in this book require very few tools. The average woodshop should have most of these. Basic hand tools will be needed, along with the following power tools:

+ Table saw or radial-arm saw
+ Router and/or shaper
+ Jigsaw or saber saw
+ Lathe (optional, see below)
+ Sander
+ Planer (optional, but handy)

It goes without saying, but always utilize *extreme caution* when using any tools and maintain safe practices to avoid any accidents.

If you do not have a lathe for some of the special turnings, write to River Bend Turnings (the address is in Appendix A). They will make up anything you need. Just send them a copy of the page that illustrates the part for a price quote.

Using the Drawings

Project plans are located after the instructions for each project. A two-view or three-view drawing is provided for each design. One view is the FRONT VIEW and the other is the RIGHT-SIDE VIEW. The third view, if provided, is the TOP VIEW. In general, the views are positioned in a standard way exactly as they are positioned on drawings used in industry. The front view is always the most important view and should be your starting point when studying the drawings. The right-side view is always located directly to the right of the front view, the top view is always located directly above the front view. All features in the front view are projected directly over into the right-side view and projected directly up to the top view. The top views are usually drawn as a section view (see below).

Dash lines on the drawing indicate that there is a hidden surface or hidden feature *within* the object that you cannot see from the outside. Think of these hidden lines as X-rays showing what the inside will look like or indicating a hidden surface you can't see.

A thin line consisting of a long dash, a short and long dash, and so forth, is the centerline. It indicates the exact center of the clock or part. All features are the same on either side of the centerline. Sometimes the centerline is marked "C/L."

Important: All drawings are fully dimensioned. The actual required size is called-off and is the distance between the tips of the arrowheads.

SECTION VIEWS are sometimes used to further illustrate a particular feature of the clock or to illustrate how an area is assembled. The section view is usually only a small section of the clock and illustrates only a portion of it. On the drawing two arrows are drawn with an A or B at the tips of the arrow—this is where you will be viewing the part, as if it were cut in two. Someplace on the drawing is a view showing what the piece would look like if cut in two at the arrows. This view will be listed as VIEW AT A-A.

In addition, section views are sometimes used to show the shape or profile of a molding or to show how two or more parts are assembled. Parts that have a lot of unusual details or unusual shape are drawn in full. The size and shape of simple parts are listed in the parts list.

Study the drawings very carefully. Some parts must be made in right-hand and left-hand pairs. The side of a clock is a good example—both sides of the clock are the same, but you must make a *right* side and a *left* side.

Besides the regular views, each project has an EXPLODED VIEW that illustrates how the clock is to be put together and where each part goes. Again, be sure you fully understand how the clock is assembled *before* any work is started.

Parts List

Each clock has a complete parts list specifying every part used in the clock, located after the step-by-step instructions and right before the project plans. The number at the left is the same number noted on the drawing, so each and every part can be easily found and copied.

Important: All efforts have been made to ensure that all dimensions of parts are correct; however, it is always best to recheck each part with the mating part by dry-fitting all parts as you proceed.

Section II

PROJECTS

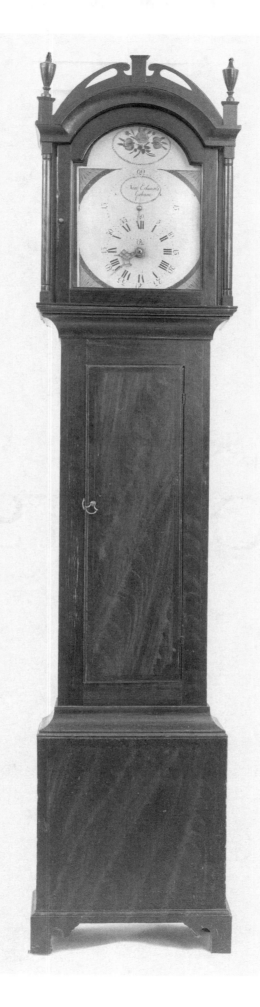

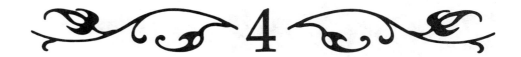

Grandfather Clock

ONCE CALLED THE LONG CLOCK, TALL-CASE CLOCK, OR EVEN COFFIN CLOCK, THE grandfather clock has always been particularly popular. Through the years it has been known as an excellent timekeeper. The term "grandfather clock" came from a song of the same name written by Henry Clay in 1876. The original tall-case clock is said to have been developed in London around 1650. The earliest tall-case clock to be made here in America was made by Abel Cottey in 1720 or so. The tall-case clock was the first household piece to be successfully mass-produced in America and was manufactured by Eli Terry.

In early America most grandfather clocks were made with flat tops. By 1740 however, during the Queen Anne period, clocks were made with round tops. The Chippendale style then became popular, followed by the most popular design, the Federal "swan-neck" top. As glass was very expensive in those days, grandfather clocks were made with solid wooden front doors. Also, in those days, the 42-inch-long pendulum and cast-iron weights were very crude, so the solid door hid them.

The long-case clock consists of the case, the movement, and accessories such as a winding key (for keywind clocks) and case door key.

The Case

Tall-case clock cases consist of the base, waist, and hood. Some original designs included feet, waist columns and door columns, hood fret work, and finials. Cases were made of many kinds of woods, although hardwoods such as maple, cherry, walnut, and mahogany were usually used. Other lower-cost clocks were made of pine, which usually had a painted grain added to simulate the more desired and expensive hardwood (Fig. 4-2).

Many cases were very elegant and beautiful, while others were extremely crude. In their heyday, many tall-case clocks were built over 9 feet tall. Today, most range from 6 feet to 7 feet, 6 inches in height. Cases shorter than 6 feet are considered grandmother clocks.

These cases reflected the styles of the period, including Chippendale, Sheraton, and Hepplewhite.

Fig. 4-1. Opposite: Grandfather clock made by Sam Edwards Jr., circa 1820.

Fig. 4-2. Painted-grain case to simulate a more desired and expensive wood.

The Movement

The brass movement of most original clocks consists of two brass plates approximately 1/8 inch thick and 5 by 7 inches in size. The plates are spaced about 2 inches apart and contain nine shafts called *arbors*. These arbors hold seven large gears, called *wheels*, and six smaller pinion gears. Mounted on the front plate are two pinion gears that regulate the movement of the two hands. Located outside the plates, just below the two front gears, is a mechanism to index the correct number of striking blows to the bell above. The pendulum length of a tall-case clock is 42 inches.

Accessories

Accessories for very early tall-case clocks, such as dials, hands, weights, pendulum bobs, finials, winding keys, case, and door locks, and door keys were usually purchased from England.

The Dial

Tall-case clock dials were divided into two basic kinds: brass dials and painted dials. Brass dials were very elaborately engraved with raised numbers and were used exclusively in America until 1775. White-painted dials with painted decorations were then imported from England and by 1800 had just about replaced the brass dials. These painted dials were much cheaper to produce, and therefore, more popular with clockmakers. As time went by, America produced painted dials of their own.

Roman numbers were used on most dials of the early period, Arabic numbers were very seldom used and are rare.

Samuel Edwards Jr.

The tall-case clock featured in this chapter was made by Samuel Edwards Jr. of Gorham, Maine, around 1820. Samuel came from a family of clockmakers who originally settled in Ashby, Massachusetts. He lived in Ashby from 1800 to 1808 and moved to Gorham, Maine in 1808 until his death in 1830. Samuel's clocks are rather simple; most were made of pine with painted grain cases. His clocks had 30-hour wooden movements and had pull wind movements (Fig. 4-3). Many of Samuel's dial faces were very unusual—the second hand ring is as large as the

Fig. 4-3. An Edward's wood movement with dial in place.

minute ring (Fig. 4-4). This is somewhat rare and, I believe, found only on his dial faces. The Bristol Clock Museum in Bristol, Connecticut moved his clock shop from Gorham, Maine and has a few of his original movements and dial faces.

Because this dial face is so unusual and not reproduced for purchase, a detailed drawing of his clock is provided. It is a rather simple dial, so it would be a good one to try your hand at making. Refer to Fig. 4-4 for details.

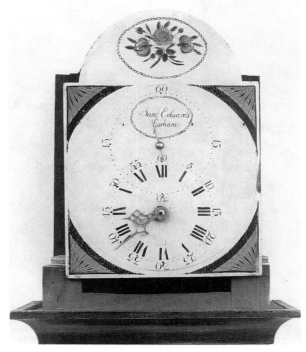

Fig. 4-4. Edward's dial face with its very unusual second-hand ring as large as the minute-hand ring.

Instruction / Tall-Case Clock

This clock is actually no different to make than any shelf or wall clock, except you will be using a few more pieces and the pieces will be larger than the other clocks. Study all drawings and try to purchase all wood and hardware before starting—*including* the movement. The original was made of pine and had a painted-grain finish to look like more expensive wood.

Think of this clock as two different assemblies, a case (parts 1 through 26) and a hood (parts 27 through 55). The hood (see Fig. 4-5) only slides in place over the case and is not fastened at all. It is important that you maintain the $17^3/_8$-inch and $8^{11}/_{16}$-inch sizes at the top of the case where the hood slides into place. (See the assembly of parts 35, 36, 38, and 39). Also be sure to maintain the $17^7/_{16}$-inch and $8^3/_4$-inch dimensions to allow clearance between the case and the hood.

Fig. 4-5. Back view of hood assembly. Notice its somewhat crude construction; everything is nailed together.

STEP 1.
Cut all parts to general overall sizes using the Parts List (Table 4-1). Cut all parts slightly larger than called for just in case you have to adjust some parts.

STEP 2.
Make up the back using parts 1, 2, and 3. Notch for the sides, (part 4). Make up the subassembly for the front using parts 6, 7, and 8.

STEP 3.
Make up the basic case using parts 1 through 12. Dry-fit all parts. If correct, glue and nail the case together. Keep everything square as you go. Add the remaining parts to the basic case—parts 13 through 24. Parts 25 and 26 can be cut to size later to fit to the hood. Sand all over, keeping all edges sharp. This completes the case construction.

STEP 4.
Assemble parts 35, 36, 38, and 39, and fit the subassembly to the case assembly. It should slide over the moldings (parts 17 and 18) on the case. From there, build

the hood. Be sure to add the two columns (part 43) as you assemble the hood. The hood is a little tricky, so be sure to dry-fit all parts as you proceed.

STEP 5.

Check that the door (parts 48, 49, 50, and 52) fits correctly before adding the glass and knob. Sand all over, keeping all edges sharp. This completes the hood construction.

Painting the Dial Face

Because the original dial is very different than most dials, you will have to paint it yourself or have it painted (see Appendix B). Because the movement has a very special 4 5/16-inch distance between the hour/minute hand shaft and the second hand shaft, you must obtain an old original style movement before you can use a dial like the one illustrated. You will have to use a standard purchased dial if you cannot find a movement with special 4 5/16-inch distance. The Parts List calls for a standard *brass* movement that is very close to an original old clock of this time. Note that the original clock had a 30-hour wooden gear movement.

Finishing

See Section III for finishing the clock case and hood. If you choose to include a painted grain, refer to your local library for books that explain this method.

PARTS LIST

No.	Name	Size	Req'd.	
1	Back	¾ × 12½ — 77 Long	1	
2	Top Filler	¾ × ⅞ — 14⅞ Long	2	
3	Bottom Filler	¾ × 1¹⁵⁄₁₆ — 16⅜ Long	2	
4	Side	¾ × 6¼ — 45½ Long	2	
5	Glue Block	¾ × ¾ — 2½ Long	12	
6	Front Stile	¾ × 2⁷⁄₁₆ — 45½ Long	2	
7	Top Rail	¾ × 6 — 9⅛ Long	1	
8	Bottom Rail	¾ × 6¼ — 9⅛ Long	1	
9	Bottom	¾ × 7⁷⁄₁₆ — 16⅜ Long	1	
10	Spacer Side	¾ × 1³⁄₁₆ — 8⅛ Long	2	
11	Spacer Front	¾ × 1³⁄₁₆ — 15⅝ Long	1	
12	Front-Base	¾ × 17⅞ — 17⅛ Long	1	
13	Side-Base	¾ × 8¹³⁄₁₆ — 17⅛ Long	2	Case
14	Skirt Front	1 × 4⅜ — 18⅝ Long	1	
15	Skirt Side	1 × 4⅜ — 9⁹⁄₁₆ Long	2	
16	Foot Rear	¾ × 3⅝ — 5½ Long	2	
17	Molding-Front	¾ × 2¾ — 18¹¹⁄₁₆ Long	1	
18	Molding-Side	¾ × 2¾ — 9⅜ Long	2	
19	Molding-Front	¾ × 3¼ — 17 ⅞ Long	1	
20	Molding-Side	¾ × 3¼ — 8¹⁵⁄₁₆ Long	2	
21	Door	¾ × 9⅝ — 31 Long	1	
22	Hinge (Iron)	1" × 1" Long	2	
23	Latch	Merritt P-109	1	
24	Board-Movement	¾ × 5½ — 14 Long	1	
25	Dial Face	¼ × 12 — 17⅝ Long	1	
26	Dial Support	¾ × 1 — 12 Long	2	

27	Hood Side	3/4 × 81/16 — 18 Long	2	
28	Rear Arch	3/4 × 57/8 — 18 Long	1	
29	Side Spacer	3/4 × 2 — 83/4 Long	2	
30	Front Arch	3/4 × 57/8 — 18 Long	1	
31	Ear	1/4 × 13/4 — 151/4 Long	2	
32	Stile	1/4 × 13/8 — 137/8 Long	2	
33	Bottom Rail	1/4 × 11/2 — 12 Long	1	
34	Top Rail	1/4 × 73/8 — 12 Long	1	
35	Center Base	3/4 × 11/2 — 177/16 Long	1	
36	Side Base	3/4 × 11/2 — 71/4 Long	2	
37	Knob	Merritt P-22A	1	
38	Molding	5/8 × 1 — 1811/16 Long	1	
39	Molding	5/8 × 1 — 93/8 Long	2	
40	Cap	1/4 × 71/2 — 18 Long	1	Hood
41	Arch Molding	5/8 × 57/8 — 191/4 Long	1	
42	Side Molding	5/8 × 2 — 10 Long	2	
43	Column	1 × 1 — 163/4 Long	2	
44	Splat	1/4 × 3 — 9 Long	2	
45	Trim	3/4 × 15/16 — 2 Long	3	
46	Top Trim	1/4 × 15/16 — 111/16 Long	3	
47	Finial (Wood)	11/2 × 11/2 — 5 Long	2	
48	Door Stile	3/4 × 15/8 — 151/4 Long	2	
49	Door Arch	3/4 × 51/2 — 15 Long	1	
50	Door Rail	3/4 × 15/8 — 15 Long	1	
51	Glass	3/32 × 121/2 — 16 Long	1	
52	Hinge	Merritt P325	2	
53	Movement	See Below	1	
54	Hands	Merritt P-169	1	
55	Hand (Second)	Merritt P-839	1	

Movement: Brass, Merrit P-54
         LaRose 084069
         Mason & Sullivan 3224-X
   Quartz, Klockit 11913-A

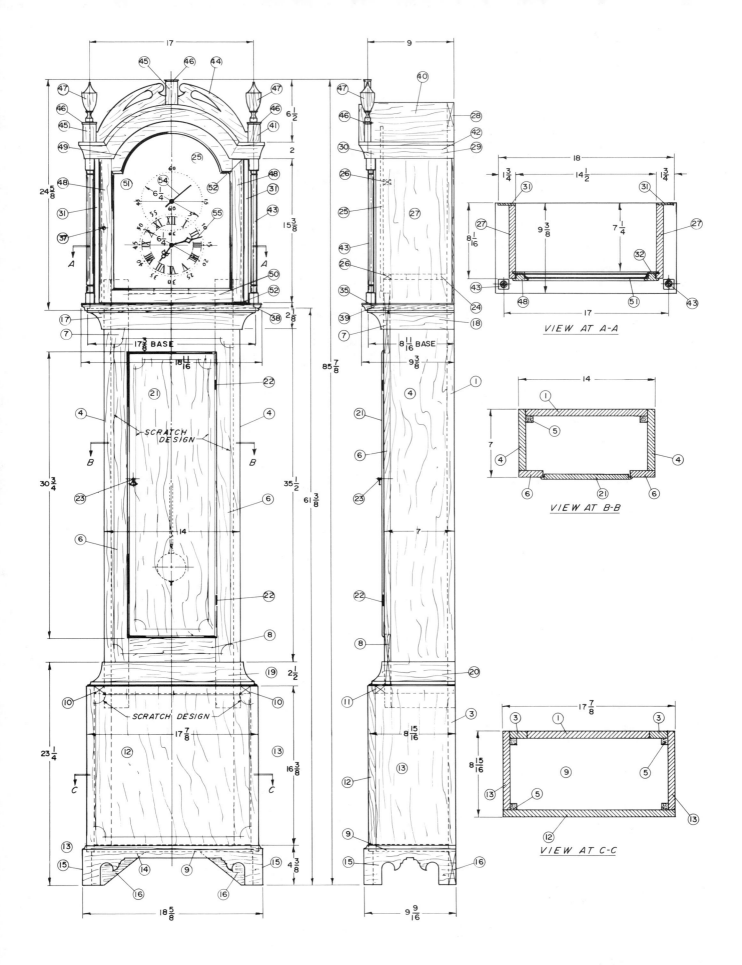

VIEW AT A-A

VIEW AT B-B

VIEW AT C-C

SCRATCH DESIGN

SCRATCH DESIGN

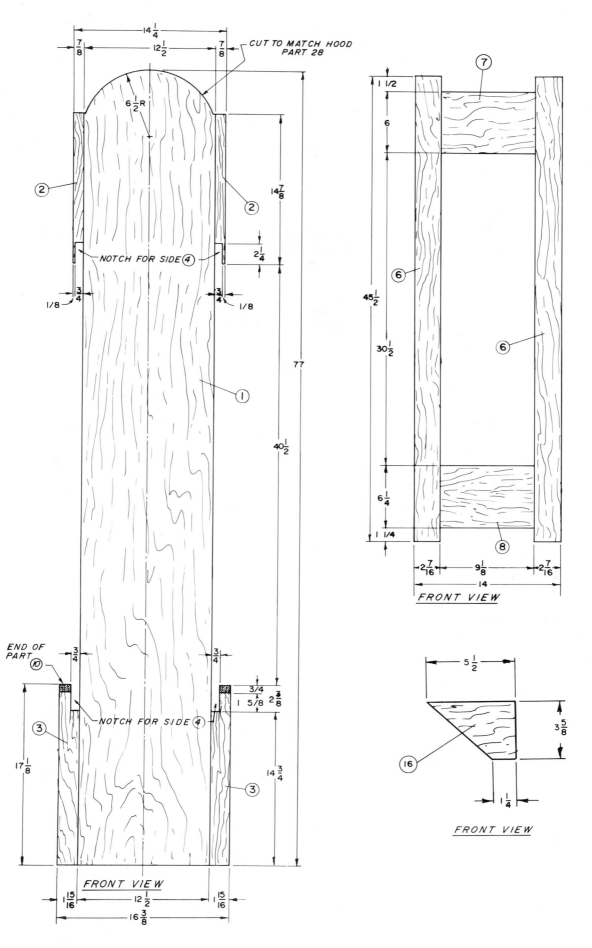

CUT TO MATCH HOOD
PART 28

14 1/4
12 1/2
7/8
7/8

6 1/2 R

2

2

14 7/8

NOTCH FOR SIDE 4

2 1/4

3/4

3/4

1/8

1/8

1

77

40 1/2

END OF
PART 10

3/4

3/4

3/4
1 5/8

2 3/8

NOTCH FOR SIDE 4

3

3

17 1/8

14 3/4

FRONT VIEW

1 15/16

12 1/2

1 15/16

16 3/8

1 1/2

7

6

6

45 1/2

30 1/2

6 1/4

1 1/4

8

2 7/16

9 1/8

2 7/16

14

FRONT VIEW

5 1/2

16

3 5/8

1 1/4

FRONT VIEW

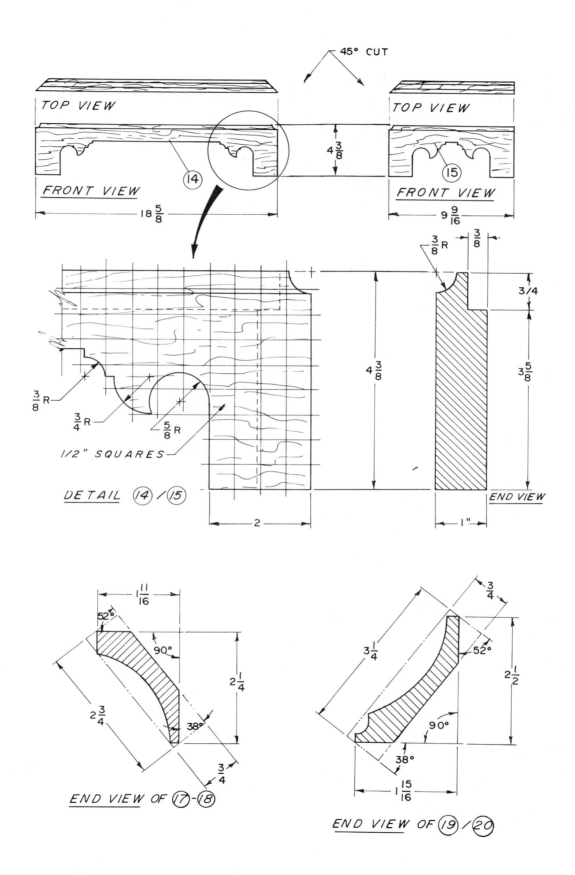

45° CUT

TOP VIEW

FRONT VIEW

(14)

4 3/8

18 5/8

TOP VIEW

FRONT VIEW

(15)

9 9/16

3/8 R

3/8

3/4

4 3/8

3 5/8

1"

END VIEW

3/8 R

3/4 R

5/8 R

1/2" SQUARES

DETAIL (14)/(15)

2

1 11/16

52°

90°

2 1/4

2 3/4

38°

3/4

END VIEW OF (17)-(18)

3/4

3 1/4

52°

2 1/2

90°

38°

1 15/16

END VIEW OF (19)/(20)

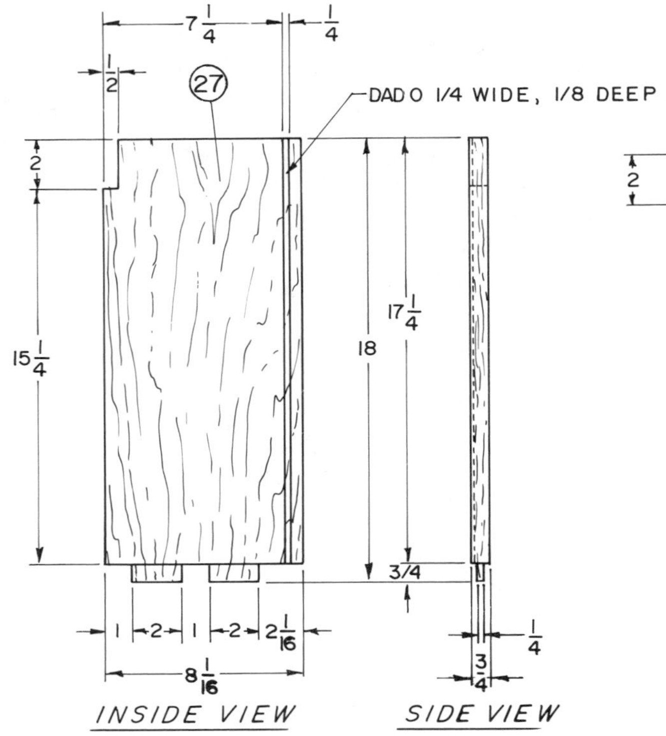

27
DADO 1/4 WIDE, 1/8 DEEP
7 1/4
1/4
1/2
2
15 1/4
18
17 1/4
3/4
1
2
1
2
2 1/16
8 1/16
1/4
3/4
INSIDE VIEW
SIDE VIEW

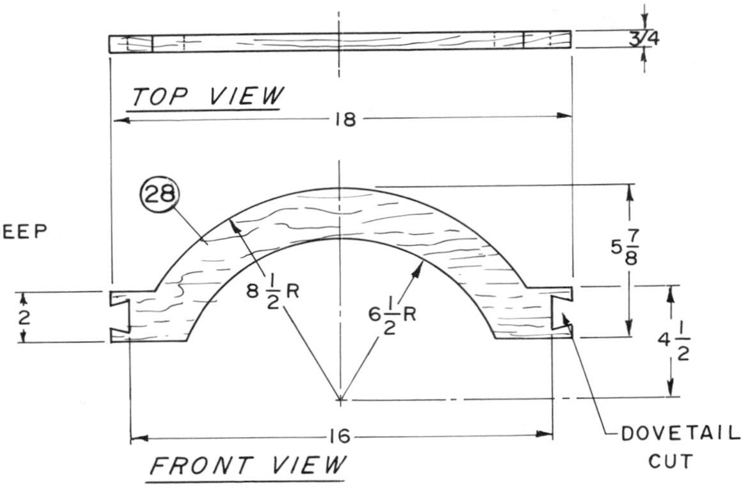

3/4
TOP VIEW
18
28
5 7/8
2
8 1/2 R
6 1/2 R
4 1/2
16
DOVETAIL CUT
FRONT VIEW

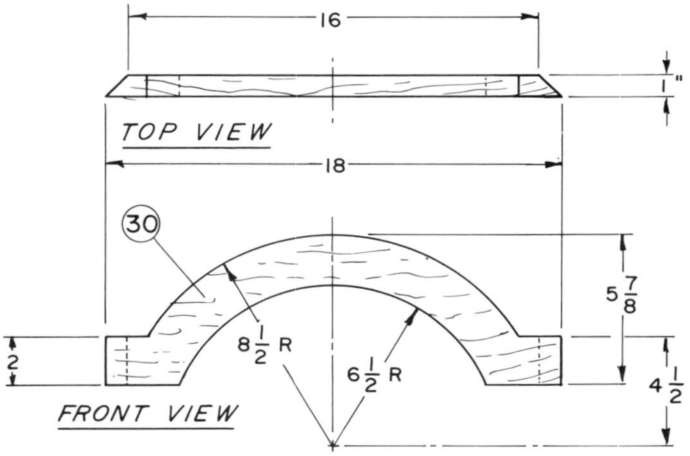

16
1"
TOP VIEW
18
30
5 7/8
2
8 1/2 R
6 1/2 R
4 1/2
FRONT VIEW

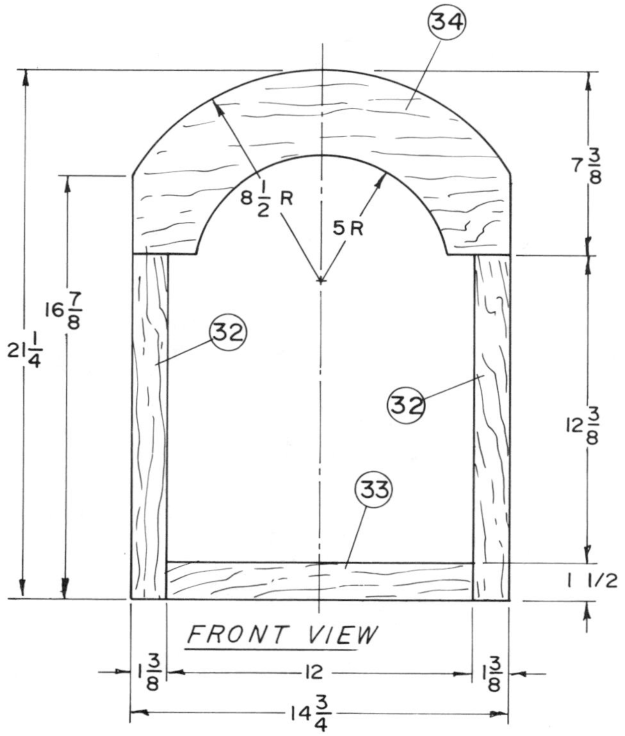

34
7 3/8
8 1/2 R
5 R
16 7/8
21 1/4
32
32
12 3/8
33
1 1/2
FRONT VIEW
1 3/8
12
1 3/8
14 3/4

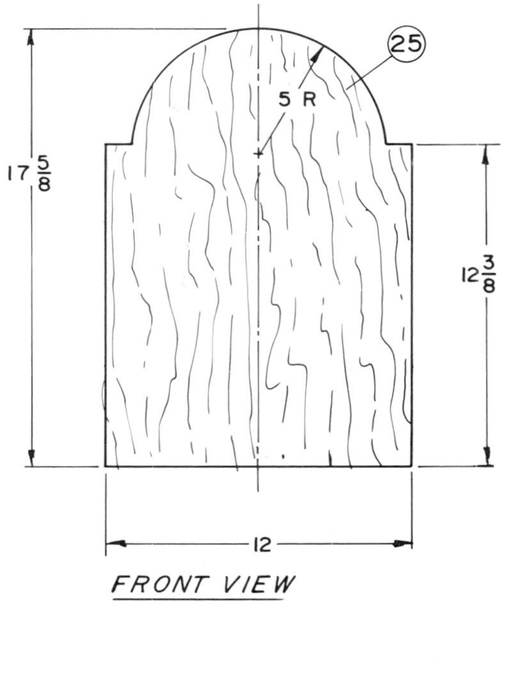

25
5 R
17 5/8
12 3/8
12
FRONT VIEW

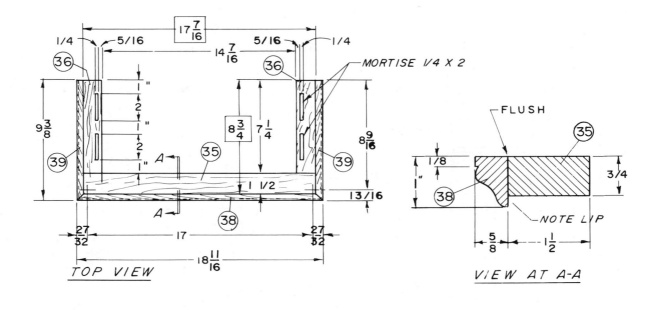

TOP VIEW

MORTISE 1/4 X 2

FLUSH

NOTE LIP

VIEW AT A-A

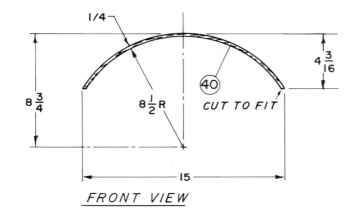

FRONT VIEW

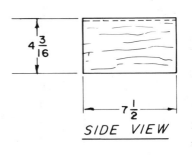

SIDE VIEW

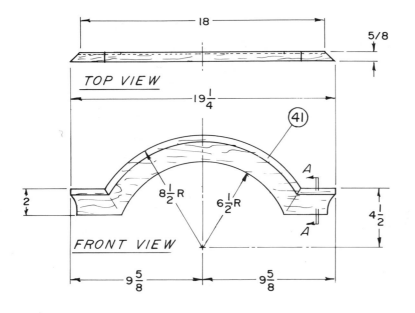

TOP VIEW

FRONT VIEW

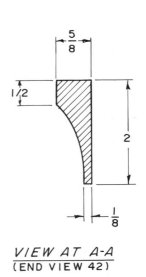

VIEW AT A-A
(END VIEW 42)

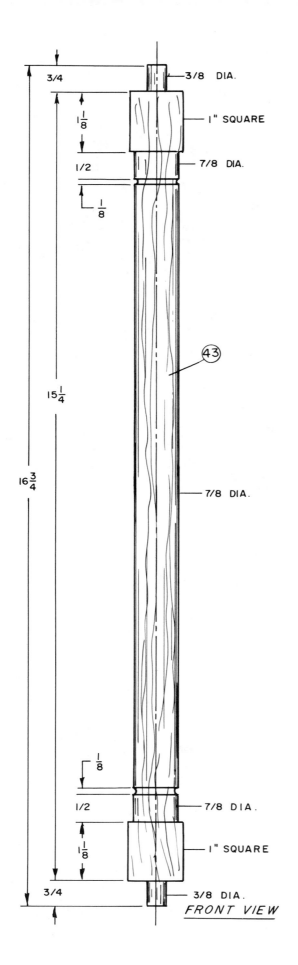

3/4

3/8 DIA.

1⅛

1" SQUARE

1/2

7/8 DIA.

⅛

43

15¼

7/8 DIA.

16¾

⅛

1/2

7/8 DIA.

1⅛

1" SQUARE

3/4

3/8 DIA.

FRONT VIEW

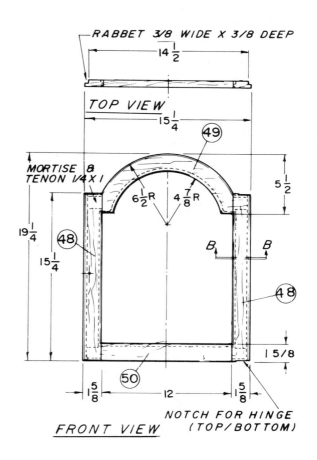

RABBET 3/8 WIDE X 3/8 DEEP

14½

TOP VIEW

15¼

49

MORTISE 8
TENON 1/4 X 1

5½

6½ R   4⅞ R

19¼

48

15¼

B   B

48

1 5/8

48

50

1 5/8   12   1 5/8

FRONT VIEW

NOTCH FOR HINGE
(TOP/BOTTOM)

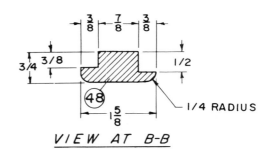

3/8   7/8   3/8

3/4 3/8   1/2

48   1/4 RADIUS

1 5/8

VIEW AT B-B

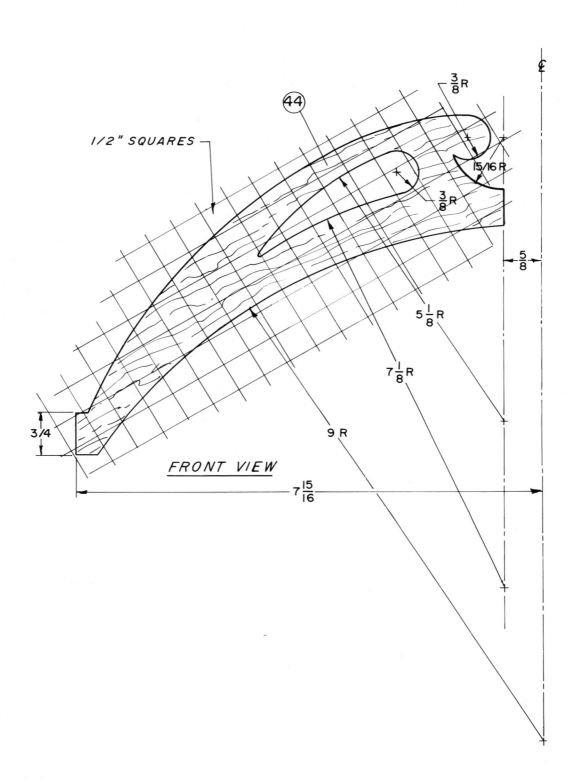

1/2" SQUARES

44

3/8 R

3/8 R

15/16 R

5/8

5 1/8 R

7 1/8 R

9 R

3/4

FRONT VIEW

7 15/16

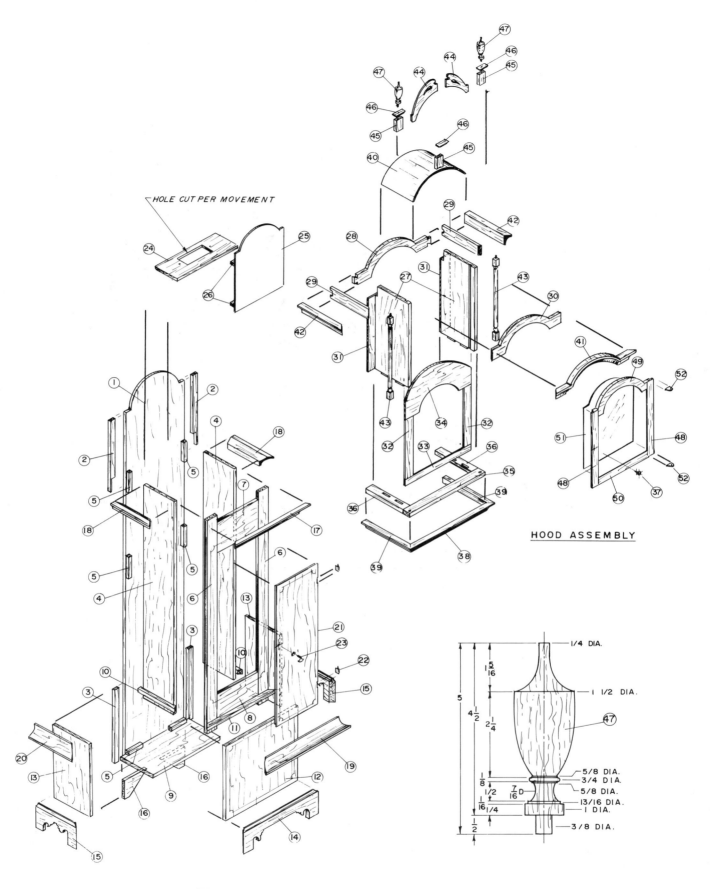

HOLE CUT PER MOVEMENT

HOOD ASSEMBLY

CASE ASSEMBLY

1/4 DIA.

1 1/2 DIA.

5/8 DIA.
3/4 DIA.
5/8 DIA.
13/16 DIA.
1 DIA.
3/8 DIA.

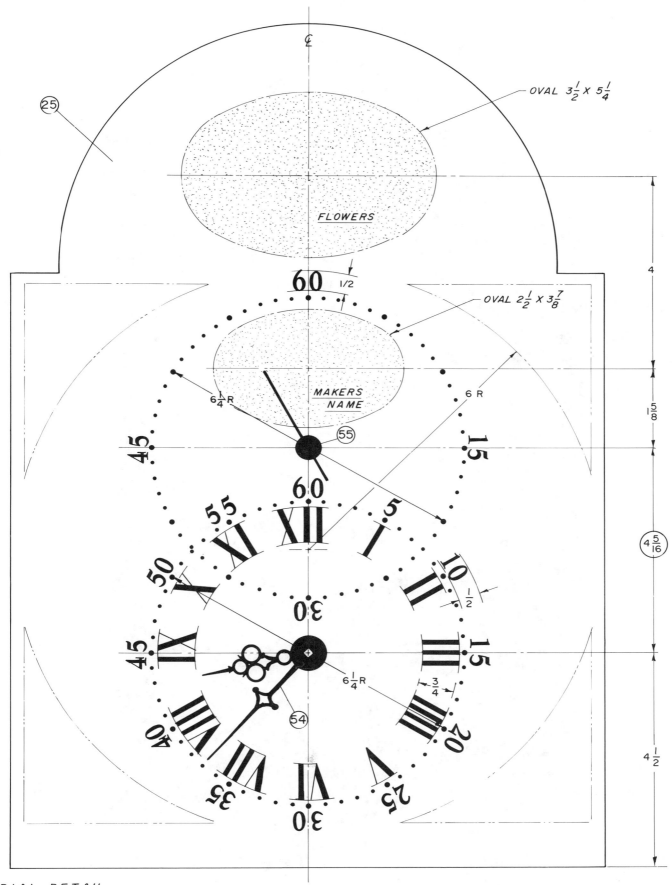

DIAL DETAIL

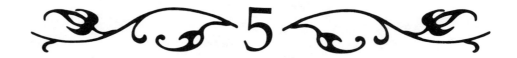

Pillar and Scroll

THE BEAUTIFUL PILLAR AND SCROLL IS AMERICA'S FIRST MASS-PRODUCED CLOCK. Most of the original pillar and scroll clocks used 30-hour wooden, weight-driven, key-wound movements to power them. A very few had 8-day wooden movements (Fig. 5-1).

From 1814 to 1822 the original pillar and scroll varied slightly in design and movements. There were five slightly different wooden movements used during that time (Fig. 5-2).

This particular model was made about 1820 by Eli Terry and Sons of Plymouth, Connecticut. It has a 30-hour, wooden, weight-driven movement, so it is one of the original designs. This clock also has an original paper that gives running instructions and the maker's name and address.

For years, many other clock companies copied the pillar and scroll clock design. In fact, they are still copied and made today.

The depth of this clock as dimensioned is the exact size of the original. It is a little narrow for most replacement movements available today, so check the movement depth before starting and thicken the depth of the case if necessary. You may consider either a quartz movement with a pendulum or an original wooden geared movement purchased from a clock repair shop. Most wooden gear movements are only 30-hour movements and must be wound each day. However, by installing a wooden movement, you will be making a conversation piece as well as a timepiece. Also, by using either the original wooden geared or quartz movement you will be able to retain the original depth as dimensioned.

If you do not have a lathe, columns can be purchased from Mason and Sullivan or from S. LaRose Inc. (see Appendix B). Premade columns will have to be reworked slightly to match the original column. Reversed paintings, close to the original, can also be purchased from LaRose.

Eli Terry

Eli Terry is referred to as the Father of American clock manufacturing. He was born in 1772, in South Windsor, Connecticut just before the Revolutionary War.

Fig. 5-1. Opposite: Pillar and scroll clock, circa 1822.

Fig. 5-2. View with door open and dial removed, showing the wood movement and original paper.

He received only a little formal education before becoming a clock apprentice at the age of 14. In time, he set himself up in the clockmaking business, making clocks on special order. Because of his high-quality workmanship, he was able to sell everything he made.

During his 60 years of clockmaking he completely transformed the industry. Although he developed and made many tall-case clocks, his most famous clock was the pillar and scroll clock, which he developed in 1812. In 1807 he started work on the standardization of clock parts and the use of waterpower to drive the machinery at his Watertown, Connecticut factory. He actually was one of the first people to develop mass production.

At his factory he hired people such as Seth Thomas, Silas Hoadley, and Chauncey Jerome, who later became very famous clockmakers themselves. He also taught his two sons, Eli Jr. and Henry the art of making clocks.

In 1818 Eli Terry sold Seth Thomas permission or rights to make and sell the pillar and scroll model clock for 50 cents each. In 1822 Seth Thomas paid Eli Terry $1,000 for all rights to use the design.

Instructions / Pillar and Scroll Clock

Study all drawings before starting. Be sure to buy the movement for this clock *before* starting because the original used a thin wooden gear movement and most new, brass, replacement movements are too thick for the thin case. If you use a quartz movement, there should be no problem with thickness of the case. You may have to adjust the thickness of the case slightly if you use a brass movement.

When making a pillar and scroll, keep in mind that this clock is very elegant and formal. Try to make all parts so that they have a thin, graceful appearance. You might want to keep the parts slightly thinner than the given dimensions.

STEP 1.
Cut all parts to overall size and sand all over.

STEP 2.
Carefully lay out and cut each piece as shown. Parts 22, 12, and 16 should be shaved from the *rear* at a slight angle to give the appearance of a thin graceful skirt and goose neck. A rasp works nicely for this.

STEP 3.
Carefully locate and cut the dadoes in parts 2 and 3 as shown. This is the key step in assembling the case.

STEP 4.
If you do not have a lathe, commercial, ready-made columns (part 10) very close to the dimensions can be purchased (see note at bottom of Parts List). They will have to be reworked slightly. A better option would be to have a custom turner make up columns (see address of River Bend Turnings in Appendix B).

STEP 5.
The clock case should go together like a simple box—keep everything square as you assemble the case.

STEP 6.
Make and add the door using the special hinges (part 31), again keeping everything square. Add a spline at the four corners, as shown, for strength.

STEP 7.
The skirts, parts 11 and 12, along with the top trim, parts 16 and 21 are held in place and supported by the braces, parts 13, 14, 15 and 33 (Fig. 5-3).

STEP 8.
Commercial dials, very close to the original can be purchased. The dial is held in place by part 9.

Finishing
See Section III for finishing the clock case.

Fig. 5-3. Back view of top section of case showing glue blocks in place.

No.	Name	Size	Req'd.
1	Side	3/4 × 3 7/8 — 21 5/16 Long	2
2	Top	7/16 × 4 1/4 — 16 1/2 Long	1
3	Bottom	3/4 × 4 5/8 — 17 1/4 Long	1
4	Dial Support	1/4 × 2 1/2 — 21 1/4 Long	2
5	Ear	1/4 × 1 1/2 — 22 Long	2
6	Back-Bottom	1/4 × 10 7/8 — 13 1/4 Long	1
7	Back-Center	1/4 × 6 7/8 — 13 1/4 Long	1
8	Back-Top	1/4 × 3 1/16 — 13 1/4 Long	1
9	Dial Top/Bottom	1/4 × 1/4 — 12 1/2 Long	2
**10	Column	1 × 1 — 21 9/16 Long	2
11	Front Skirt	7/16 × 2 1/2 — 17 1/8 Long	1
12	Side Skirt	7/16 × 2 1/2 — 4 1/2 Long	2
13	Brace-Large	3/4 × 3/4 — 2 Long	7
14	Brace-Center	5/8 × 5/8 — 2 Long	4
15	Brace-Small	1/2 × 1/2 — 2 Long	2
16	Goose Neck	3/8 × 4 3/8 — 7 1/16 Long	2
17	Center Post	15/16 × 1 — 2 29/32 Long	1
18	Face-White Wood	1/16 × 1 — 2 29/32 Long	1
19	End Post	15/16 × 1 — 1 1/8 Long	2
20	Face-White Wood	1/16 × 1 — 1 1/8 Long	2
21	Side Trim	1/4 × 1 1/8 — 3 3/8 Long	2
22	Cap	3/32 × 1 3/16 — 1 3/16 Long	3
*23	Dial	1/4 × 11 3/4 — 12 1/2 Long	1
24	Door Stile	11/16 × 1 3/16 — 20 3/4 Long	2
25	Door Rail	11/16 × 1 3/16 — 13 1/4 Long	2
26	Center Rail	11/16 × 11/16 — 11 3/8 Long	1
27	Top Glass	3/32 × 11 1/4 — 11 1/4 Long	1
28	Bottom Glass	LaRose 126-8036	1
29	Escutcheon	1/16 × 1/2 — 1 3/8 Long	1
30	Door Lock w/Key	LaRose 089001	1
31	Door Hinge	LaRose 125-8700	2
32	Finial Brass	LaRose 117-8206	3
33	Center Post Block	5/8 × 5/8 — 1" Long	1
34	Screw-Rd. Hd.	No. 4 — 1/2 Long	4
35	Movement	See Below	1
36	Hands	LaRose FL-9-8150	1 pr.
37	Paper	T.E.C. Terry No. 1	1

*Purchased Dial: LaRose 126-8037

**Purchased column: LaRose 126-8042 (must be reworked)

Movement: Brass, S.C.S. No. IM-22/4
        Quartz, LaRose 812073

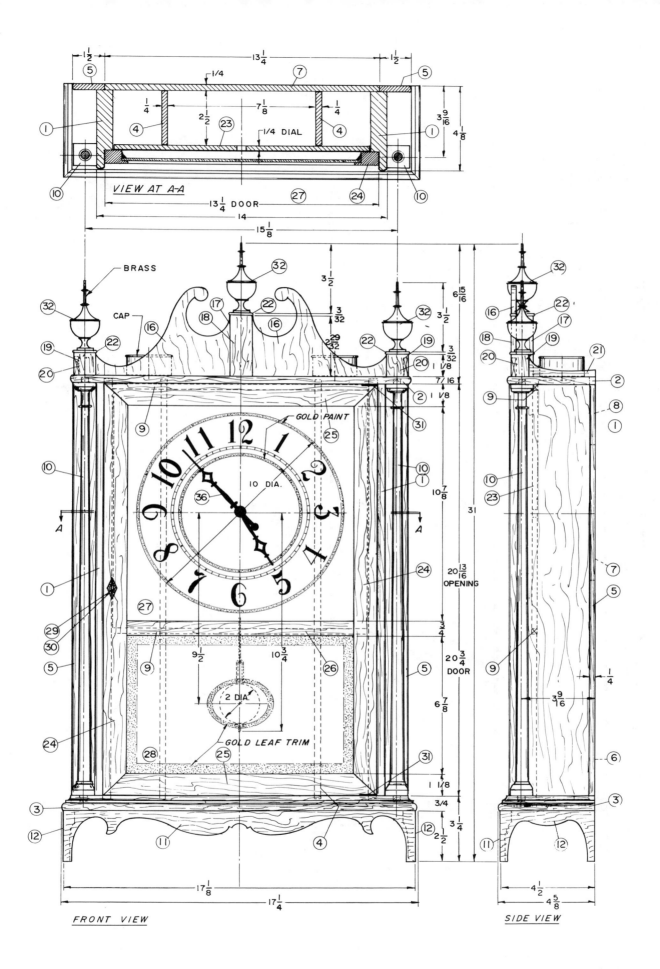

VIEW AT A-A

FRONT VIEW

SIDE VIEW

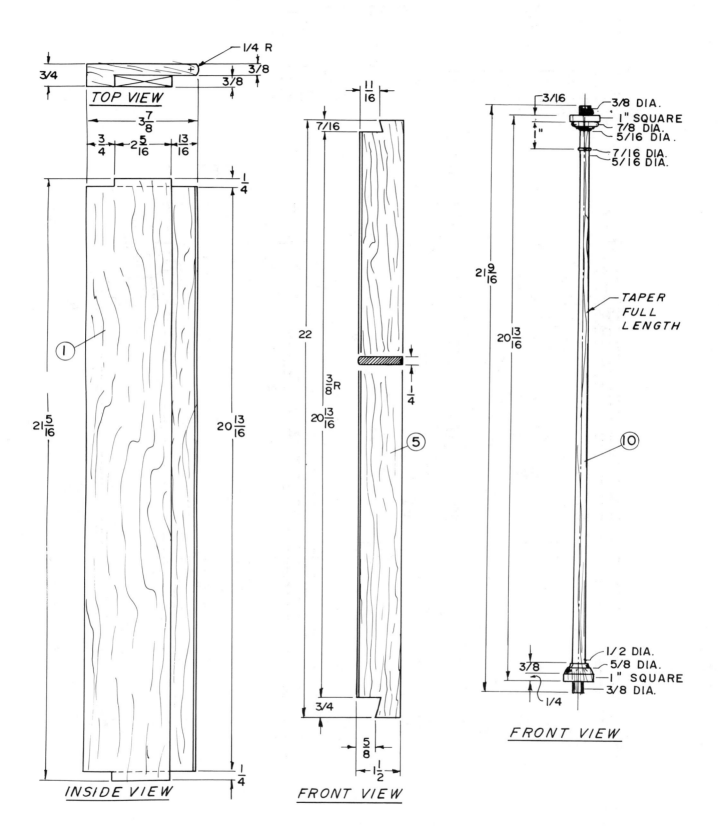

1/4 R

3/4

3/8
3/8

TOP VIEW

3 7/8

3/4 2 5/16 13/16

1/4

①

21 5/16

20 13/16

1/4

INSIDE VIEW

11/16

7/16

22

3/8 R

20 13/16

1/4

⑤

3/4

5/8
1 1/2

FRONT VIEW

3/16 3/8 DIA.
1" SQUARE
1" 7/8 DIA.
5/16 DIA.
7/16 DIA.
5/16 DIA.

21 9/16

20 13/16

TAPER FULL LENGTH

⑩

1/2 DIA.
5/8 DIA.
1" SQUARE
3/8 DIA.

3/8

1/4

FRONT VIEW

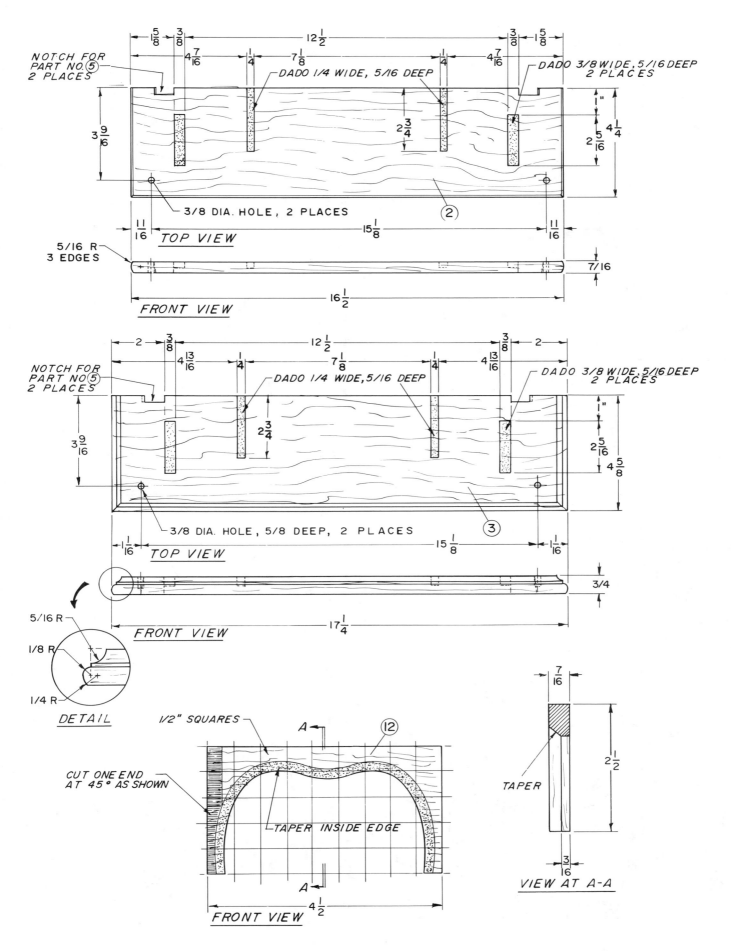

NOTCH FOR PART NO.⑤ 2 PLACES

DADO 1/4 WIDE, 5/16 DEEP

DADO 3/8 WIDE, 5/16 DEEP 2 PLACES

3/8 DIA. HOLE, 2 PLACES

TOP VIEW

5/16 R 3 EDGES

FRONT VIEW

②

NOTCH FOR PART NO ⑤ 2 PLACES

DADO 1/4 WIDE, 5/16 DEEP

DADO 3/8 WIDE, 5/16 DEEP 2 PLACES

3/8 DIA. HOLE, 5/8 DEEP, 2 PLACES

TOP VIEW

③

5/16 R
1/8 R
1/4 R

DETAIL

FRONT VIEW

1/2" SQUARES

CUT ONE END AT 45° AS SHOWN

TAPER INSIDE EDGE

A — A

⑫

FRONT VIEW

TAPER

VIEW AT A-A

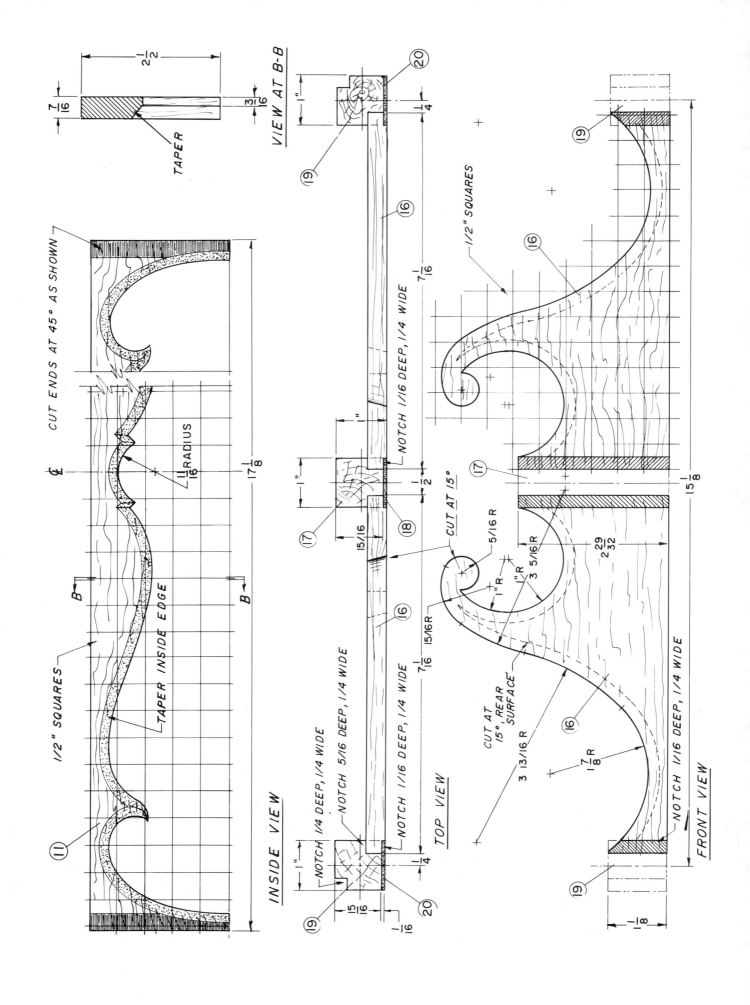

CUT ENDS AT 45° AS SHOWN

1/2" SQUARES

TAPER INSIDE EDGE

11/16 RADIUS

17 1/8

B

B

INSIDE VIEW

TAPER

2 1/2

7/16

3/16

VIEW AT B-B

1"

1/4

7 1/16

NOTCH 1/16 DEEP, 1/4 WIDE

1"

15/16

1"

1/2

NOTCH 1/4 DEEP, 1/4 WIDE

NOTCH 5/16 DEEP, 1/4 WIDE

15/16

1/16

NOTCH 1/16 DEEP, 1/4 WIDE

7 1/16

CUT AT 15°

5/16 R

1" R

3 5/16 R

15/16 R

CUT AT 15°, REAR SURFACE

3 13/16 R

1 7/8 R

NOTCH 1/16 DEEP, 1/4 WIDE

TOP VIEW

1/2" SQUARES

15 1/8

2 29/32

NOTCH 1/16 DEEP, 1/4 WIDE

1 8

FRONT VIEW

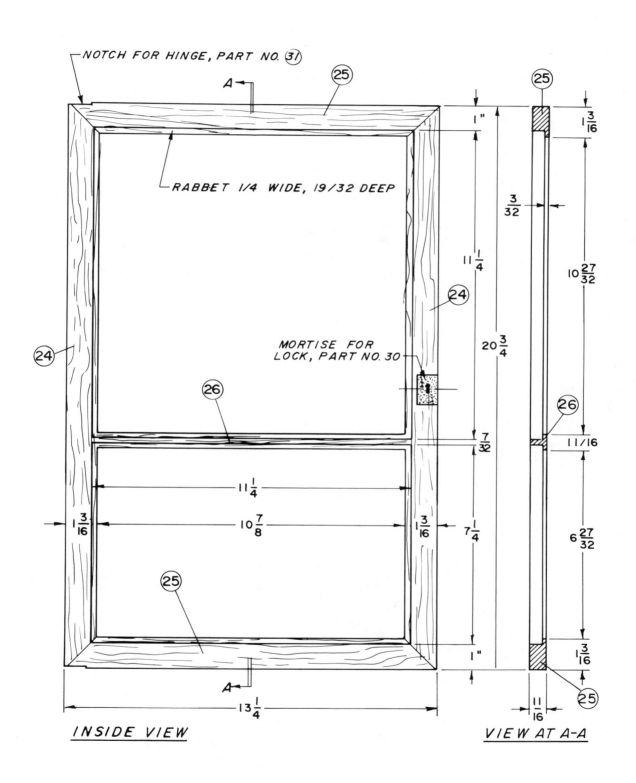

NOTCH FOR HINGE, PART NO. (31)

A

(25)

(25)

RABBET 1/4 WIDE, 19/32 DEEP

$1''$

$\frac{3}{16}$

$\frac{3}{32}$

$11\frac{1}{4}$

(24)

$10\frac{27}{32}$

MORTISE FOR
LOCK, PART NO. 30

$20\frac{3}{4}$

(24)

(26)

(26)

$\frac{7}{32}$

$11/16$

$11\frac{1}{4}$

$1\frac{3}{16}$

$10\frac{7}{8}$

$1\frac{3}{16}$

$7\frac{1}{4}$

$6\frac{27}{32}$

(25)

$1''$

$1\frac{3}{16}$

A

(25)

$13\frac{1}{4}$

$\frac{11}{16}$

INSIDE VIEW

VIEW AT A-A

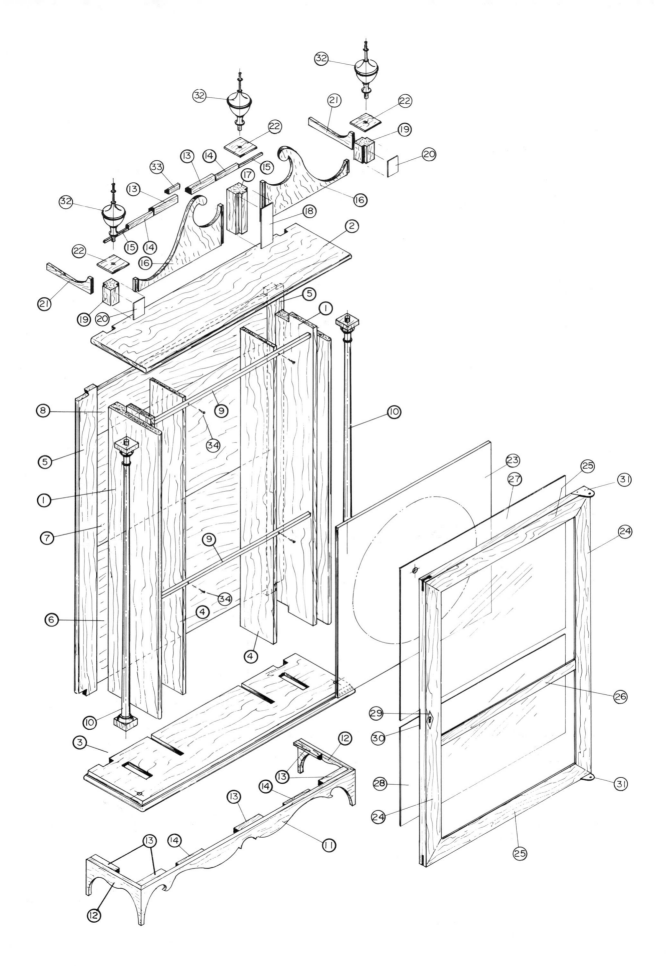

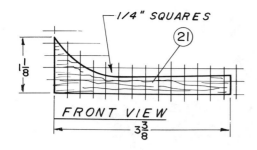

1/4" SQUARES

(21)

1⅛

FRONT VIEW

3⅜

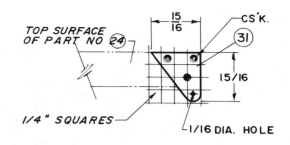

15/16

TOP SURFACE
OF PART NO (24)

CS'K.

(31)

15/16

1/4" SQUARES

1/16 DIA. HOLE

Column and Splat

IN ORDER TO COMPETE WITH THE PILLAR AND SCROLL CLOCK, IN 1828 GEORGE Mitchell hired a cabinetmaker by the name of Elias Ingraham to develop a competitive clock case design. Within a year Elias created a new clock design with columns, lion-paw feet, a reversed painting on the door and a patriotic eagle splat top (Fig. 6-1). It was called a "patent mantel clock." The term "splat" refers to the decorator piece at the top of the clock case.

In its day, other clockmakers such as Jerome, Darron and Mash took off on the design and made their own copies of it. Some added a looking glass in the door in place of the reverse painting. Even Eli Terry developed a model of his own that he called the "transitional model." His version had some pillar and scroll characteristics.

At least 19 clockmakers produced the column and splat and in time the pillar and scroll model was replaced by this new model which was very popular from 1829 to 1845 (Fig. 6-2).

Daniel Pratt Jr.

The model shown in this chapter was made by Daniel Pratt Jr. of Reading, Massachusetts. It was made in 1840 and has a 30-hour wooden, weight-driven, key-wound movement, and a painted wooden dial face. Daniel was associated with many clockmakers of the day.

This particular model had a looking glass in place of the reversed painting.

Instructions / Column and Splat

Study all drawings before starting. As always, purchase the movement *before* starting this clock because many originals of this model had a thin wooden geared movement—most new, brass replacement movements are too thick for the thin case. If you use a quartz movement, you should have no problem with thickness of the case. You may have to adjust the thickness of the case slightly if you use a brass movement. Adjust all parts accordingly. Try to make all parts to

Fig. 6-1. Opposite: Column and splat clock, circa 1840.

Fig. 6-2. Original Daniel Pratt Jr. paper.

have a thin, graceful appearance. You might want to make the parts slightly thinner than the given dimensions.

STEP 1.
Cut all parts to overall size and sand all over. Lay out and cut to shape each piece as shown.

STEP 2.
Carefully locate and cut the mortises in parts 4 and 5 for the sides (part 1) as shown. This is the key step for assembling the case. Cut the tenons on each end of the sides to fit the mortises in parts 4 and 5.

STEP 3.
If you do not have a lathe, have a custom turner make up columns (refer to Appendix B for address of River Bend Turnings). Remember, these turnings are *split* turnings—that is, they are only *half* round.

STEP 4.
The clock case goes together like a simple box, keep everything square as you assemble the case. Make and add the door using the special hinges, part 20. Add a spline at the four corners as shown for strength.

STEP 5.

The top trim (parts 11 and 12) are held in place and supported by the braces (parts 13 and 14).

STEP 6.

Commercial dials very close to the original can be purchased. The dial is held in place by part 16.

Finishing

See Section III for finishing the clock case. Add a clock paper to make your clock look like the original.

PARTS LIST

No.	Name	Size	Req'd.
1	Side	¾ × 3⅞ — 27 Long	2
2	Front	¾ × 1⁹⁄₁₆ — 26½ Long	2
3	Back	¼ × 15¼ — 26½ Long	1
4	Bottom	1″ × 4⅞ — 16¼ Long	1
5	Top	½ × 4⅞ — 16¼ Long	1
6	Bottom Trim	¾ × 1⁹⁄₁₆ — 1¾ Long	2
7	Column (Split)	1⅜ Dia. × 24½ Long	1
8	Top Trim	¾ × 1⁹⁄₁₆ — 1¼ Long	2
9	Door Trim	⁷⁄₁₆ × 1 — 26½ Long	2
10	Trim Top Block	⅞ × 2 — 2⅛ Long	2
11	Splat	⅜ × 3½ — 12½ Long	1
12	Side Splat	⅜ × 1¹⁵⁄₁₆ — 3⅞ Long	2
13	Large Glue Block	¾ × ¾ — 1″ Long	2
14	Small Glue Block	½ × ½ — 1¾ Long	2
15	Top Molding	⅜ × 1¼ — 2¾ Long	2
16	Dial Support	½ × ½ — 12⅞ Long	1
17	Door Side	¾ × 1¼ — 26½ Long	2
18	Door Top/Bottom	¾ × 1¼ — 12 Long	2
19	Door Rail	¾ × 1 — 12 Long	1
20	Hinge (Steel)	¹⁄₃₂ × 1⅛ — 1⅛ Long	2
21	Door Lock	Merritt P-183	1
22	Glass	³⁄₃₂ × 10 Square	1
23	Mirror	10 × 14	1
24	Dial Face (9″ Size)	LaRose 126-8037	1
25	Movement	See Below	1
26	Hands 4½″ Size	LaRose FL9-8150	1 pr.
27	Paper (Optional)	T.E.C. Gilbert No. 1	1
28	Pulley Wood	Merritt P-555	2

Movement: Brass: LaRose No. 084053
　　　　　Quartz: Klockit No. 12115-A w/Hands 66967-A

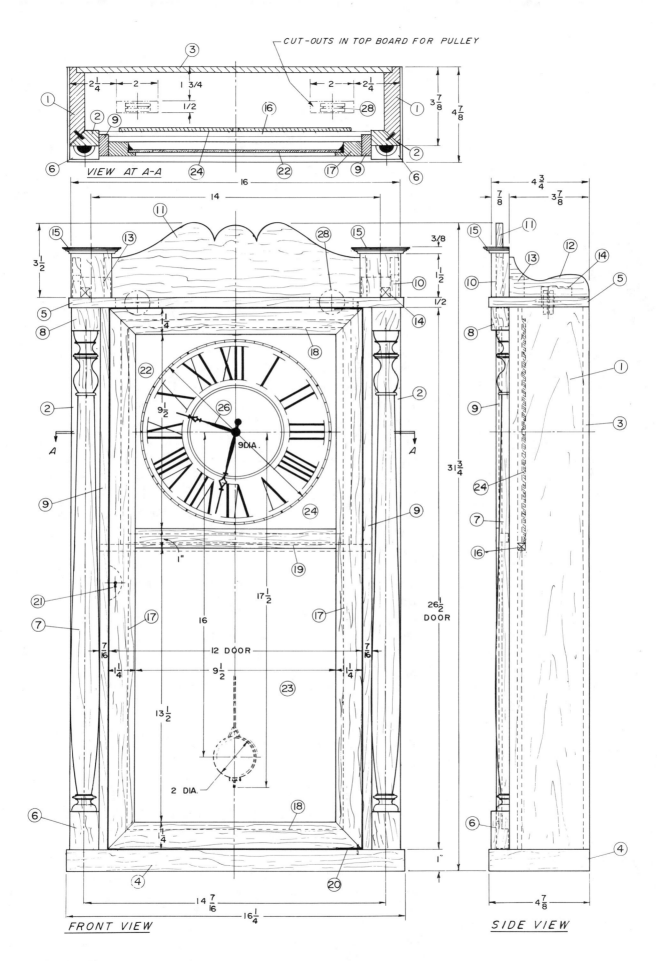

CUT-OUTS IN TOP BOARD FOR PULLEY

VIEW AT A-A

FRONT VIEW

SIDE VIEW

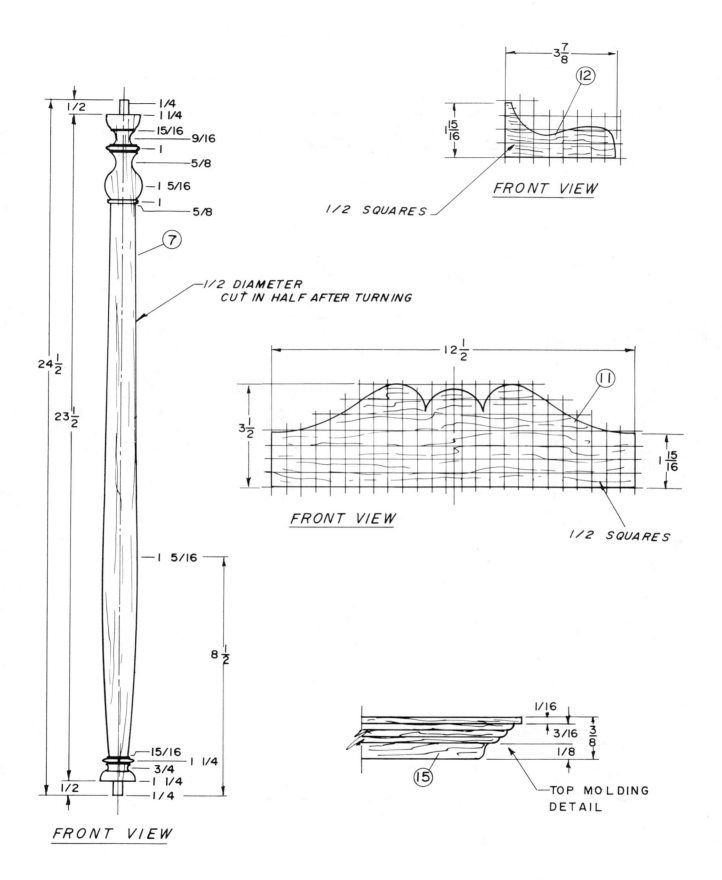

3 7/8

12

1 15/16

FRONT VIEW

1/2 SQUARES

1/4
1 1/4
15/16   9/16
1
5/8
1 5/16
1
5/8

7

1/2 DIAMETER
CUT IN HALF AFTER TURNING

12 1/2

11

3 1/2

1 15/16

FRONT VIEW

1/2 SQUARES

24 1/2

23 1/2

1 5/16

8 1/2

1/16
3/16   3/8
1/8

15

TOP MOLDING
DETAIL

15/16   1 1/4
3/4
1 1/4
1/2
1/4

FRONT VIEW

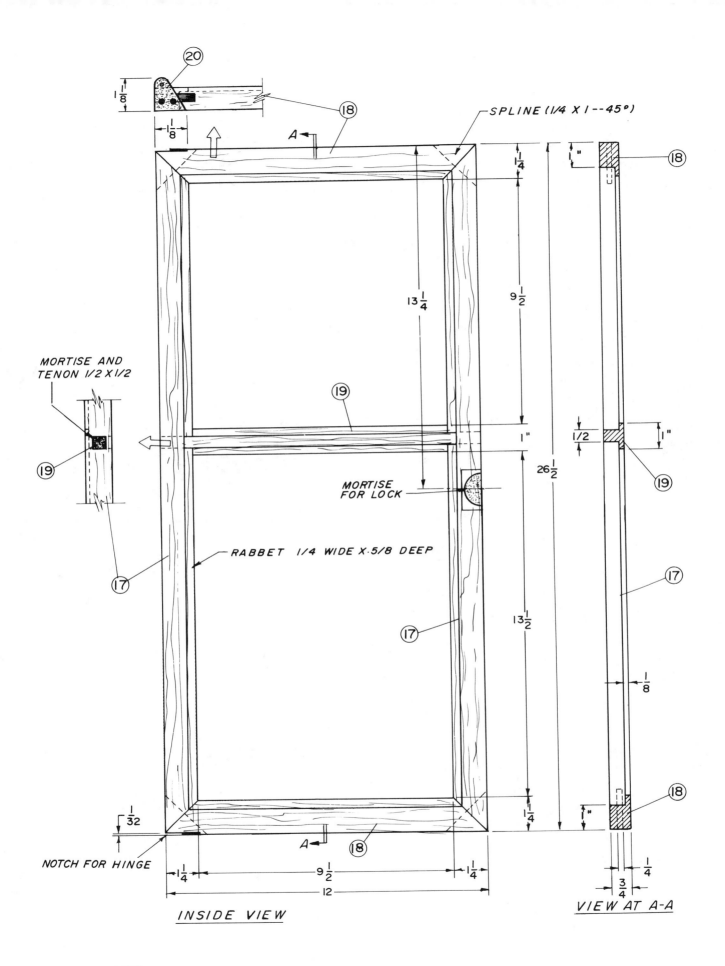

MORTISE AND
TENON 1/2 X 1/2

SPLINE (1/4 X 1--45°)

13¼

9½

1"

26½

13½

MORTISE
FOR LOCK

RABBET 1/4 WIDE X·5/8 DEEP

NOTCH FOR HINGE

1¼ 9½ 1¼

12

INSIDE VIEW

1"

½

1"

⅛

¾ ¼

VIEW AT A-A

1⅛

⅛

1/32

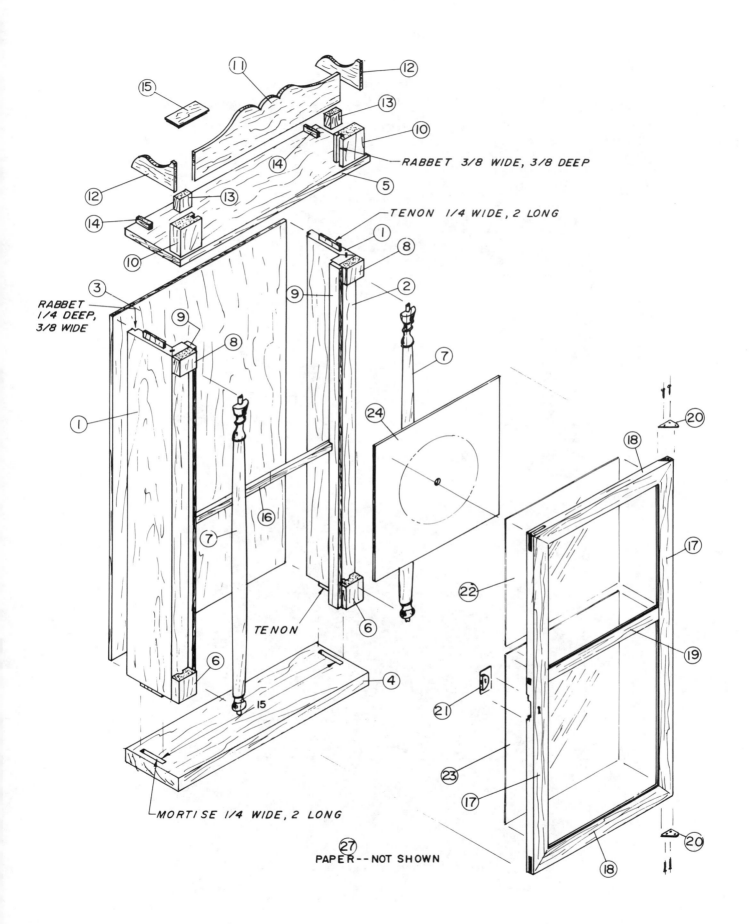

15

11

12

13

10

RABBET 3/8 WIDE, 3/8 DEEP

14

5

TENON 1/4 WIDE, 2 LONG

1

8

2

12

13

9

14

7

10

24

3

RABBET
1/4 DEEP,
3/8 WIDE

9

8

11

20

18

1

8

17

16

22

7

19

21

6

TENON

6

23

17

4

6

15

18

20

MORTISE 1/4 WIDE, 2 LONG

27
PAPER -- NOT SHOWN

18

7

Column Clock

A POPULAR CLOCK DURING THE VICTORIAN PERIOD WAS THE COLUMN CLOCK, (Fig. 7-1), sometimes referred to as the "gilt column clock" because of its gold gilded columns. Note the classical influence and empire base. Column clocks were made in Connecticut, New York, and Massachusetts, as early as 1824 and as late as 1885. They reflect the styles of furniture popular around 1850. Some of the column clocks were made with two or even three doors with both a looking glass *and* reversed painting.

Most early column clocks were more expensive than other shelf clocks of the day because some of them had the somewhat new, 8-day, brass, spring-driven movement. Herman Clark, who developed the first mass-produced, spring-driven movements, used this style of clock to house most of his first movements.

These clocks usually had tin, white-painted dial faces, and some had open dial faces so the brass movement could be seen. This also allowed the oiling of the verge and escapement wheel (Fig. 7-2).

Seth Thomas

This model was produced by Seth Thomas, in Plymouth Hollow, Connecticut, around 1850. It had a paper label glued inside on the backboard printed by steam presses. It uses the older, 8-day, weight-driven, brass movement. This model cost $12 when new—a lot of money in those days.

Instructions / Column Clock

Study all drawings before starting. Be sure to purchase the movement *before* starting this clock because many originals of this model had a thin wooden geared movement—most new, brass, replacement movements are too thick for the thin case. If you use a quartz movement, you should have no problem with thickness of the case. The thickness of the case may have to be adjusted slightly if you use a brass movement. Adjust all part sizes accordingly. Try to shape all parts so that they have a thin, graceful appearance. You might want to keep the parts slightly thinner than the given dimensions.

Fig. 7-1. Opposite: Column clock, circa 1850.

Fig. 7-2. Eight-day, weight-driven brass movement. Note also the original paper.

STEP 1.

Cut all parts to overall size and sand all over. Lay out and cut to shape each piece as shown.

STEP 2.

Carefully locate and cut the mortises in parts 1 and 2 for the sides (part 3) as shown. This is the key step for assembling the case. Cut the rabbets in the ends of the sides to fit the mortises in parts 1 and 2.

STEP 3.

If you do not have a lathe, have a custom turner make up a column (part 18). See Appendix B for the address of River Bend Turnings. Remember, these turnings are *split* (half round) turnings. You should prime these turnings two or three times with a light sanding between coats to get an extra-smooth surface. Apply two or more coats of bright gold gild paint to the columns *before* assembling the clock.

STEP 4.

The clock case goes together like a simple box. Keep everything square as you assemble the case. Make and add the door using the hinges (part 21).

STEP 5.
Commercial dials, very close to the original, can be purchased. The dial is held in place by part 16.

STEP 6.
See Section III for finishing the clock case.

STEP 7.
Add a clock paper to make your clock look like the original.

PARTS LIST

No.	Name	Size	Req'd.
1	Bottom Board	7/8 × 4 3/8 — 14 3/4 Long	1
2	Top Board	3/4 × 4 3/8 — 15 1/8 Long	1
3	Side	5/8 × 3 — 23 7/8 Long	2
4	Back	3/8 × 6 11/16 — 23 7/8 Long	2
5	Front	3/8 × 1 3/16 — 23 3/16 Long	2
6	Base Bottom	3/4 × 1 7/8 — 3 1/2 Long	2
7	Glue Block	1/4 × 1 — 3 1/2 Long	2
8	Face-Bottom	3/4 × 3 1/2 — 10 3/8 Long	1
9	Column Support	3/8 × 1 — 2 3/16 Long	4
10	Filler	3/8 × 11/16 — 9 5/8 Long	2
11	Trim-Front	3/8 × 1/2 14 3/8 Long	1
12	Trim-Side	3/8 × 1/2 — 4 1/8 Long	2
13	Base-Top	3/4 × 1 7/8 — 2 7/16 Long	2
14	Glue Block	1/4 × 1 — 2 7/16 Long	2
15	Face-Top	5/8 × 2 7/16 — 10 3/8 Long	1
16	Door Trim	3/8 × 3/4 — 16 1/8 Long	2
17	Door Stop	1/4 × 1/2 — 1 Long	2
18	Column (Split)	1 1/2 Dia. — 16 1/8 Long	1
19	Dial Support	3/8 × 2 1/4 — 14 1/2 Long	2
20	Dial	8 3/8 Square	1
21	Hinge Brass	3/4 × 3/4 Long	2
22	Door Stile	1/2 × 7/8 — 16 1/16 Long	2
23	Door Rail	1/2 × 7/8 — 9 5/8 Long	2
24	Door Rail Ctr.	1/2 × 3/4 — 8 7/8 Long	1
25	Door Glass Top	3/32 × 8 1/8 — 8 1/4 Long	1
26	Door Glass-Bottom	3/32 × 6 1/8 — 8 1/4 Long	1
27	Decal (Lower)	Shipley T.A.-23	1
28	Glass Insert	1/16 × 3/16 — 80 Long	1
29	Knob w/Latch	Merritt P-72	1
30	Movement	See Below	1
31	Hands (O.G. Style)	Merritt P-276	1 pr.

Movement: Brass, LaRose No. 084052
　　　　　Quartz, Merritt No. P-160
Paper: (*Optional*) T.E.C. No. S.T.7

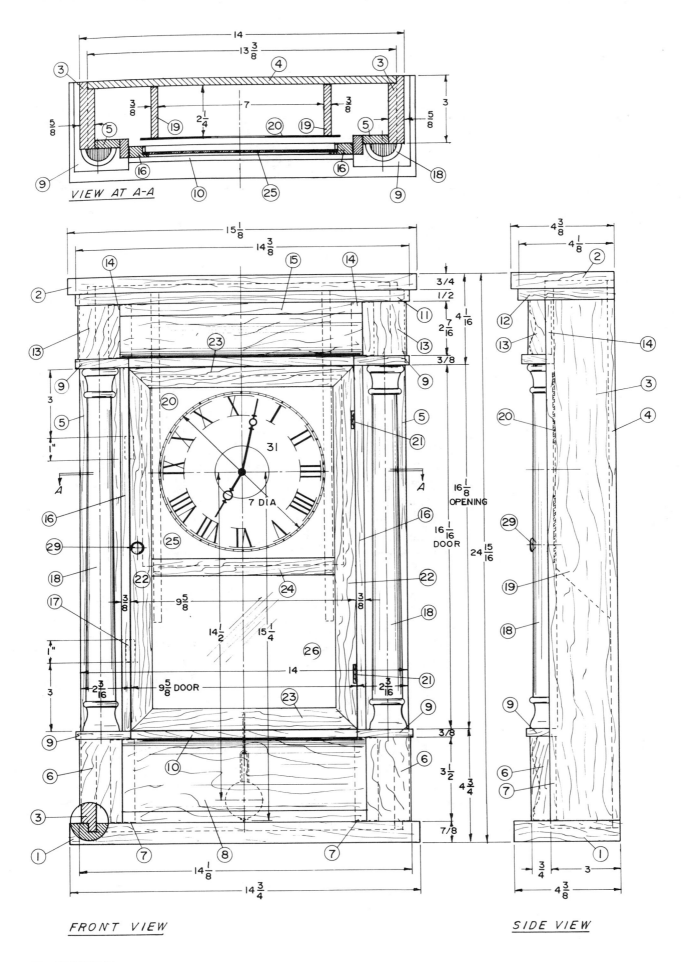

VIEW AT A-A

FRONT VIEW

SIDE VIEW

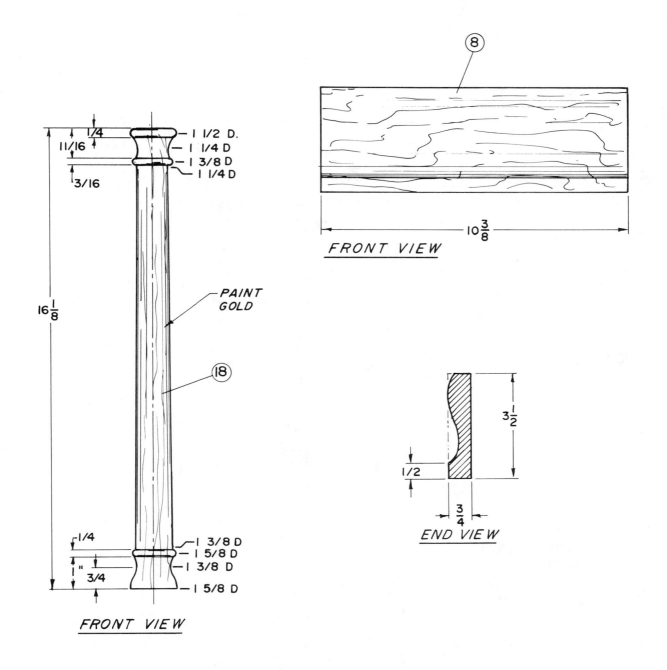

⑧

FRONT VIEW

$10\frac{3}{8}$

$\frac{1}{4}$
$1\frac{1}{2}$ D.
$11/16$
$1\frac{1}{4}$ D
$1\frac{3}{8}$ D
$3/16$
$1\frac{1}{4}$ D

PAINT
GOLD

⑱

$16\frac{1}{8}$

$1/4$
$1\frac{3}{8}$ D
$1\frac{5}{8}$ D
$1\frac{3}{8}$ D
"
$3/4$
$1\frac{5}{8}$ D

FRONT VIEW

$3\frac{1}{2}$

$1/2$

$\frac{3}{4}$

END VIEW

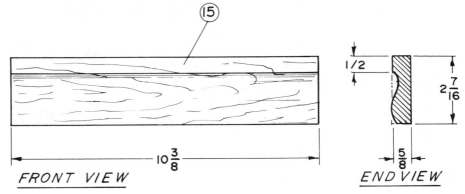

⑮

FRONT VIEW

$10\frac{3}{8}$

$1/2$

$2\frac{7}{16}$

$\frac{5}{8}$

END VIEW

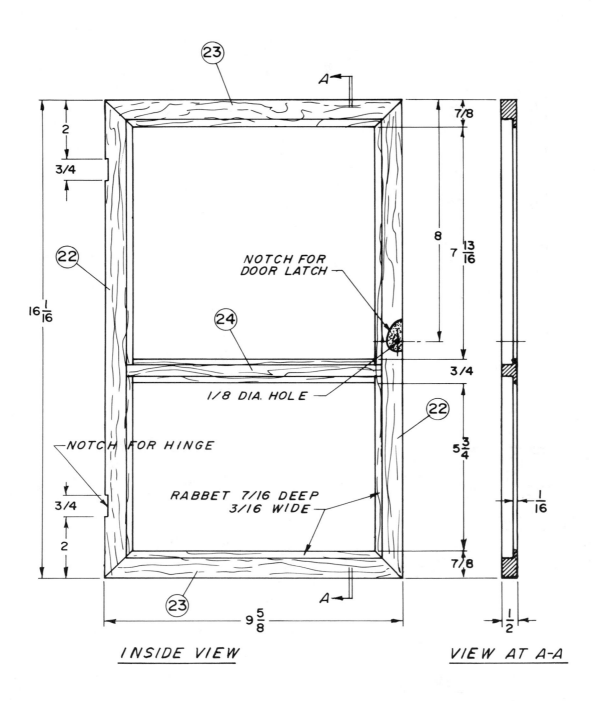

NOTCH FOR
DOOR LATCH

1/8 DIA. HOLE

NOTCH FOR HINGE

RABBET 7/16 DEEP
3/16 WIDE

2

3/4

16 1/16

3/4

2

9 5/8

7/8

8   7 13/16

3/4

5 3/4

7/8

1/16

1/2

INSIDE VIEW

VIEW AT A-A

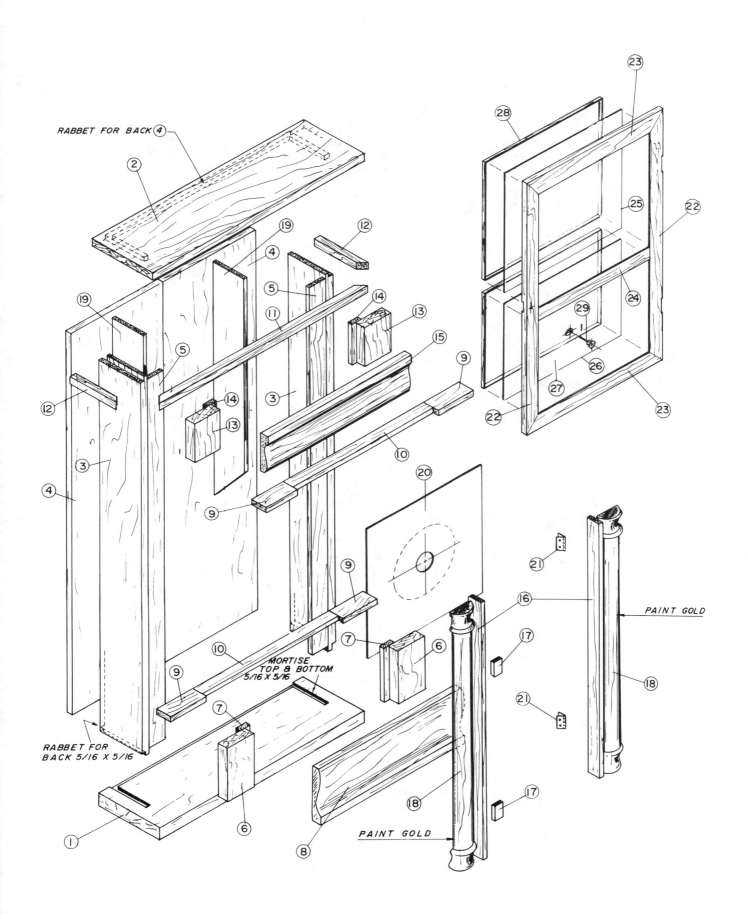

RABBET FOR BACK (4)

MORTISE TOP & BOTTOM 5/16 X 5/16

RABBET FOR BACK 5/16 X 5/16

PAINT GOLD

PAINT GOLD

Ogee Clock

MANY CLOCK COLLECTIONS GOT STARTED WITH A SIMPLE OGEE (FIG. 8-1). There is just something about this clock that everyone likes. I once went to an auction and watched one person buy five of them; he wasn't a collector or dealer—he simply liked them! It has a simple weight-driven brass works that just about anyone can take apart and repair. Its name is derived from the simple curved molding used in its construction. This simple, reversed-curved, S-shaped molding is referred to as an Ogee molding—hence, the clock's name. This clock is a very simple rectangular, box-like clock with a door, nothing fancy or false. It is among the most versatile of clock cases.

Very early models had wooden geared movements but most had a simple 30-hour, weight-driven brass movement (Fig. 8-2). In addition, some ogee clocks had a mirror in the door, as this one does. Others had reversed paintings on the door in place of the mirror. They came in all sizes, from the very small, 4 inches deep, 11½ inches wide, and 18 inches high, to the very large model, 5½ inches deep, 18 inches wide, and 31 inches high. This one is the standard size of a 4½ inches deep, 15½ inches wide, and 25¾ inches high, most were this size.

These simple clocks were made as early as 1827. They were moderately priced clocks and were popular from 1830 to 1859 or so. It is said they helped revive the clock industry after the panic of 1837. They remained in production up to 1915.

Some ogee clocks have a flat molding in place of the ogee molding. These clocks are referred to as "beveled-case clocks" or "flat ogee clocks."

It is not known just who designed the ogee clock, although many speculate that it was Chauncey Jerome.

George Vaugham

The paper inside the model shown, indicates that it was made by George Vaugham of Laight, New York. I cannot find a thing on George Vaugham and have no idea who he was. It has a weight-driven alarm, which is rather unusual.

Fig. 8-1. Opposite: Ogee clock, circa 1850.

Fig. 8-2. Thirty-hour, weight-driven brass movement.

Instructions / Ogee Clock

As always study all drawings before starting. Purchase the movement for this clock before starting, because many originals of this model had a thin, wooden geared movement. Most new, brass, replacement movements are too thick for the thin case. If you use a quartz movement, you should have no problem with the thickness of the case. You may have to adjust the thickness slightly if you use a brass movement. Adjust all parts accordingly.

STEP 1.

Cut all parts of overall size and sand all over. Lay out and cut to shape each piece as shown. The only part that might be a problem is the ogee molding (parts 4 and 5). You might be able to purchase ogee molding at a local lumberyard.

STEP 2.

This clock case goes together like a simple box—in fact, it *is* a box. Keep everything square as you assemble the case. Make and add the door using hinges (part 22). Again, keep everything square. If you wish, you can add a spline at the four corners as shown for strength.

STEP 3.

Commercial dials, very close to the original can be purchased. The dial is held in place by part 8.

STEP 4.
See Section III for instructions on finishing the clock case.

STEP 5.
Add a clock paper to make your clock look like the original.

─────────────── PARTS LIST ───────────────

No.	Name	Size	Req'd.	
1	Side	¾ × 4¹⁄₁₆ — 25¾ Long	2	
2	Top/Bottom	¾ × 4¹⁄₁₆ — 15½ Long	2	
3	Back	¼ × 15 — 25¼ Long	1	
4	Molding-Side	¾ × 2¹⁵⁄₁₆ — 24¼ Long	2	
5	Molding-Top·Bottom	¾ × 2¹⁵⁄₁₆ — 14 Long	2	
6	Trim–Side	¹⁄₁₆ × ⅞ — 25¾ Long	2	
7	Trim-Top·Bottom	¹⁄₁₆ × ⅞ — 15½ Long	2	
8	Dial Support	⅜ × 2 — 13 Long	2	
9	Dial 7½ Dia.	Merritt O.G-3	1	
*10	Wheel (Weight)	Merritt P-555	2	
*11	Box Nail	8d	2	
12	Paper	T.E.C. S.T. No 7	1	
13	Door-Side	⅜ × ½ — 19⅛ Long	2	
14	Door-Top·Bottom	⅜ × ½ — 8⅞ Long	2	
15	Door-Center	⅜ × ½ — 8⅞ Long	1	
16	Trim-Door Side	¹⁄₁₆ × ¾ — 19½ Long	2	
17	Trim Door Top	¹⁄₁₆ × ¾ — 9¼ Long	2	
18	Trim Door Center	¹⁄₁₆ × ¾ — 7¾ Long	1	
19	Glass	³⁄₃₂ × 8 Sq.	1	
20	Mirror or Glass	Merritt NG-1 (3 or 5)	1	(8 × 10)
21	Latch	Merritt P-109	1	
22	Hinge ¾ × ¾	Merritt P-93	2	
23	Hands 3½ (O.G.)	Merritt P-276	1 pr.	
24	Movement	See Below	1	
25	Gong–Base	Merritt P-112	1	
26	Gong	Merritt P-231	1	
*27	Dust Cover	Merritt P-554	2	
*28	Weight	Merritt P-820	2	

*Parts 10, 11, 27, 28 are not necessary unless weight-drive movement is used.

Movement: Brass, Merritt No. P-286
　　　　　Quartz, Merritt No. P-160

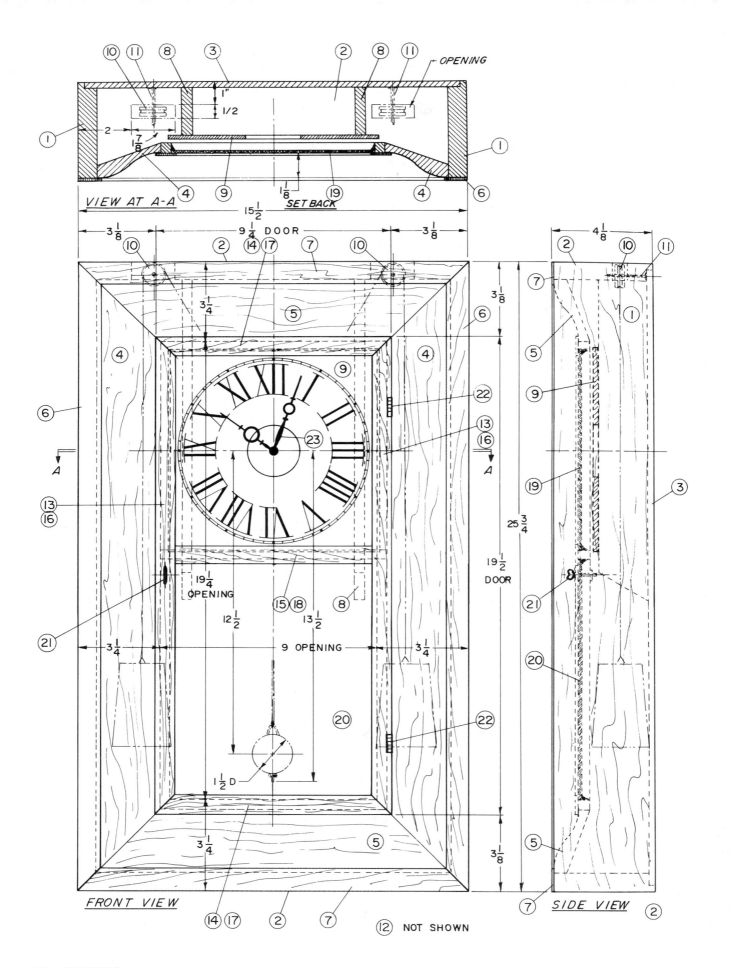

VIEW AT A-A

SET BACK

FRONT VIEW

SIDE VIEW

NOT SHOWN

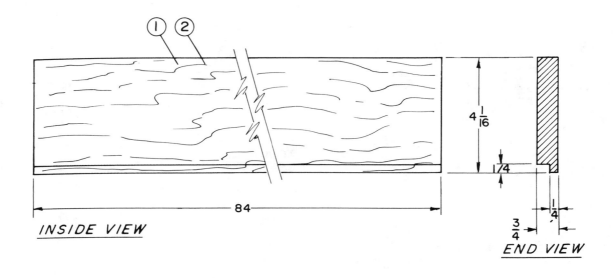

INSIDE VIEW

4 1/16

1/4

3/4

1/4

84

END VIEW

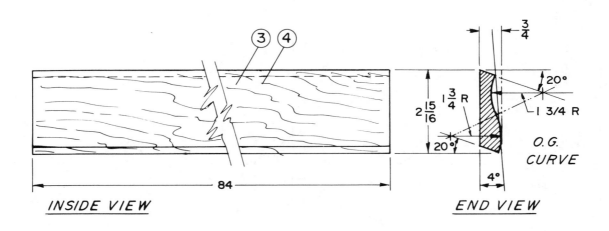

INSIDE VIEW

3/4

20°

1 3/4 R

1 3/4 R

2 15/16

O.G.
CURVE

20°

4°

84

END VIEW

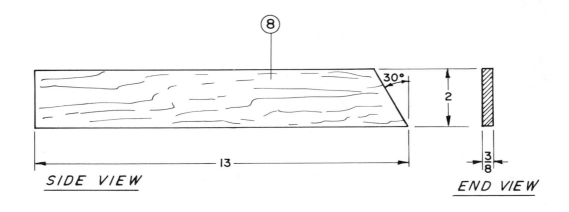

30°

2

SIDE VIEW

13

3/8

END VIEW

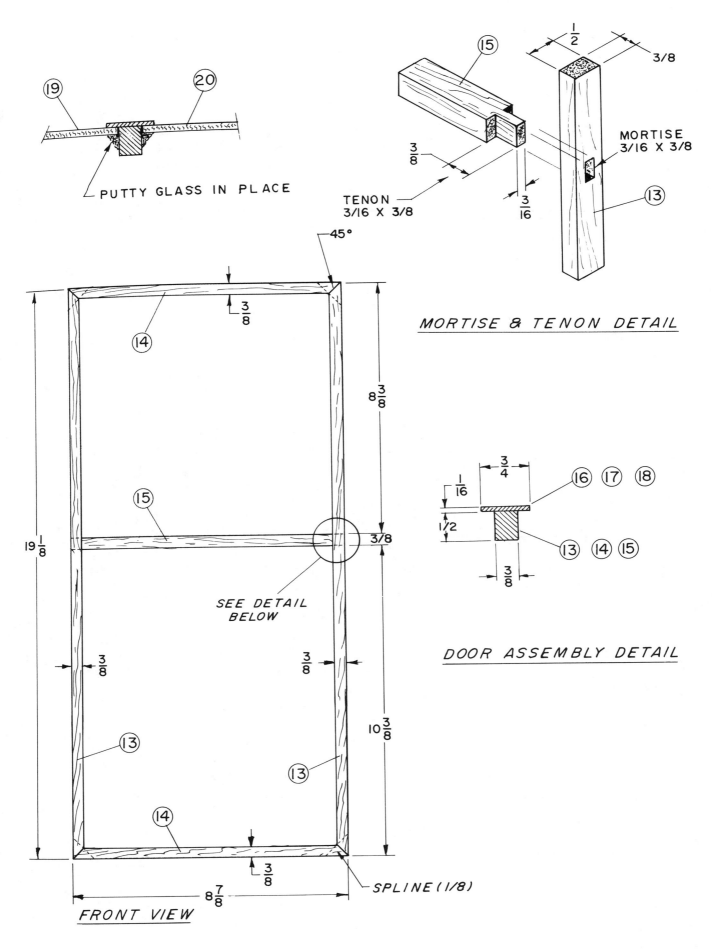

PUTTY GLASS IN PLACE

MORTISE 3/16 X 3/8

TENON 3/16 X 3/8

MORTISE & TENON DETAIL

DOOR ASSEMBLY DETAIL

45°

SEE DETAIL BELOW

SPLINE (1/8)

FRONT VIEW

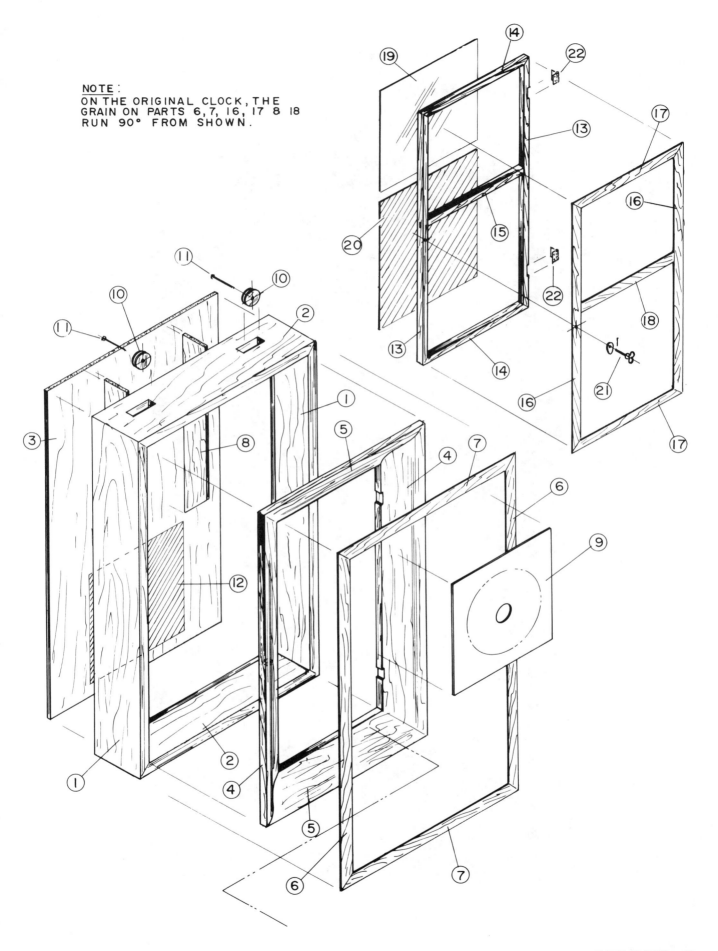

NOTE:
ON THE ORIGINAL CLOCK, THE
GRAIN ON PARTS 6, 7, 16, 17 & 18
RUN 90° FROM SHOWN.

Calendar Clock

IN 1850, CLOCKMAKERS DEVELOPED A TIMEPIECE THAT PROVIDED THE HOUR OF the day, day of the week, day of the month, and the month of the year (Fig. 9-1). Some models even indicated the phase of the moon, as well as high and low tides. Every 24 hours, at midnight, a pin on a gear turns once, putting the calendar mechanism into operation. This simple idea was adopted to fit many other clock cases such as the schoolhouse clock.

In its day, this clock afforded its owner a method of long-range planning. Today we rely on a desk calendar; an electric, or quartz, watch or clock; a radio, or the television set. Remember, in 1870 and before the adoption of standard time, this information was not readily available.

In 1860, Seth Thomas bought the patents for the calendar clock and built this double-dial-face clock (Fig. 9-2). For a very little more than the cost of a regular wall or shelf clock, members of the middle class could own a calendar clock.

By 1880, clock companies such as Ithaca Clock Company, Ansonia Brass and Copper Company, and Waterbury Clock Company started making their own calendar clocks. These clocks were very popular until right up to 1910. Today calendar clocks are sought after by almost all clock collectors.

Seth Thomas

This is another model manufactured by Seth Thomas and patented on December 28th, 1875. It is a pedimented, partial-octagon clock and the style in Victorian with some Gothic influence. It strikes out the hours, on the hour, and rings once on the half hour.

Instructions / Calendar Clock

Study all drawings before starting. With this clock you *must* have the movement before starting. An exact replacement copy of this movement cannot be purchased at this time from any suppliers that I could find. If you wish to build this clock, you will have to find an original movement from a clock dealer. If you can-

Fig. 9-1. Opposite: Calendar clock, circa 1865.

Fig. 9-2. Mechanism for calendar below regular dial. The upper movement trips the lower mechanism at 12 o'clock midnight.

not find a local clock repairer or dealer that has a calendar movement, try Merritt's Antiques (see Appendix B). They carry antique clock movements and might have a calendar movement. Be sure to get one that has exactly 8 inches between dial shaft centers.

A movement (#21004) very close to the original is available from Armor Products, but the connecting shaft between dials will have to be shortened from the 9 1/4-inch distance to the required 8-inch distance. This movement and calendar comes already mounted on a board, which will also have to be redone slightly to fit. Be sure to purchase the movement before starting and adjust the case dimensions accordingly.

STEP 1.
Cut all parts to overall size and sand all over.

STEP 2.
The only real challenge for you is the making of a wooden bezel (part 16). Turn it as shown in the view at A-A. Be sure the glue has set before turning. Assemble the door with the two bezels (part 16) and ears (part 17).

STEP 3.
Carefully lay out and cut each piece as shown. Parts 1 and 2 must be cut at exactly 18 degrees so the case will go together correctly. You might wish to add splines between the parts for strength. It was impossible to tell if the original had splines in it. I doubt it did, but you might want to add them anyway. Once the case and door are made up, the clock can easily be assembled.

STEP 4.

See Section III for instructions on finishing the clock case.

---------------------------PARTS LIST----------------------------

No.	Name	Size	Req'd.
1	Side	¾ × ¾ — 15¾	2
2	Top	¾ × 3¾ — 3½ Long	4
3	Back	¼ × 9¾ — 19⅛ Long	1
4	Face-Side	⅜ × 2⅛ — 15⅝ Long	2
5	Face-Bottom/Top	⅜ × 2⅛ — 9¼ Long	1
6	Face-Top	⅜ × 2⅛ — 9¼ Long	1
7	Platform	¾ × 1 — 9 Long	1
8	Base-Front	1¼ × 1½ — 12⅛ Long	1
9	Base-Side	1¼ × 1½ — 5¼ Long	2
10	Molding-Front	¾ × 1⅜ — 12¾ Long	1
11	Molding-Side	¾ × 1⅜ — 5⅜ Long	2
12	Bottom	¾ × 3⅝ — 9 Long	1
13	Brace	⅜ × ¾ — 3⅝ Long	2
14	Molding-Side	⅞ × 1 — 13⅞ Long	2
15	Molding-Top	⅞ × 1 — 3½ Long	4
16	Bezel Segment	¾ × 1⅛ — 3⁹⁄₁₆ Long	16
17	Ear	⅜ × 2⅛ — 2⅞ Long	2
18	Knob-Right	⁹⁄₁₆ Diameter × ⅝ Long	1
19	Knob-Left	⁹⁄₁₆ Diameter × 1¼ Long	1
20	Pin-Locking	³⁄₃₂ Dia. — ⅝ Long	1
21	Hinge-Brass	¾ × ¾ Long	2
22	Upper Dial 7⅛ D.	T.E.C. 7-CFS	1
23	Lower Dial 7⅛ D.	T.E.C. 7⅛ CA	1
24	Movement	See Below	1
25	Hands 3½ Size	M&S 4908X	1 pr.
26	Hand	Merritt P-156-A	1
27	Glass	³⁄₃₂ × 7⅝ Diameter	2
28	Glass Support	¹⁄₁₆ × ¼ — 27 Long	2
29	Calendar Mech.	See Below	1
30	Paper (Optional)	T.E.C. S.T. No. 1	1

Movement: Brass, Mason and Sullivan 3398X

        Quartz, Mason and Sullivan 3609X-18 w/Hands 4808X

Calendar Mech: Brass, An original—See clock repairer

        Quartz, R.V. Tapp Imports 715/33 (dial face must be drawn special)

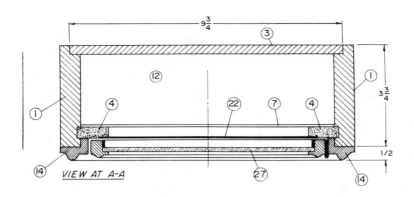

VIEW AT A-A

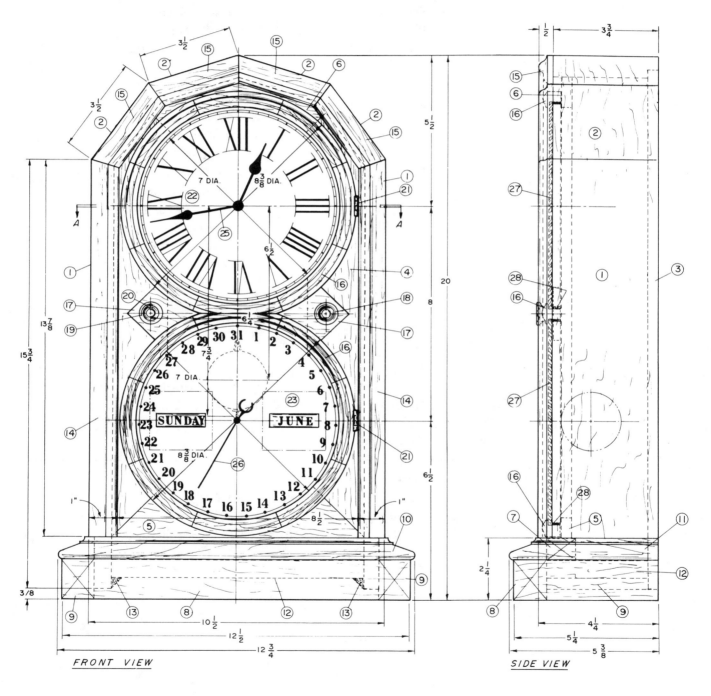

FRONT VIEW

SIDE VIEW

7 DIA.

$8\frac{3}{8}$ DIA.

SUNDAY   JUNE

7 DIA.

$8\frac{3}{8}$ DIA.

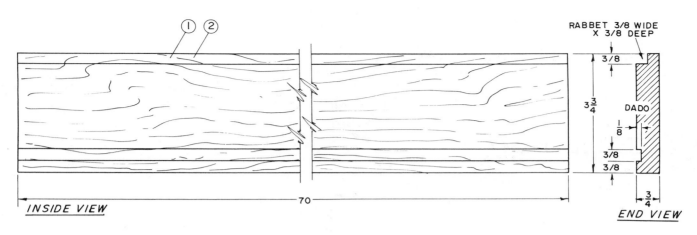

① ②

RABBET 3/8 WIDE
X 3/8 DEEP

3/8

3¾

DADO

⅛

3/8

3/8

¾

INSIDE VIEW

70

END VIEW

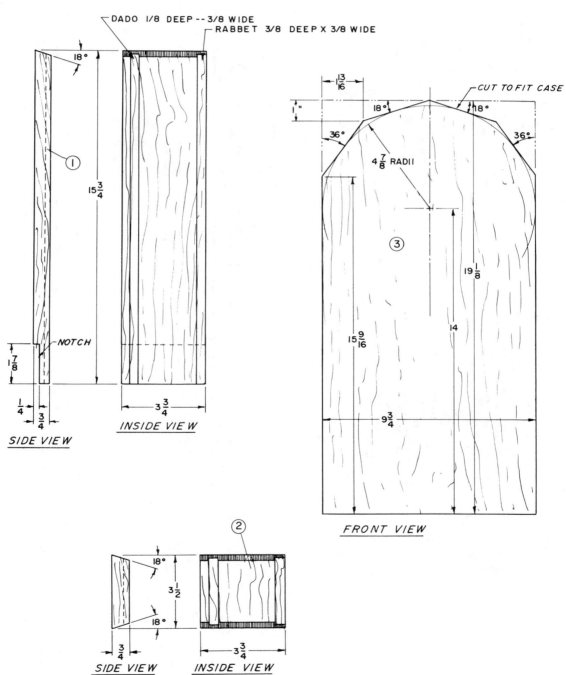

DADO 1/8 DEEP -- 3/8 WIDE

RABBET 3/8 DEEP X 3/8 WIDE

18°

①

15¾

NOTCH

1⅞

¼

¾

SIDE VIEW

INSIDE VIEW

1 13/16

1"

18°

CUT TO FIT CASE

18°

36°

36°

4 7/8 RADII

③

19⅛

14

15 9/16

9¾

FRONT VIEW

②

18°

3½

18°

¾

3¾

SIDE VIEW

INSIDE VIEW

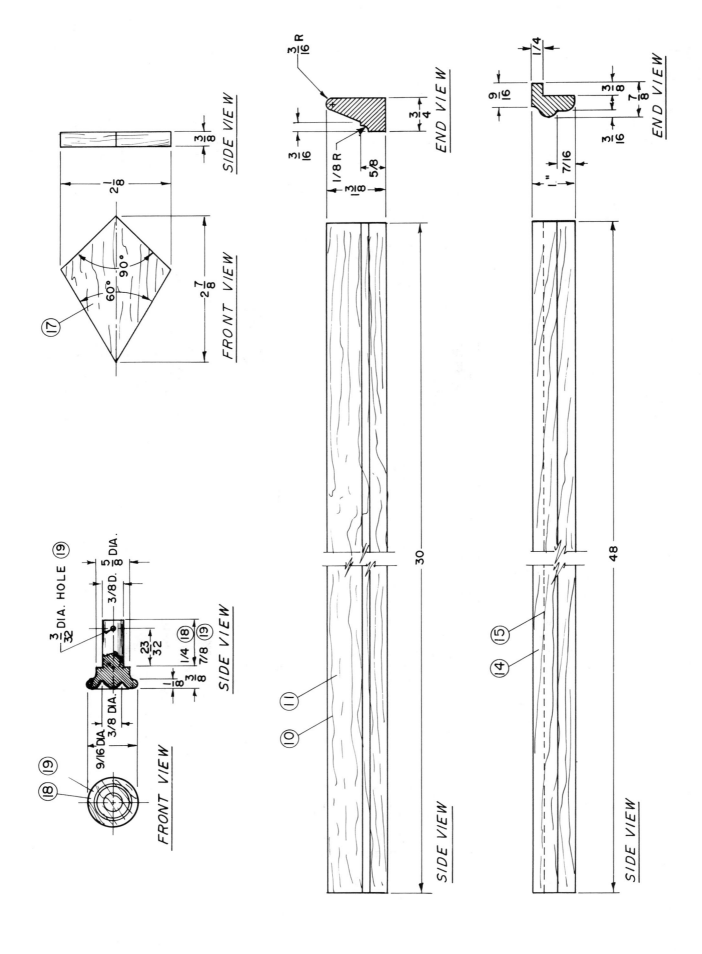

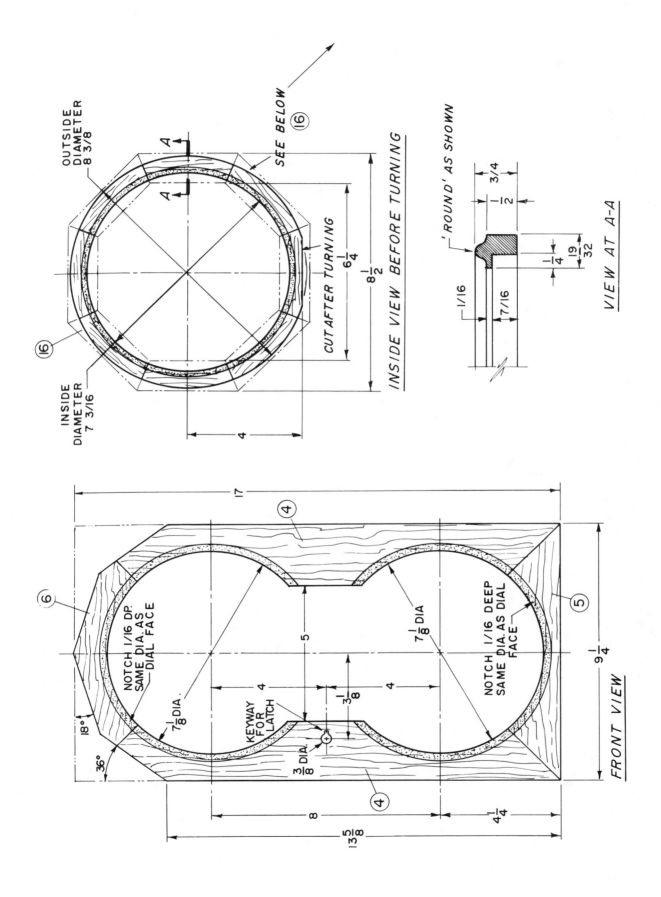

OUTSIDE DIAMETER 8 3/8

INSIDE DIAMETER 7 3/16

CUT AFTER TURNING

6 1/4

8 1/2

4

(16)

(16)

A   A

SEE BELOW

(16)

INSIDE VIEW BEFORE TURNING

'ROUND' AS SHOWN

3/4

1/2

1/16

7/16

1/4

19/32

VIEW AT A-A

17

(4)

(6)

NOTCH 1/16 DP. AS SAME DIA. AS DIAL FACE

7 1/8 DIA.

KEYWAY FOR LATCH

3/8 DIA.

18°

36°

5

3 1/8

4

4

7 1/8 DIA

NOTCH 1/16 DEEP SAME DIA. AS DIAL FACE

(5)

(4)

9 1/4

8

4 1/4

13 5/8

FRONT VIEW

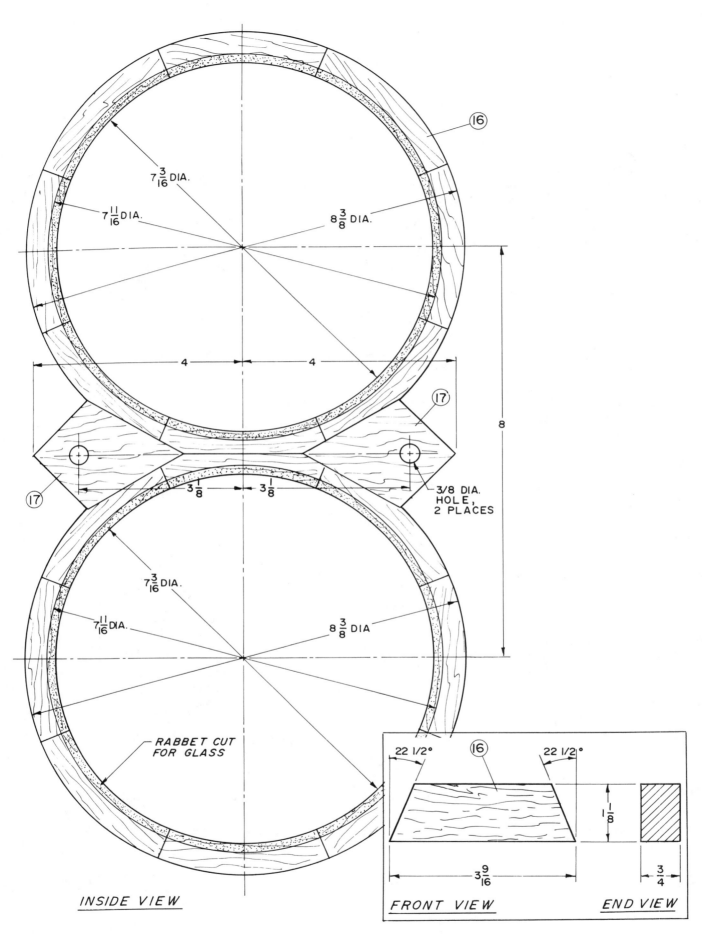

7 3/16 DIA.

7 11/16 DIA.

8 3/8 DIA.

16

4   4

17

17

3 1/8   3 1/8

3/8 DIA.
HOLE,
2 PLACES

8

7 3/16 DIA.

7 11/16 DIA.

8 3/8 DIA

RABBET CUT
FOR GLASS

INSIDE VIEW

22 1/2°   16   22 1/2°

1 1/8

3 9/16

3/4

FRONT VIEW   END VIEW

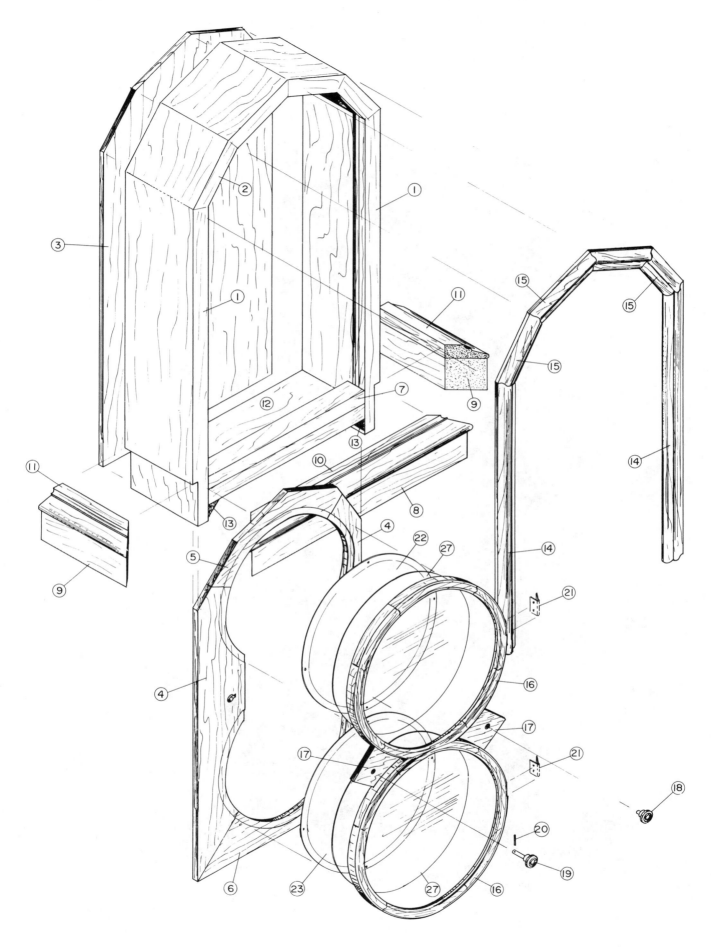

10

Steeple Clock

Elias Ingraham of Bristol, Connecticut was a skilled cabinetmaker. He designed and produced many fine clock cases. In 1845, he designed the "sharp" gothic clock case—today called the steeple clock (Fig. 10-1). These clocks are topped with church-like spires. This design is one of the most popular clock models ever made, and it is still being reproduced today. Even in its day this clock was copied by most all existing clock companies. Everyone wanted one.

The Ingraham Clock Company, named E. Ingraham and Company, was started in 1857 by Elias and his son, Edward, in Bristol, Connecticut. McGraw-Edison Company purchased the E. Ingraham Company in 1967 and is still producing clocks in North Carolina.

Many of the earlier steeple clocks contained a 30-hour brass movement. The 8-day movements are somewhat rare and therefore, cost more today. Steeple clocks range in height from $10^{1/2}$ to 23 inches.

This model is a mystery clock—a real puzzler. The label on the back of the case reads "Jerome and Company, New Haven, Conn.," with the number 251 above (Fig. 10-2). The movement is stamped New Haven. Research done by W.L. Wadleigh, Jr. for the National Association of Watch and Clock Collectors (NAWCC) showed that Jerome Manufacturing Company, issued their catalog in 1853. The catalog contained only standard steeple clocks. In 1857, the company was taken over by the New Haven Clock Company, which used Jerome and Company's name from 1880 to 1904. It is believed this clock was actually made by New Haven Clock Company under the Jerome company name. New Haven's 1880 catalog did not contain this model, either; it is assumed that this clock was made sometime between 1880 and 1904. This model is a *very* unusual steeple clock.

New Haven Clock Company

New Haven Clock Company was started on February 17, 1853 with only $20,000. Hiram Camp was its first president. The company produced cheap brass movements for the Jerome Manufacturing Company. New Haven later bought out

Fig. 10-1. Opposite: Steeple clock, circa 1856.

Fig. 10-2. Back view showing original Jerome paper. The clock has an original New Haven movement.

Jerome Manufacturing, and began manufacturing more complete clocks. They made many different model clocks and by 1880 started making pocket watches. In 1917 they began making wristwatches. In 1956 the New Haven Clock Company ceased production.

Instructions / Steeple Clock

Be sure to study all drawings before starting. Always have the movement before starting this clock in order to check for fit. Try to make all parts so that they have a thin, graceful appearance. You might want to keep the parts slightly thinner.

STEP 1.
Cut all parts of overall size and sand all over. Lay out and cut to shape each piece.

STEP 2.
Assemble the case as shown in Assembly A on p. 90. Add the parts as noted in Assembly B also on p. 90. Then add the door and remaining parts as illustrated in Assembly C on p. 91.

STEP 3.
If you do not have a lathe, have a custom turner make up finials, parts 16 and 21. (See Appendix B for the address of River Bend Turnings.) These turnings can be made into one piece as shown and then cut in two to make parts 16 and 21. Be sure to cut the turnings in two as noted on the drawing, leaving the 1/4-inch-diameter stub attached to the top finial (part 21). You will have to remove a 1/4 sector from part 16, so that it will fit up and into the side trim (part 14).

STEP 4.
A special hinge (part 27) will have to be custom-made from a thin piece of metal—*not brass*. The door is held closed by a small piece of metal that applies a little friction to the left side of the door.

STEP 5.
Commercial dials that are very close to the original can be purchased. The dial is screwed to parts 10 and 11.

STEP 6.
See Section III for instructions on finishing the clock case.

STEP 7.
This clock uses a dial in the *back* of the glass as illustrated in the photograph. A decal very similar to the original is listed in the materials list; you might have to scrape some of the design off so it will fit correctly. Some suppliers noted in Appendix B, will make up special reversed designs especially for this clock. Write for details and prices.

STEP 8.
Add a clock paper to make your clock look like the original.

PARTS LIST

No.	Name	Size	Req'd.
1	Side	½ × 3 — 11¼ Long	2
2	Top	½ × 3 — 6⁷⁄₁₆ Long	2
3	Base	⁵⁄₁₆ × 3⁵⁄₁₆ — 7¹⁵⁄₁₆ Long	1
4	Back	¼ × 7¹⁄₁₆ — 16½ Long	1
5	Front Skirt	⅝ × 1⅞ — 9½ Long	1
6	Side Skirt	⅝ × 1⅞ — 4⅜ Long	2
7	Corner Block	¾ × ¾ — 1 Long	2
8	Front-Molding	⅜ × ⅝ — 8¾ Long	1
9	Side-Molding	⅜ × ⅝ — 4 Long	2
10	Dial Side Support	¼ × ¾ — 3 Long	2
11	Dial Top Support	1 × 1 — 2⅛ Long	1
12	Glue Block	¼ × ½ — 2 Long	2
13	Trim Top	⁷⁄₁₆ × ⁹⁄₁₆ — 5⅝ Long	2
14	Trim Side	⁷⁄₁₆ × ⁹⁄₁₆ — 8⅞ Long	2
15	Block	¾ × 1⅛ — 1¹¹⁄₁₆ Long	2
16	Bottom Finial	1 Dia. — 1 Long	2
17	Dial	¹⁄₁₆ × 6⁷⁄₁₆ — 9¼ Long	1
18	Top Molding	¹¹⁄₁₆ × 1⅛ — 5¾ Long	2
19	Front Molding	¹¹⁄₁₆ × 1⅛ — 2⅛ Long	2
20	Side Molding	¹¹⁄₁₆ × 1⅛ — 1¼ Long	2
21	Top Finial	1⅜ Dia. — 3¼ Long	2
22	Door Side	½ × ¾ — 8⅞ Long	2
23	Door Bottom	½ × ¾ — 6⁷⁄₁₆ Long	1
24	Door Top	½ × ¾ — 5½ Long	2
25	Glass	³⁄₃₂ × 5⁷⁄₁₆ — 12⅛ Long	1
26	Decal For Door	Shipley No. SG-44	1
27	Top Hinge	¹⁄₃₂ × ⅞ — 1 Long	1
28	Bottom Hinge	¹⁄₃₂ × ¹³⁄₁₆ — ¹³⁄₁₆ Long	1
29	Movement	See Below	1
30	Hands	3½ Size	1 pr.

Movement: Brass: Southwest Clock Supply IM-22/9 w/1H-17 Hands
 Quartz: Klockit 11008-A w/66927-A Hands
Paper (*Optional*): T.E.C. Jerome No. 1
(*Glue to lower back No. 3 outside*)

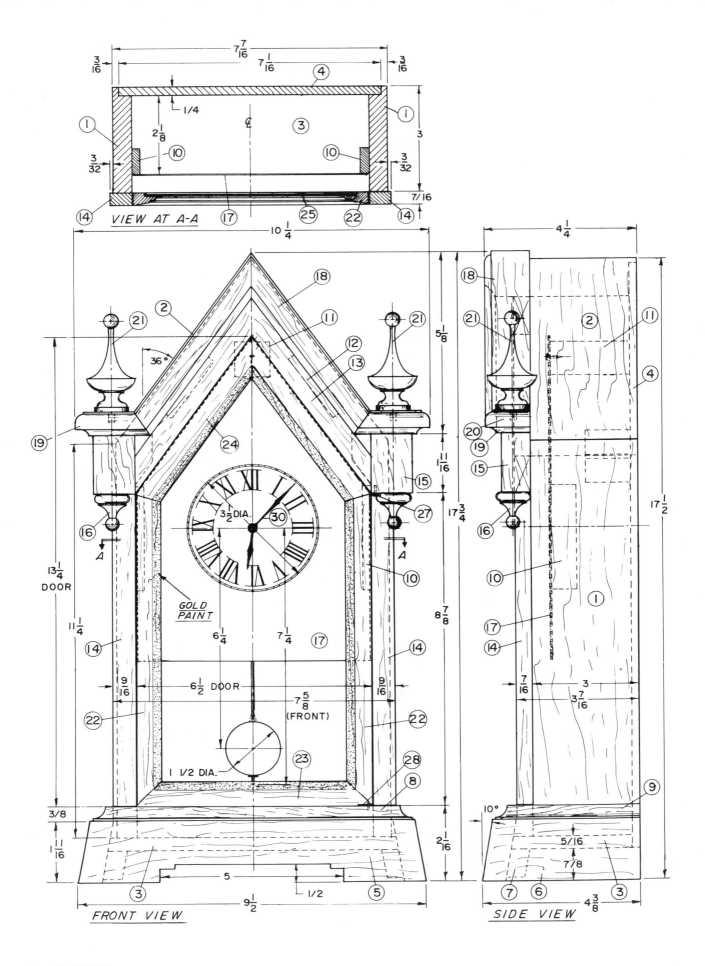

VIEW AT A-A

GOLD
PAINT

FRONT VIEW

SIDE VIEW

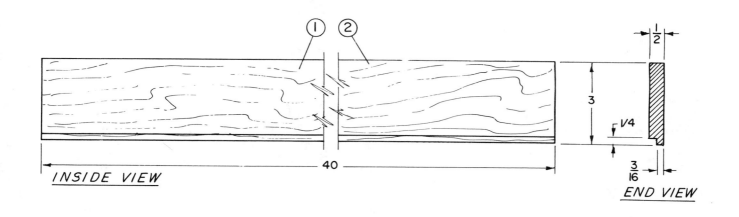

INSIDE VIEW

END VIEW

40

3

½

¼

3/16

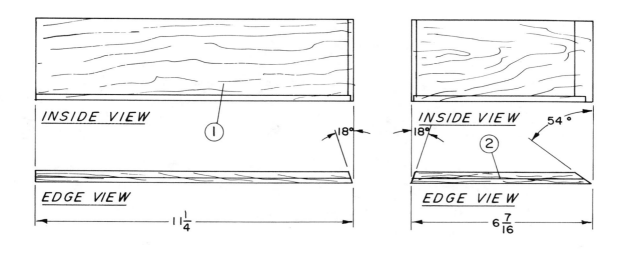

INSIDE VIEW

①

EDGE VIEW

11¼

18°

INSIDE VIEW

②

EDGE VIEW

18°

54°

6 7/16

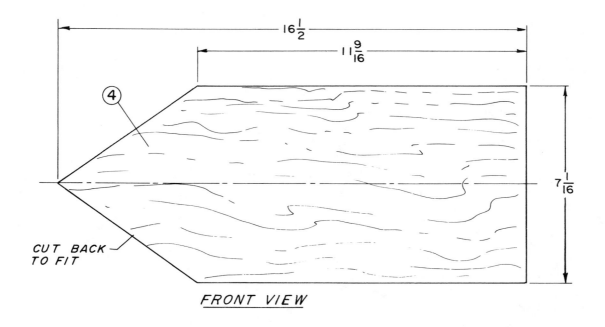

16½

11 9/16

④

CUT BACK
TO FIT

7 1/16

FRONT VIEW

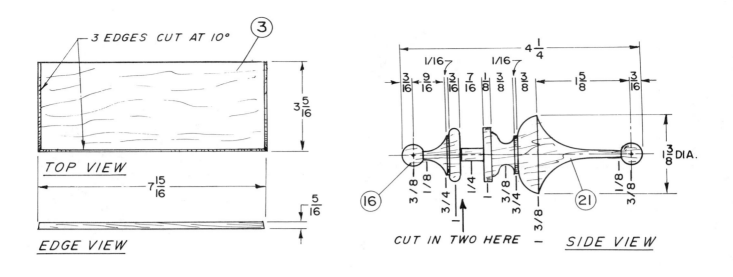

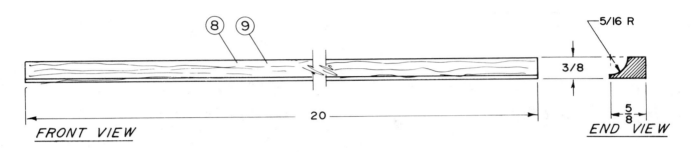

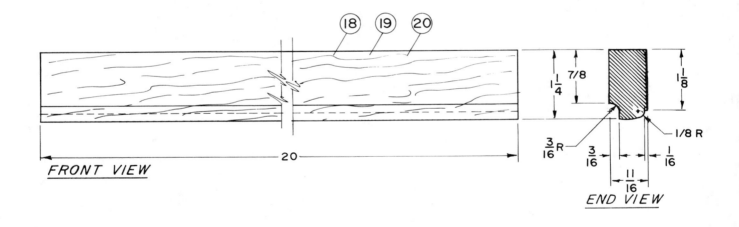

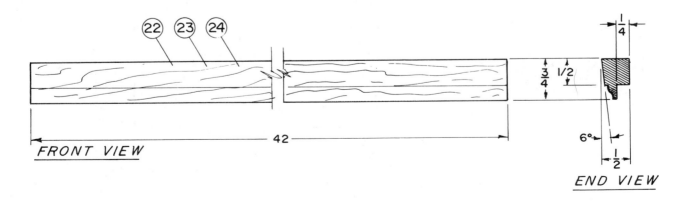

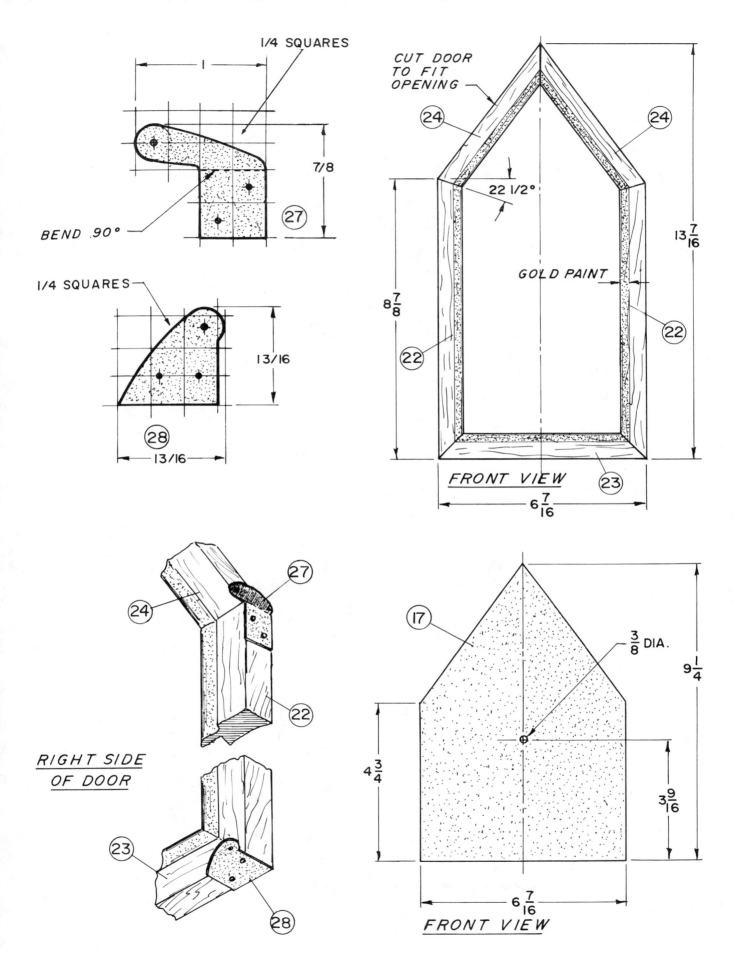

1/4 SQUARES

1

7/8

BEND .90°

27

1/4 SQUARES

13/16

13/16

28

CUT DOOR
TO FIT
OPENING

24   24

22 1/2°

13 7/16

GOLD PAINT

8 7/8

22   22

23

FRONT VIEW

6 7/16

24   27

22

RIGHT SIDE
OF DOOR

23

28

17

3/8 DIA.

9 1/4

4 3/4

3 9/16

6 7/16

FRONT VIEW

STEEPLE CLOCK   89

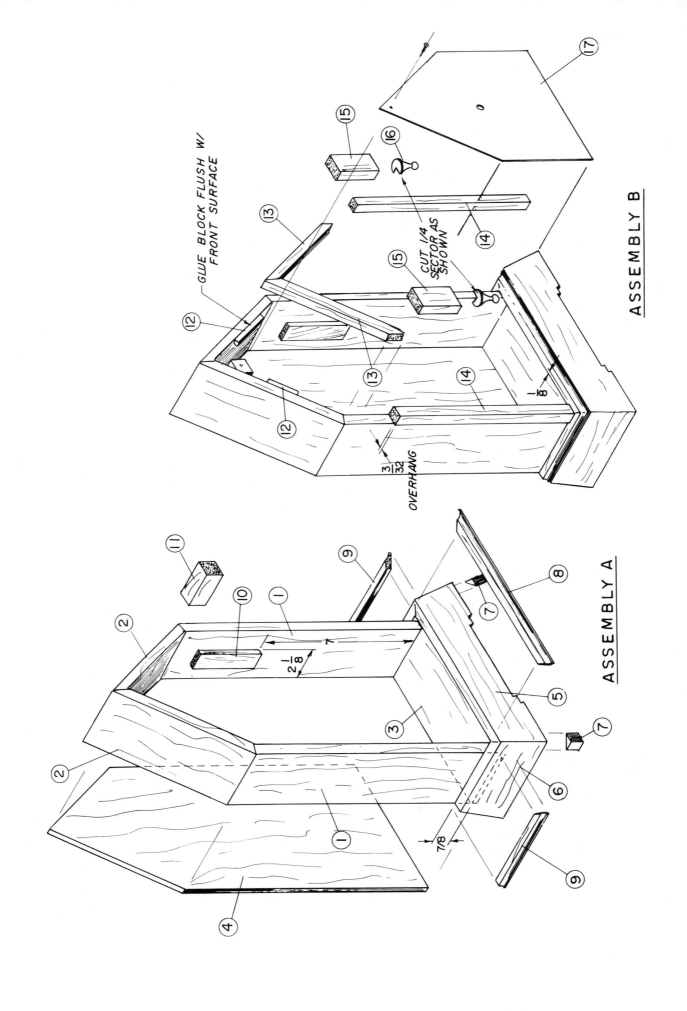

GLUE BLOCK FLUSH W/
FRONT SURFACE

CUT 1/4
SECTOR AS
SHOWN

$\frac{1}{8}$

$\frac{3}{32}$
OVERHANG

ASSEMBLY B

$2\frac{1}{8}$

7

7/8

ASSEMBLY A

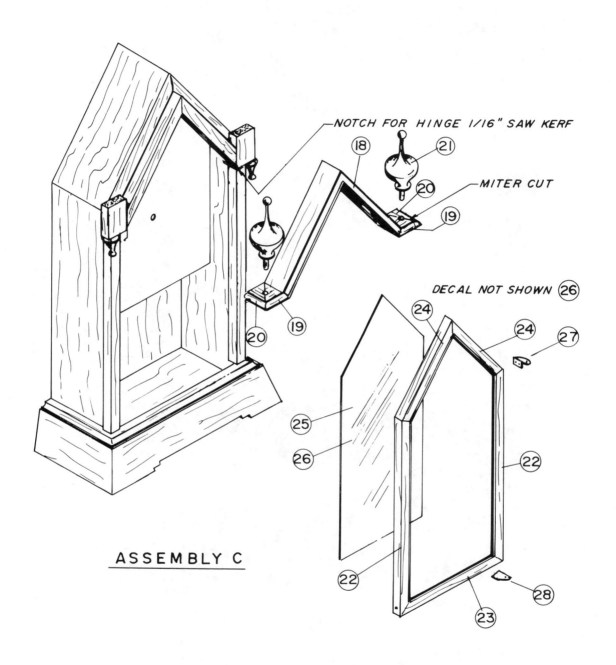

NOTCH FOR HINGE 1/16" SAW KERF

MITER CUT

DECAL NOT SHOWN 26

ASSEMBLY C

Cottage Clock

THE COTTAGE CLOCK (FIG. 11-1) IS A SIMPLE, RATHER PLEASANT FORM OF THE Connecticut shelf clock. It was popular during the Victorian age and replaced the somewhat larger, more expensive box clock. It was a very small, usually less than 12 inches high. Most models had an uncomplicated simple 30-hour movement, some even had alarms (Fig. 11-2). They were made in great volume from 1865 through to 1895 and were identified by their decorated doors. Today they are fairly popular, but their 30-hour movement limits their value, as they are a nuisance to wind every day.

Maker

This model had no markings whatsoever, but many experts believe it was made by E.N. Welch around 1865. It has a small 30-hour movement with an alarm. The alarm is set by turning the 1-inch brass selector knob, located at the center of the dial. The early alarms were not set to ring at a precise *time*. Instead, they were set for the number of hours before the alarm would sound. For instance, if you went to bed at 11:00 P.M. and wanted to get up at 7:00 A.M., you would set the indicator at 8. This would give you 8 hours before the alarm would ring.

Instructions / Cottage Clock

This is a rather simple clock to build. If you are just starting out, this one should be a good one to try. Try to shape all parts so that they have a thin, graceful appearance. You might want to keep the parts slightly thinner than the given dimensions.

Study all drawings before starting. Remember to purchase the movement before starting this clock. If you use a quartz movement you should have no problem, but be sure it has a pendulum.

The only challenging part of this clock is the door assembly, the case itself is very simple and is actually nailed together. If you nail your clock together, be sure to use square-cut nails, available from Tremont Nail Company (see Appendix A).

Fig. 11-1. Opposite: Cottage clock, circa 1865.

Fig. 11-2. Thirty-hour, spring-driven movement.

STEP 1.
Carefully lay out and cut each piece as shown.

STEP 2.
The clock case goes together like a simple box, keep everything square as you assemble the case. Make and add the door using the special hinges (part 15).

STEP 3.
Commercial dials that are very similar to the original can be purchased, but it is more fun to make your own. Try it. If you do not like it you can always glue a commercial paper dial over yours. Handmade dials look so much more authentic than the commercial ones. The dial is screwed directly to the sides (part 1).

STEP 4.
See Section III for instruction on finishing the clock case.

STEP 5.
Add a paper so that your clock will really look old.

No.	Name	Size	Req'd.
1	Side	½ × 2⅝ — 10⅝ Long	2
2	Bottom	¼ × 2¹⁵/₁₆ — 7⅛ Long	1
3	Back	¼ × 6⅝ — 11 Long	1
4	Top Board	⁵/₁₆ × 3⁹/₁₆ — 7½ Long	1
5	Base-Front	½ × 2⅝ — 7¾ Long	1
6	Base-Side	½ × 2⅝ — 3⁹/₁₆ Long	2
7	Brace	¼ × ¼ — 2¾ Long	2
8	Dial Base	¹/₁₆ × 6⅝ — 6¼ Long	1
9	Door Stile	½ × ¾ — 8¹¹/₁₆ Long	2
10	Door Rail	½ × ¾ — 6⅞ Long	2
11	Door Ctr. Rail	½ × ½ — 5⅝ Long	1
12	Glass-Top	³/₃₂ × 5½ — 5⅝ Long	1
13	Glass-Bottom	³/₃₂ × 1⁹/₁₆ × 5⅝ Long	1
14	Glass Support	⅛ × ¼ — 5⅝ Long	2
15	Door Hinge	¹/₁₆ × ⁵/₁₆ — ¹⁷/₃₂ Long	2
16	Brass Tack	½ Round Head	4
17	Hook-Brass	¾ Size	1
18	Scres-Rd. Hd.	For Hook No 17	2
19	Bell (If Req'd.)	1¾ Diameter	1
20	Dial Face	5″ Dial Size	1
21	Hands For Dial	2½″ Min. Hand	1 Pr.
22	Decal For Glass	Style Five	1
23	Movement	5⅝ Pendulum	1
24	Nail Square-Cut	Finish, ¾ Long	20

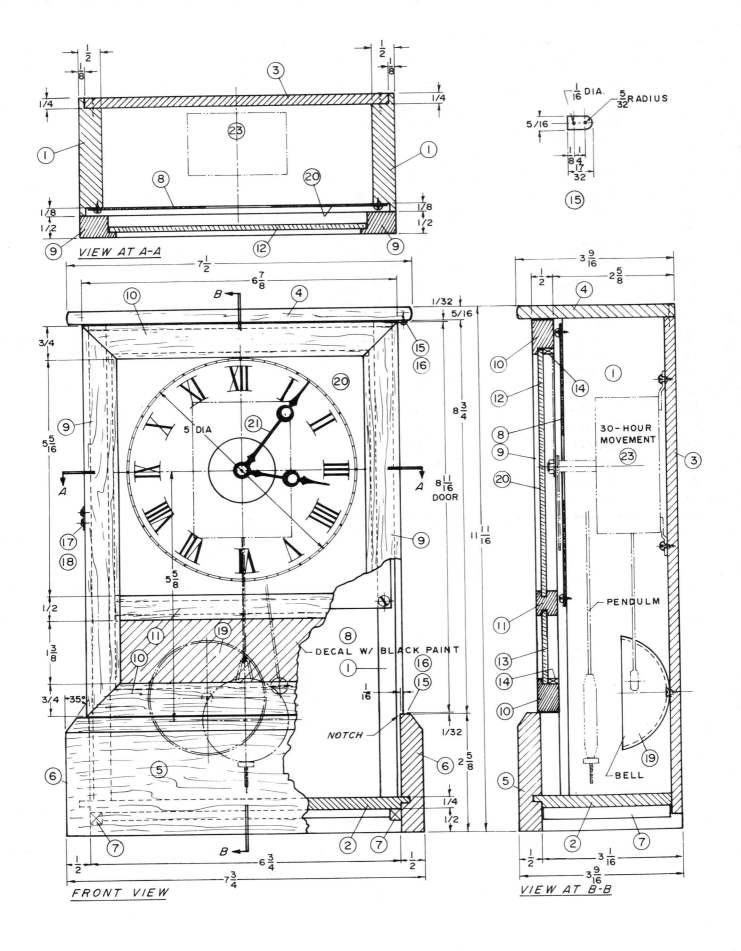

VIEW AT A-A

1/16 DIA.   5/32 RADIUS

5/16

15

FRONT VIEW

5 DIA

21

5 5/8

DECAL W/ BLACK PAINT

NOTCH

8 3/4

8 11/16 DOOR

11 11/16

VIEW AT B-B

3 9/16

2 5/8

30-HOUR MOVEMENT

PENDULM

BELL

3 1/16

3 9/16

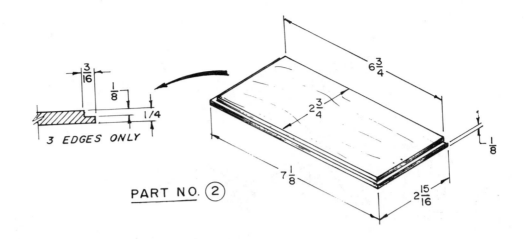

PART NO. ②

3 EDGES ONLY

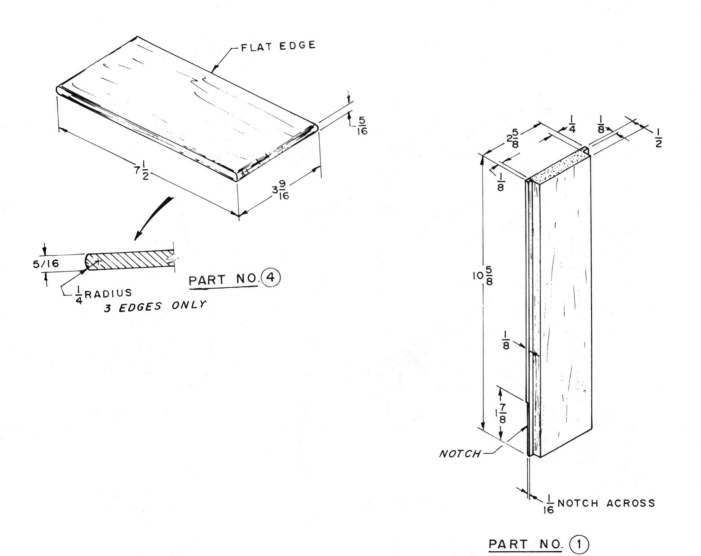

FLAT EDGE

PART NO. ④

1/4 RADIUS
3 EDGES ONLY

NOTCH

NOTCH ACROSS

PART NO. ①

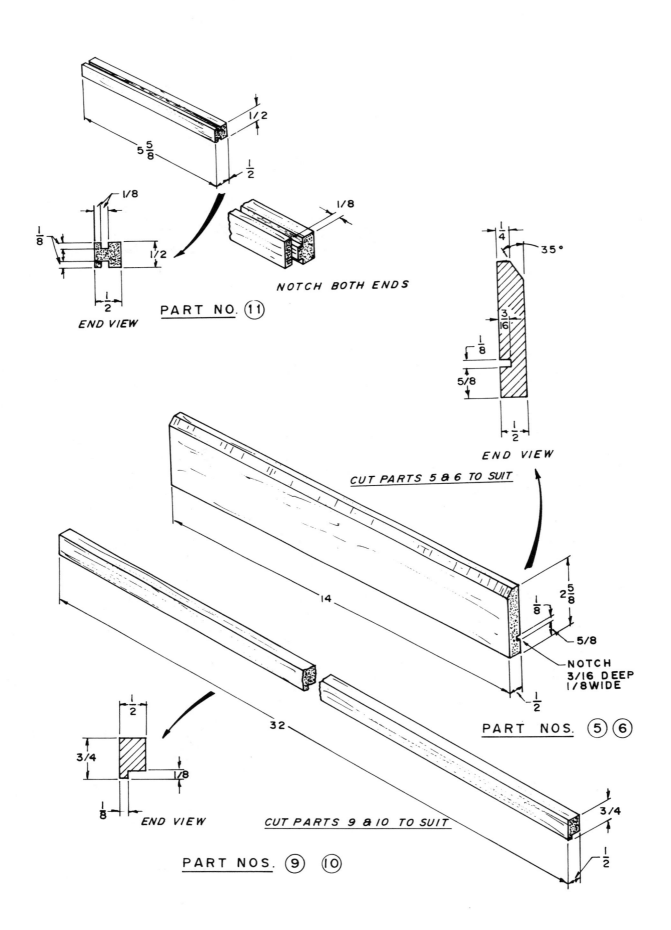

1/2

5 5/8

1/2

1/8

1/8

1/2

1/2

NOTCH BOTH ENDS

1/8

END VIEW

PART NO. ⑪

1/4

35°

3/16

1/8

5/8

1/2

END VIEW

CUT PARTS 5 & 6 TO SUIT

14

2 5/8

1/8

5/8

NOTCH
3/16 DEEP
1/8 WIDE

1/2

PART NOS. ⑤ ⑥

32

1/2

3/4

1/8

1/8

END VIEW

CUT PARTS 9 & 10 TO SUIT

3/4

1/2

PART NOS. ⑨ ⑩

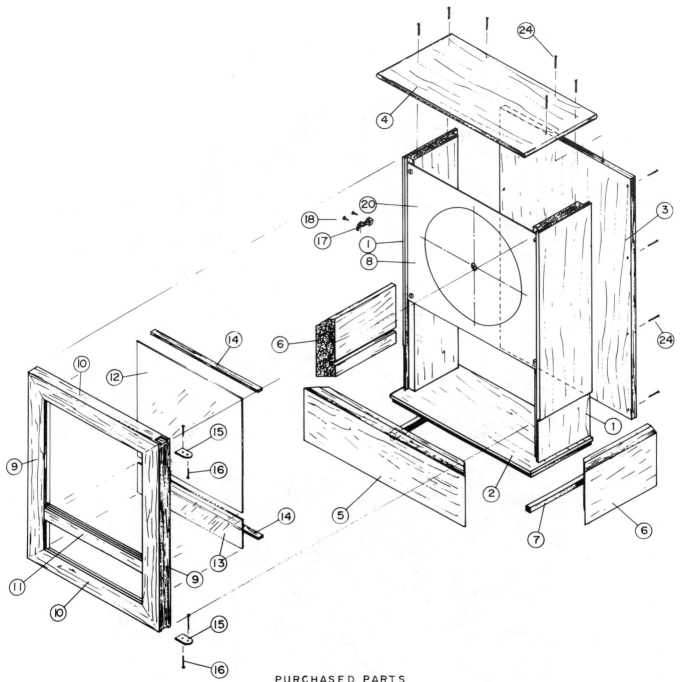

PURCHASED PARTS

⑰ HOOK - MERRITT NO. P-92C

⑲ BELL - MERRITT NO. P893

⑳ DIAL FACE - T.E.C. NO. 5-RWE, SEMI-GLOSS WHITE, 5" SIZE

㉒ DECAL - STYLE FIVE

㉓ MOVEMENT :

　　　QUARTZ, SHORT SHAFT - KLOCKIT NO. 11901-A (66936-A)

　　　SPRING, 8-DAY, TURNCRAFT NO. 400412 (GJ)

ⓧⓧ PAPER LABLE - WELCH, T.E.C. NO. 1

Connecticut Shelf Clock

THERE WERE MANY CONNECTICUT SHELF CLOCKS (FIG. 12-1) MANUFACTURED IN early America, starting with Eli Terry's famous pillar and scroll clock and followed by Ingraham's column and splat clock, and the calendar clocks made by Seth Thomas. With the invention of the coil spring in 1830 by Silas Terry, clock cases became smaller. They no longer had to be built around large weights and long pendulums, therefore, the designs that were produced were much smaller.

New tops of clocks were developed around 1860 to suggest a pitched or gabled roof. These were simple designs that were a modification of the Gothic style. Later, the "roof-pitch" was altered slightly into a hexagon or octagon top, which was a variation of the eight-sided, wall-hanging schoolhouse clocks. Through the years, cases changed to keep up with the current styles and trends. Later models had 8-day, brass movements that were very well made.

These clocks were manufactured by all the major clock companies of the time period and are still popular today. This model was manufactured by E.N. Welch Manufacturing Company of Forrestville, Connecticut (Fig. 12-1).

E.N. Welch Manufacturing Company

Elisha N. Welch was born in Forrestville, Connecticut on February 7, 1809. He became America's largest and most successful maker of clocks. In 1850 he became president of Bristol Brass and Company, and by 1854, he began making clocks. He later acquired the Manross Clock Company and J.C. Brown Company. In 1903 the E.N. Welch Company became the Sessions Clock Company.

Instructions / Connecticut Shelf Clock

Except for the wooden bezel (part 16), this is a rather simple clock to build. If you are just starting out and have a little lathe experience, this should be a good one to build.

Study all drawings before starting. Be sure to have the movement before starting this clock. If you use a quartz movement you should have no problem,

Fig. 12-1. Opposite: Connecticut shelf clock, circa 1870.

Fig. 12-2. Back-mounted, eight-day brass movement.

but make sure it has a pendulum. You should also have the dial pan (part 7) before starting. This could affect the size of the hole in part 3.

STEP 1.

The only difficult part of this clock is the door assembly; the case itself is very simple. The door is made up of parts 17 through 27. Note the notch in the bezel (part 16) sized to fit into the face board (part 19). Study the side view for details. Be sure to maintain the 3⁷/₈-inch distance from the center of the bezel to the top of the door frame (part 17) per the front view of the clock. Notch the rosettes (part 20), so they also fit up and into the face board. Be sure to make a right- and left-hand pair of rosettes.

STEP 2.

Carefully lay out and cut each piece as shown, shaping all parts so that they have a thin, elegant appearance. (You might want to keep the parts slightly thinner than the given dimensions.) The clock case goes together like a simple box, keep everything square as you assemble the case.

STEP 3.

Commercial dials very similar to the original can be purchased, but it is more fun to make your own. Give it a try. If you do not like it you can always glue a commercial paper dial over your dial. The handmade dials look much more authentic than the commercial ones. The dial is glued inside the pan. Use rubber cement to secure the paper dial in place. Screw the pan directly to the face (part 3).

STEP 4.
See Section III for finishing instructions.

STEP 5.
To make your clock really look old, add a clock paper.

STEP 6.
Place a decal to the back of the glass and paint in various areas of the design with different colors. Leave the center open so the pendulum can be seen.

PARTS LIST

No.	Name	Size	Req'd.
1	Side	¾ × 3¼ — 11¾ Long	2
2	Top	¾ × 3¼ — 4⅝ Long	2
3	Face	¼ × 6⅞ — 8⅛ Long	1
4	Back	¼ × 7⅝ — 14¾ Long	1
5	Corner Brace	¾ × 1¼ — 2⅛ Long	3
6	Face Brace	¼ × ½ — 1¼ Long	4
7	Dial Pan 5¼ Dia.	Merritt No. P-61-D	1
8	Dial Face (4" Dia.)	T.E.C. No. RS-4	1
9	Screw-Rd. Hd.	No 4 — ¼ Long	4
10	Screw-Flat Hd.	No. 6 — ¾ Long	8
11	Base-Front	1⅛ × 1⅞ — 7⅜ Long	1
12	Base-Side	1⅛ × 1⅞ — 4⅛ Long	2
13	Bottom	¼ × 3 — 7⅝ Long	1
14	Molding-Side	⅛ × ¾ — 11⅜ Long	2
15	Molding-Top	⅛ × ¾ — 4⅝ Long	2
16	Frame-Round	⅝ × 6⅛ — 6⅛ Long	1
17	Molding-Rail	½ × ⅝ — 6⅜ Long	2
18	Molding-Stile	½ × ⅝ — 4⅝ Long	2
19	Face Board	5⁄16 × 1 — 5 1⁄16 Long	1
20	Rosette	⅝ × 1⅜ Diameter	2
21	Glass	3⁄32 × 4⅛ — 5⅞ Long	1
22	Glass Support	⅛ × ¼ — 5⅞ Long	2
23	Hinge ¾ × 11⁄16	LaRose FL-22-86075	2
24	Door Lock	Merritt No. P-72	1
25	Movement	See Below	1
26	Decal	LaRose No. 082029	1
27	Glass	⅛ × 5⅝ Diameter	1
28	Hands 2" Size	LaRose No. 816015	1 pr.
29	Paper	T.E.C. No. Welch No. 1	1
30	Screw for Movement	No. 8 — ⅜ Long	4

Movement: Brass: LaRose No. 084015 (9¼ Pendulum)
Quartz: LaRose No. 812071 (Cut to 9" Long)

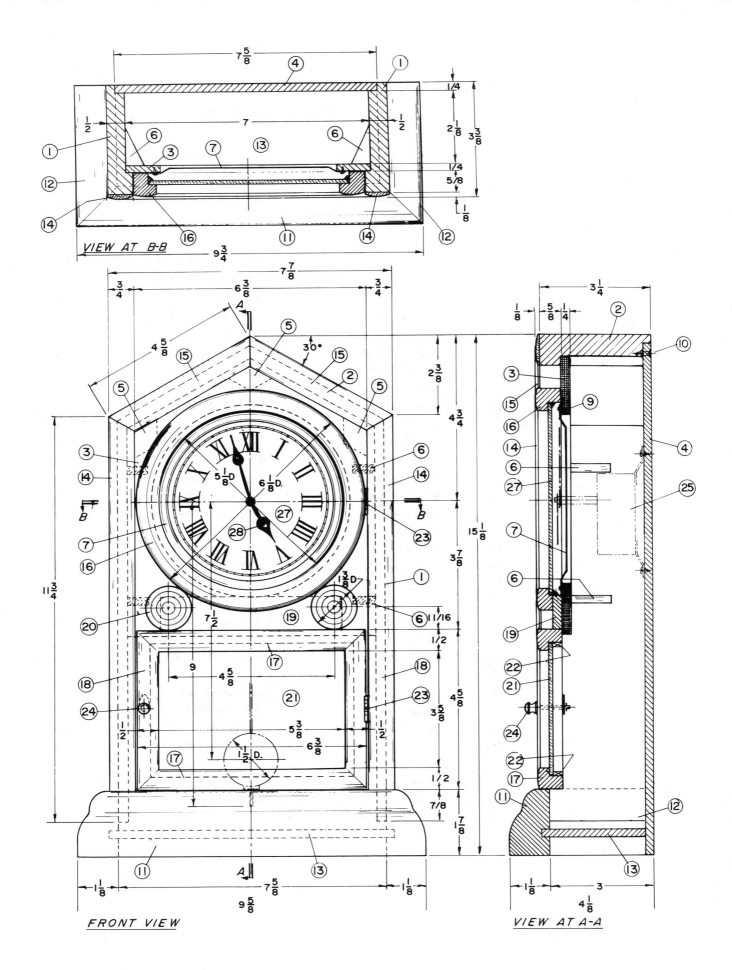

VIEW AT B-B

FRONT VIEW

VIEW AT A-A

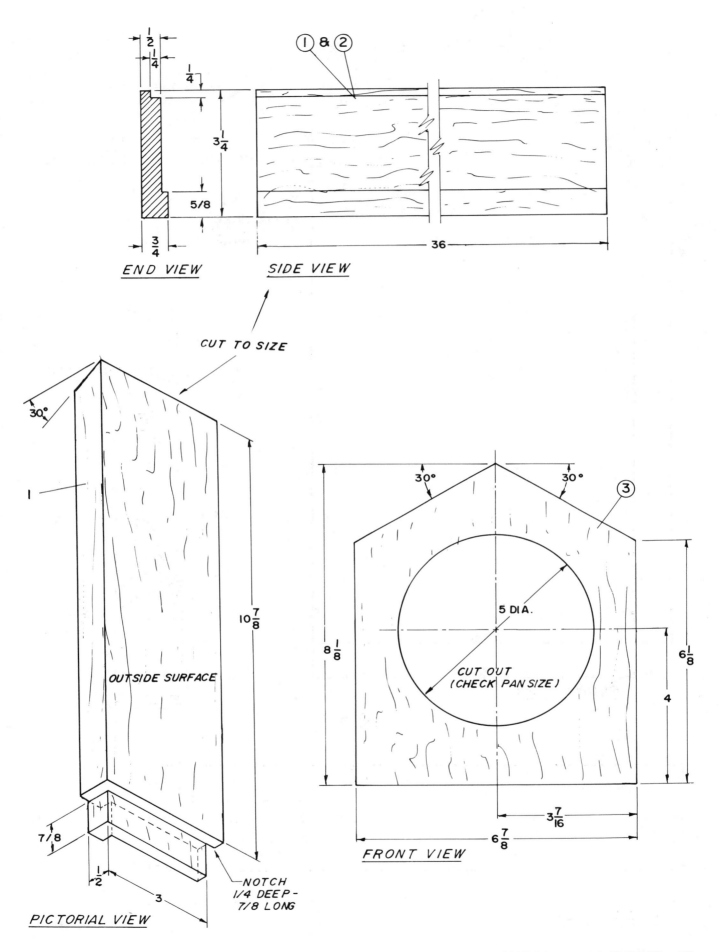

½

¼

¼

3¼

5/8

¾

END VIEW   SIDE VIEW

① & ②

36

CUT TO SIZE

30°

1

OUTSIDE SURFACE

10⅞

7/8

½

3

NOTCH
1/4 DEEP -
7/8 LONG

PICTORIAL VIEW

30°   30°

③

5 DIA.

CUT OUT
(CHECK PAN SIZE)

8⅛

6⅛

4

3 7/16

6⅞

FRONT VIEW

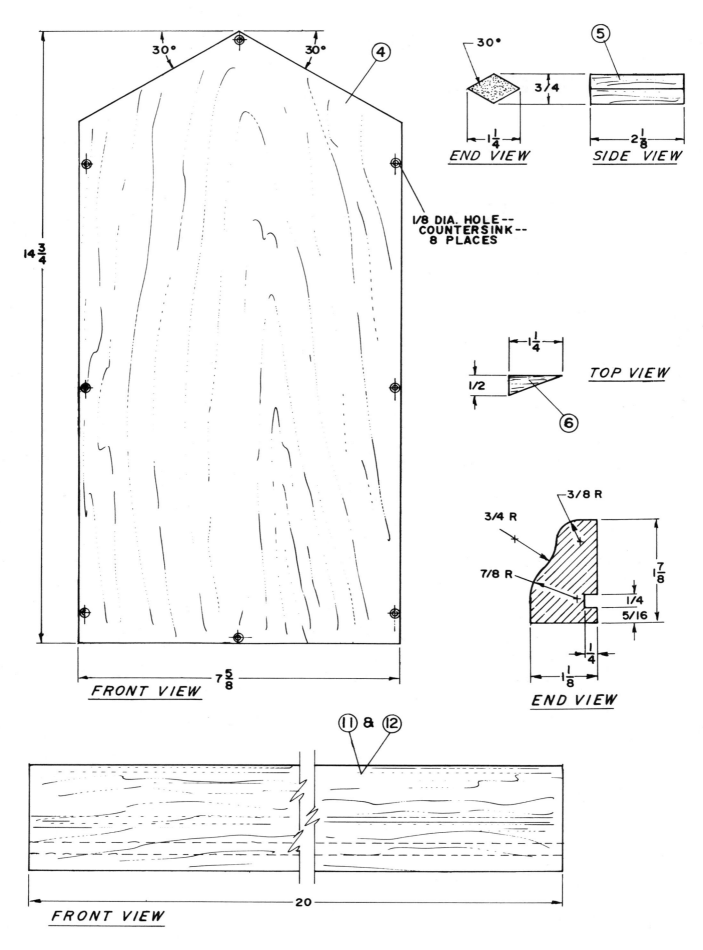

30°   30°   ④

④30°   3/4

SIDE VIEW

END VIEW   2⅛

⑤

1/8 DIA. HOLE--
COUNTERSINK--
8 PLACES

14¾

1¼

TOP VIEW

1/2

⑥

3/8 R

3/4 R

1⅞

7/8 R

1/4

5/16

1¼

1⅛

END VIEW

7⅝

FRONT VIEW

⑪ & ⑫

20

FRONT VIEW

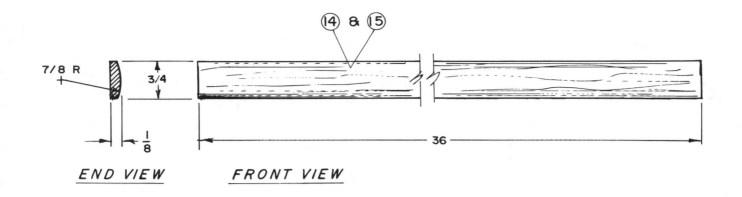

7/8 R

3/4

1/8

⑭ & ⑮

36

END VIEW   FRONT VIEW

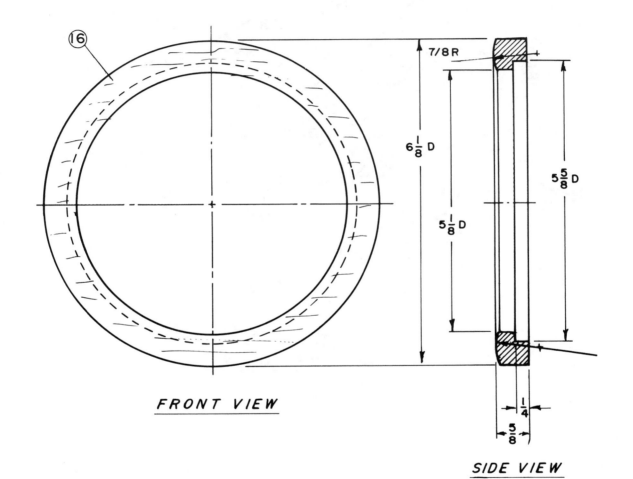

⑯

7/8 R

$6\frac{1}{8}$ D

$5\frac{1}{8}$ D

$5\frac{5}{8}$ D

$\frac{1}{4}$

$\frac{5}{8}$

FRONT VIEW

SIDE VIEW

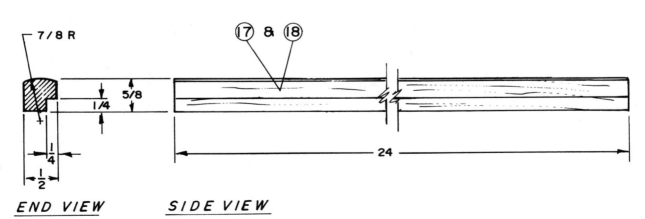

7/8 R

5/8

1/4

$\frac{1}{4}$

$\frac{1}{2}$

⑰ & ⑱

24

END VIEW   SIDE VIEW

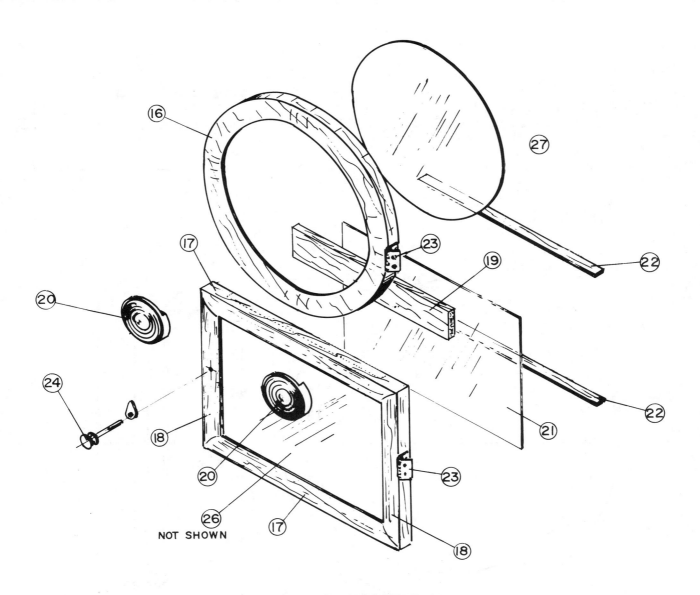

DOOR ASSEMBLY

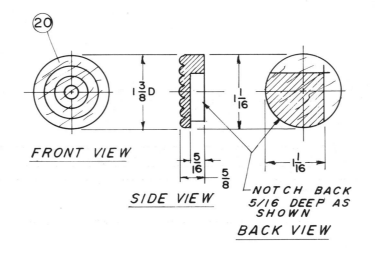

FRONT VIEW

SIDE VIEW

NOTCH BACK 5/16 DEEP AS SHOWN

BACK VIEW

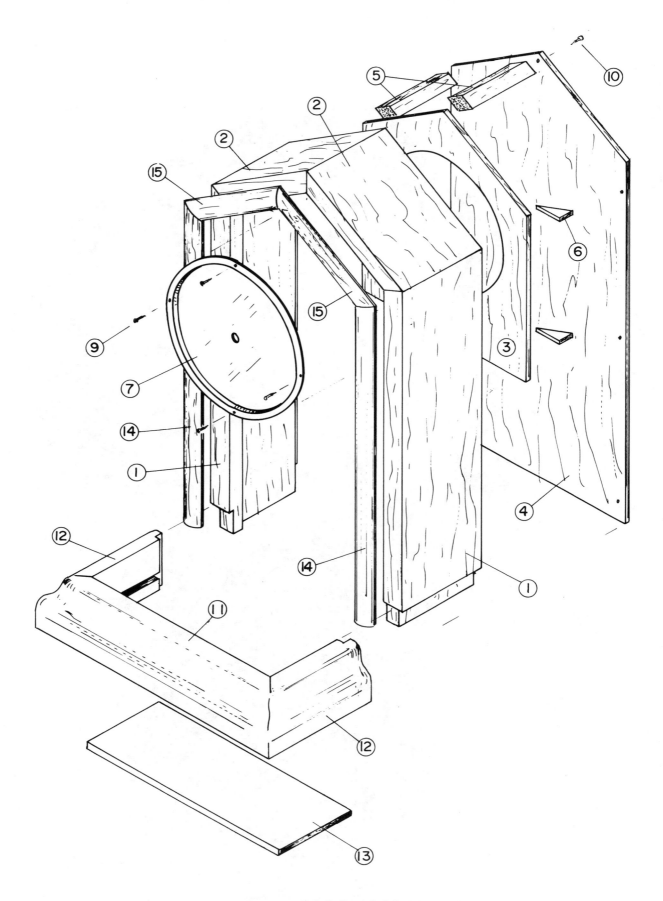

CASE ASSEMBLY

13

Figure Eight Clock

THIS CLOCK (FIG. 13-1) IS SHAPED LIKE A NUMBER EIGHT, HENCE THE NAME. Its case design is another early example of Elias Ingraham's work. He patented this design around 1862 and named it the "ionic" wall clock. At the same time, Elias hired Anson Atwood to set up and run a movement manufacturing division of the Ingraham company. This would allow the company to manufacture the complete clock—not just the case. Up to this time Elias purchased movements from Noah Pomeroy and Waterbury Brass Company.

This clock is the forerunner of the popular schoolhouse clock, developed in 1875 by Ansonia Clock Company.

The original model, as pictured, has an 8-day, time-only brass movement (Fig. 13-2). It has a rather unusual pendulum, very similar to those later used on kitchen clocks. It winds at 6:30, which is also rather unusual.

Elias Ingraham

Elias was born in 1805 in Marlborough, Connecticut. He served a 5-year apprenticeship in cabinetmaking in the early 1820s. By 1828, at the age of 23, Elias was designing and building clock cases for George Mitchell. When he was 25 years old he worked for the Chauncey and Lawson Ives Clock Company, still designing and building clock cases. The most popular clock case ever designed, the steeple clock, was designed by Elias in 1845.

He formed a new company with his brother, Andrew, in 1852, called the E. and A. Ingraham and Company, but 4 years later, it went bankrupt. A year later he formed his own company with his son, Edward. Changing the name to E. Ingraham and Company, the business began manufacturing clock cases. As noted above, by 1862 his company manufactured their own movements.

Throughout his lifetime, Elias was granted many clock case design patents, including the one shown. He died in 1885, but the company he started continued. Elias was perhaps the greatest clock case designer ever, and his clock designs are still being copied today.

Fig. 13-1. Opposite: Figure eight clock.

Fig. 13-2. Doors open showing the simple construction.

Instructions / Figure Eight Clock

Be sure to purchase the dial pan and dial (parts 17 and 18) before starting. If necessary adjust your wooden bezels to fit your brass pan.

To make this clock, you should have a lathe and be fairly good at turning, because the major parts (parts 9 through 12) require lathe work.

Study all drawings before starting. Remember to obtain the movement before starting this clock. If you use a quartz movement, you should have no problems with dimensions, but make sure it has a pendulum.

The only challenging parts of this clock are the turnings. Actually, they are not *that* difficult to make, but you will need special tools and some skill on the lathe. Be sure the glue on the segments is set thoroughly before turning parts 1 and 2.

STEP 1.

Carefully lay out and cut each piece as shown.

STEP 2.

The top drum (part 1) and bottom drum (part 2) can be made one of four different ways: you can steam-bend them, make saw kerfs close together on the interior surfaces and roll to size, glue-up thin strips of wood until the required thickness is achieved, or turn them on a lathe. Remember, they both require rabbets cut into the edges for the backs, parts 5 and 6, and the donut, part 4.

STEP 3.

Assemble the case per the front and side view with the doors removed. After the parts are made to size, the case is very simple. Be sure to maintain the 10 7/8-inch center-to-center dimension between the top and bottom doors. A flat surface in part 9 will have to be cut as shown.

STEP 4.
After the case is assembled, notch out for the two hinges (parts 13 and 14) and the hanger (part 23).

STEP 5.
Commercial dials that are very close to the original can be purchased, (see part 18) in Material List. Glue the dial directly inside the dial pan (part 17) with rubber cement.

STEP 6.
See Section III for instructions on finishing the clock case.

STEP 7.
Add a paper so your clock will really look authentic.

STEP 8.
Stick the decal to the glass and paint all the area from the rear with black paint, leaving only the center open so the pendulum can be seen.

PARTS LIST

No.	Name	Size	Req'd.
1	Drum-Top	13⅛ Diameter — 3 Deep	1
2	Drum-Bottom	7⅞ Diameter — 3 Deep	1
3	Neck	¼ × 2½ — 4⅜ Long	2
4	Donut	¼ × 13⅛ — 13⅛ Long	1
5	Back-Top	¼ × 12⅞ — 12⅞ Long	1
6	Back-Bottom	¼ × 7⅜ — 7⅜ Long	1
7	Back-Center	¼ × 2⅜ — 5⅜ Long	1
8	Center Board	¼ × 2⅜ — 5⅜ Long	1
9	Wing	2½ Diameter × 3 Long	2
10	Rosette	2⅝ Diameter × ½ Long	2
11	Door-Top	13¼ Diameter 1" Thick	1
12	Door-Bottom	8 Diameter ¾ Thick	1
13	Hinge-Brass	1¾ Size	1
14	Hinge-Brass	1⅜ Size	1
15	Door Glass	11⅛ Diameter	1
16	Door Glass	6¼ Diameter	1
17	Dial Pan 10⅛ D.	Merritt No. P61-J	1
18	Dial Face, 9 Dia.	Merritt No. R-900	1
19	Hands 5" Size	Merritt No. P89	1 pr.
20	Movement	See Below	1
21	Filler	½ × ½ — 2 Long	3
22	Filler	¼ × 1 — 2 Long	2
23	Hanger-Brass	Merritt No. P-71	1
24	Decal	Merritt No. P-572	1
25	Hook & Eye	Merritt No. P-92-A	2

Movement: Brass: Merritt No. P-287
Quartz: Merritt No. P-160

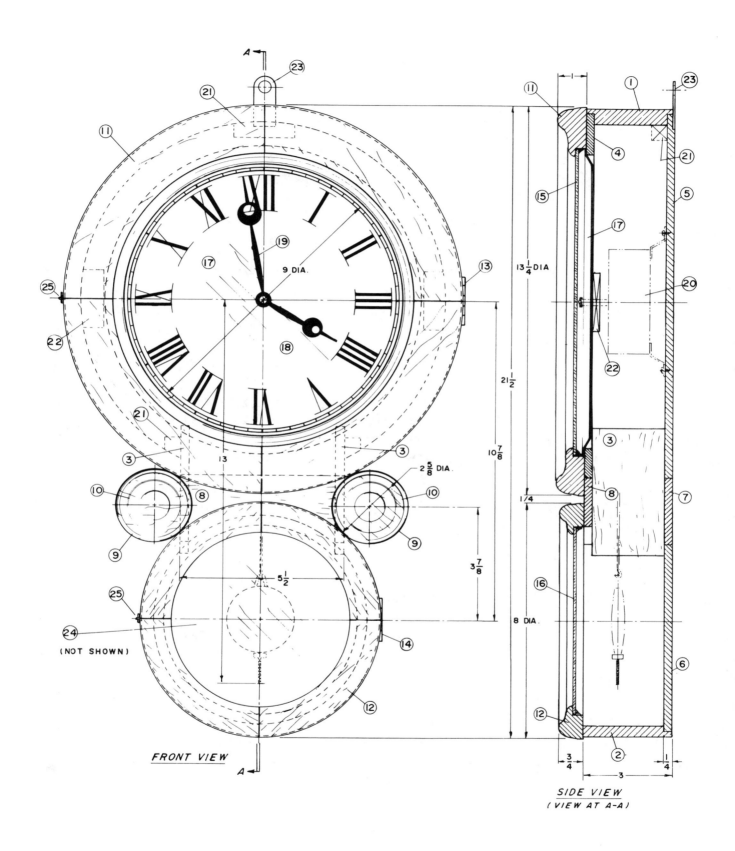

9 DIA.

13¼ DIA

21½

10⅞

2⅝ DIA.

5½

3⅞

8 DIA.

13

FRONT VIEW

A

A

(NOT SHOWN)

1

¾

3

¼

SIDE VIEW
(VIEW AT A-A)

1/4

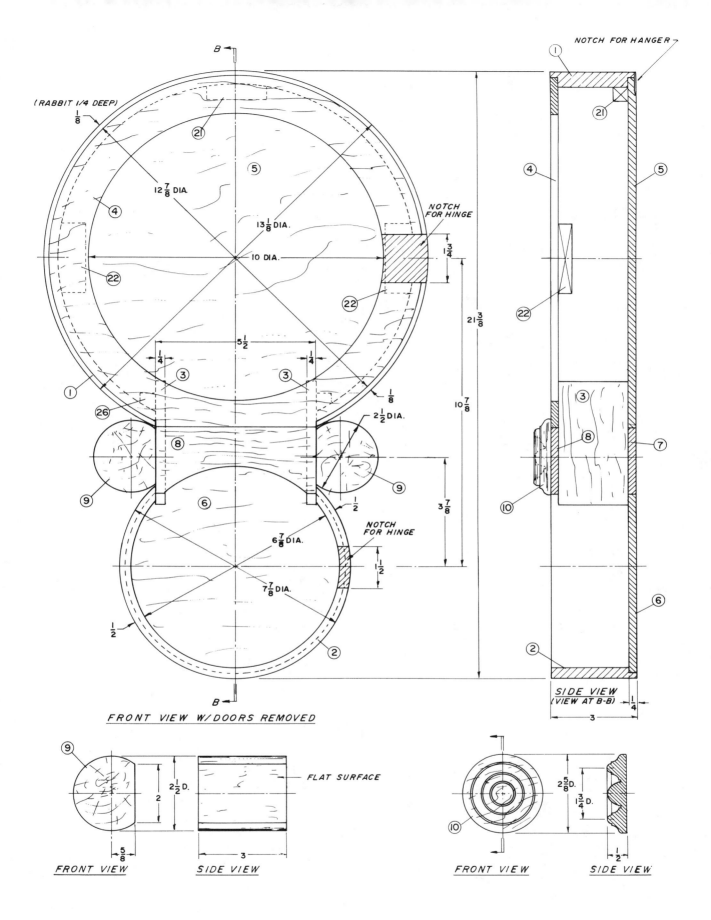

NOTCH FOR HANGER

(RABBIT 1/4 DEEP)

12 7/8 DIA.

13 1/8 DIA.

10 DIA.

NOTCH FOR HINGE

1 3/4

21 3/8

10 7/8

5 1/2

1/4   1/4

1/8

2 1/2 DIA.

3 7/8

1/2

NOTCH FOR HINGE

6 7/8 DIA.

7 7/8 DIA.

1 1/2

1/2

FRONT VIEW W/DOORS REMOVED

SIDE VIEW
(VIEW AT B-B)

1/4

3

FLAT SURFACE

2 1/2 D.

2

5/8

FRONT VIEW   SIDE VIEW

3

2 5/8 D.

1 3/4 D.

1/2

FRONT VIEW   SIDE VIEW

FIGURE EIGHT CLOCK   115

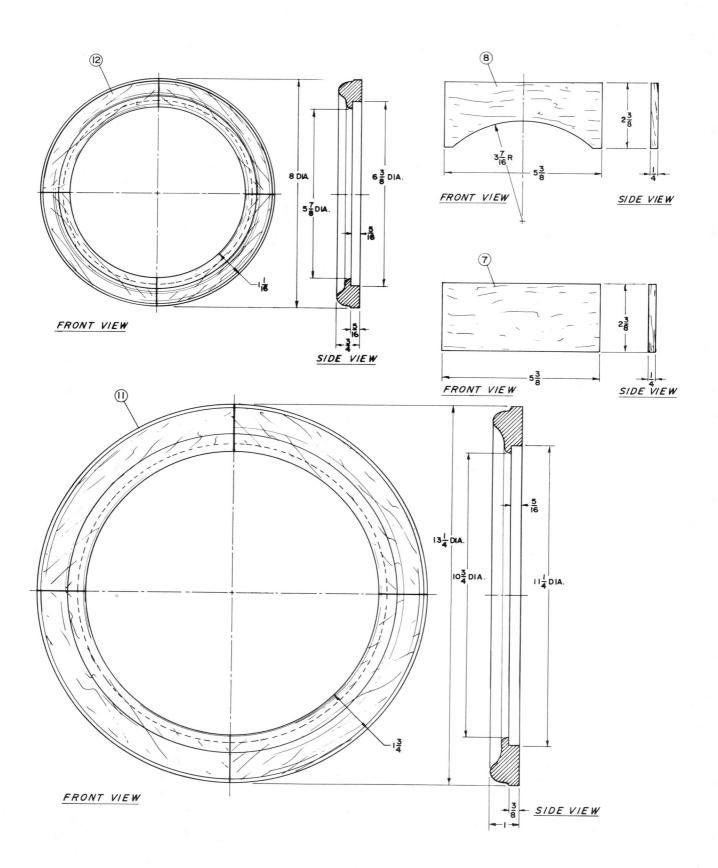

⑫

8 DIA

6 3/8 DIA.

5 7/8 DIA.

5/16

1 1/16

5/16

3/4

FRONT VIEW

SIDE VIEW

⑧

3 7/16 R

5 3/8

2 3/8

1/4

FRONT VIEW

SIDE VIEW

⑦

5 3/8

2 3/8

1/4

FRONT VIEW

SIDE VIEW

⑪

13 1/4 DIA.

10 3/4 DIA.

11 1/4 DIA.

5/16

1 3/4

3/8

1

FRONT VIEW

SIDE VIEW

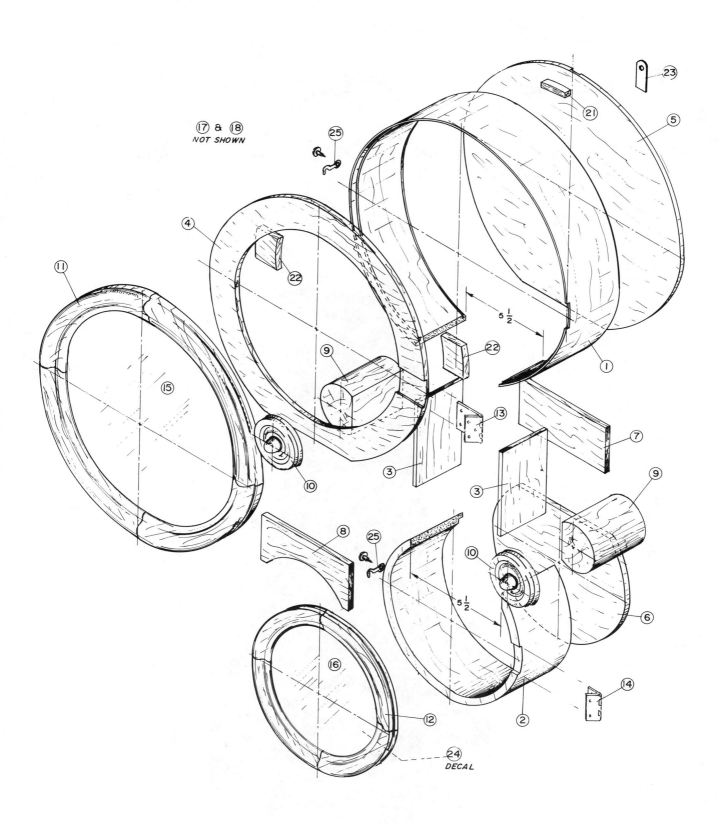

17 & 18
NOT SHOWN

5 ½

5 ½

DECAL

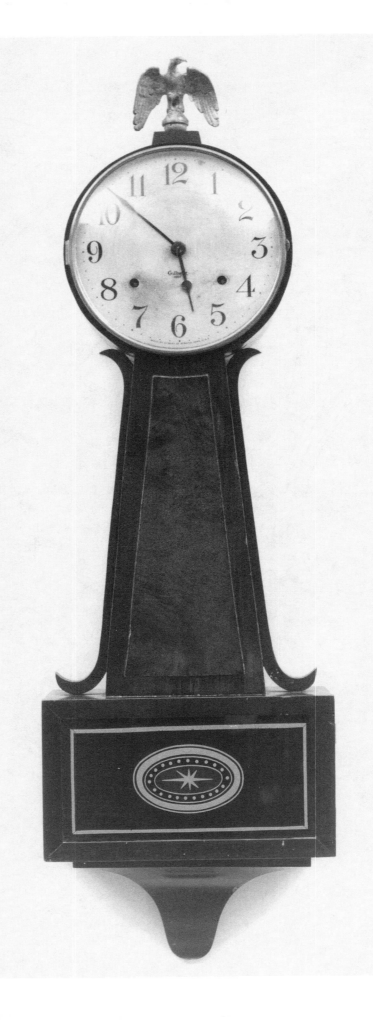

14

Banjo Clock

THE WILLARD FAMILY OF MASSACHUSETTS DESIGNED AND BUILT MANY KINDS OF beautiful clocks. Today, clocks built by Benjamin, Simon, Ephram, and Aaron Willard demand top dollar, *if* you can find one for sale. Simon Willard learned clockmaking from his older brother, Benjamin, and settled in Roxbury, Massachusetts right after the Revolutionary War. In 1795 Simon designed a totally new wall clock, which he called the "improved timepiece." He patented it in 1802, and it was an instant success with the burgeoning middle class. The case is shaped like a banjo, and it is referred to today as a banjo clock (Fig. 14-1).

The banjo clock has been very popular since 1842, and the styling of this clock has been copied and recopied by many companies. It still is a very popular model of clock—an early original Willard banjo would be almost priceless. Famous naval battles were painted on the bottom glass and the top glass panel was gold-gilded with a matching design. Some banjo clocks have brass side brackets.

An interesting place to visit is the Willard homestead in Grafton, Massachusetts. Call them at (617) 839-3500 for information.

William L. Gilbert

William Gilbert was born in 1806 and died at the age of 84 in 1890. He purchased a clockshop with his brother-in-law, George Marsh in 1828. They made cheap clocks in Bristol, Connecticut up to 1834. The company desolved in 1837, but in 1841 William purchased another factory and began making clocks again. George B. Owens served as manager for over 20 years. Owens was responsible for many of the clock case designs of the W. L. Gilbert and Company.

This banjo is a copy of a later model manufactured by the William L. Gilbert Clock Company. It is powered by an 8-day brass movement with a bim-bam hour count and a single sound on the half hour (Fig. 14-2). This banjo has a 21-inch-long pendulum. The unusual wood side panels make this an inexpensive, unique and interesting clock case to make.

Fig. 14-1. Opposite: Banjo clock, circa 1898.

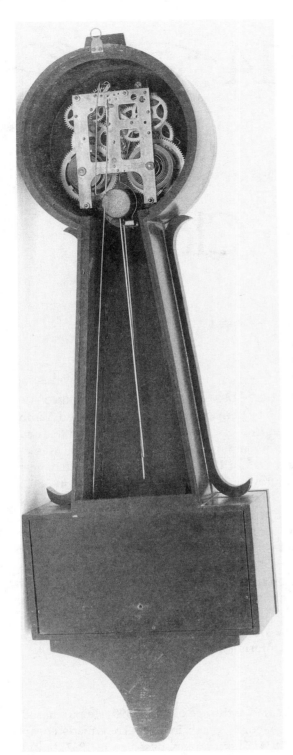

Fig. 14-2. View with back removed showing front-mounted movement and bim-bam strike rods.

Instructions / Banjo Clock

Be sure to purchase the dial pan and dial (part 20) before starting. If necessary, adjust all wooden parts (parts 1, 3, and 5) to fit your brass pan. There should be a 3/16- or 1/4-inch wood space showing all around the brass bezel.

Study all drawings before starting. It is a good idea to have the movement before starting this clock. If you use a quartz movement you should have no problem with size, but make sure it has a pendulum.

STEP 1.

The only difficult part of making this clock is bending the head (part 1). The rest of it is very easy. Make saw kerfs 5/16 inch deep and 3/8 inch apart as shown. Roll up to the 7 1/8-inch *inside* diameter as illustrated, hold in place, and add wood glue into the saw kerfs to maintain its round shape.

STEP 2.
Carefully lay out and cut all other pieces as shown.

STEP 3.
After cutting the parts to size, assemble the case per the illustrated front and side views. It should go together without any problem.

STEP 4.
Dry-fit all parts before gluing.

STEP 5.
See Section III for instructions on finishing the clock case.

STEP 6.
Add the decal to the glass and paint all the area from the rear with black paint, leaving only the center open so the pendulum can be seen.

———————————————PARTS LIST———————————————

No.	Name	Size	Req'd.
1	Head	5/8 × 3 1/4 — 25 1/8 Long	1
2	Neck	5/8 × 3 1/4 — 13 1/2 Long	2
3	Face Board	5/8 × 8 3/8 — 20 13/16 Long	1
4	Back Support	3/8 × 1/2 — 5 1/4 Long	1
5	Back-Head	3/8 Tk — 7 3/4 Diameter	1
6	Back-Neck	3/8 × 5 — 12 1/2 Long	1
7	Brace-Neck	5/8 × 5/8 — 2 3/4 Long	1
8	Base-Top/Bottom	3/4 × 10 1/2 Long	2
9	Base-Side	3/4 × 4 — 6 Long	2
10	Corner Brace	3/4 × 3/4 — 3 5/8 Long	4
11	Back-Base	3/8 × 5 1/4 × 9 3/4 Long	1
12	Door-Top/Bottom	9/16 × 11/16 — 10 1/2 Long	2
13	Door-Side	9/16 × 11/16 — 6 Long	2
14	Glass	3/32 × 5 1/4 — 9 13/16 Long	1
15	Glass Support	1/8 × 5/16 — 36 Long.	1
16	Hinge Brass	3/4 × 3/4 Long	2
17	Top Cap	11/16 × 1 7/8 Square	1
18	Side Arm	1/2 × 2 — 13 1/2 Long	2
19	Burl	1/16 × 4 — 11 Long	1
*20	Dial Face, Bezel	M/S 3415 — X	1
21	Pediment	3 3/4 × 4 7/8 — 8 3/4 Long	1
22	Eagle	Empire 250-81-143	1
23	Movement	See Below	1
24	Hanger Cut to 1" Lg.	Turncraft 272202	1
25	Hands 3" Long	See Below	1 pr.
26	Decal (not shown)	T.E.C. Style 'Ten'	1

*Or Turncraft 710988

Movement: Brass, None available
    Quartz, Klockit 12947-A   w/Hands 66927-A

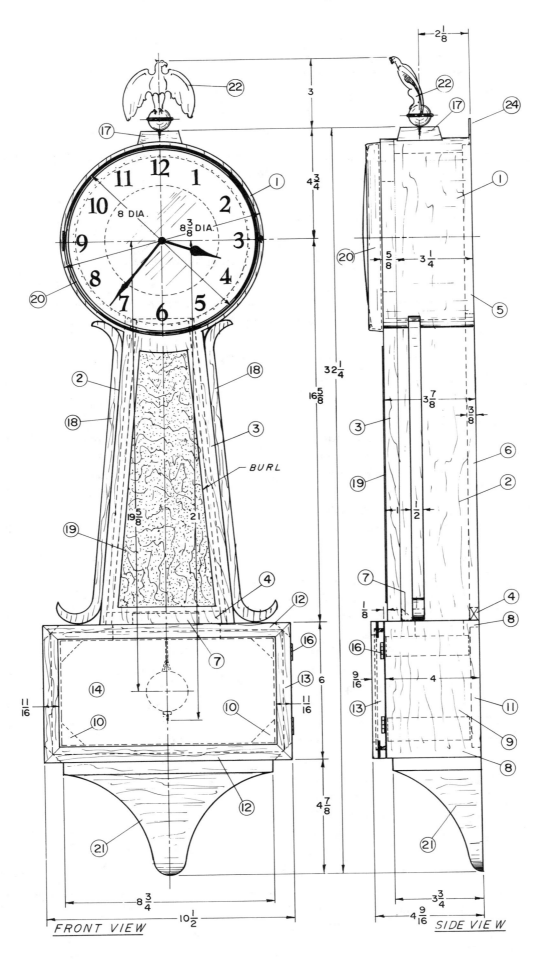

FRONT VIEW

SIDE VIEW

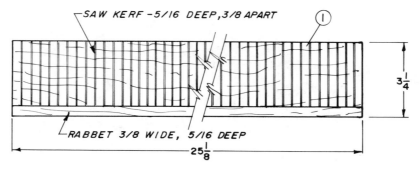

SAW KERF –5/16 DEEP, 3/8 APART

①

3 1/4

RABBET 3/8 WIDE, 5/16 DEEP

25 1/8

INSIDE VIEW (BEFORE ROLLING)

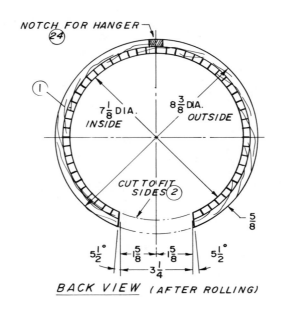

NOTCH FOR HANGER
㉔

①

7 1/8 DIA.
INSIDE

8 3/8 DIA.
OUTSIDE

CUT TO FIT
SIDES ②

5/8

5 1/2°   1 5/8   1 5/8   5 1/2°

3 1/4

BACK VIEW (AFTER ROLLING)

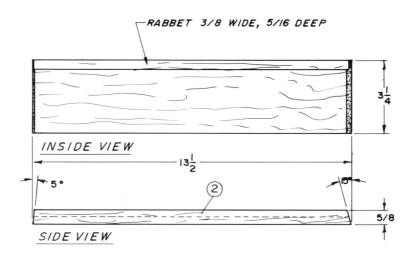

RABBET 3/8 WIDE, 5/16 DEEP

3 1/4

INSIDE VIEW

13 1/2

5°   5°

②

5/8

SIDE VIEW

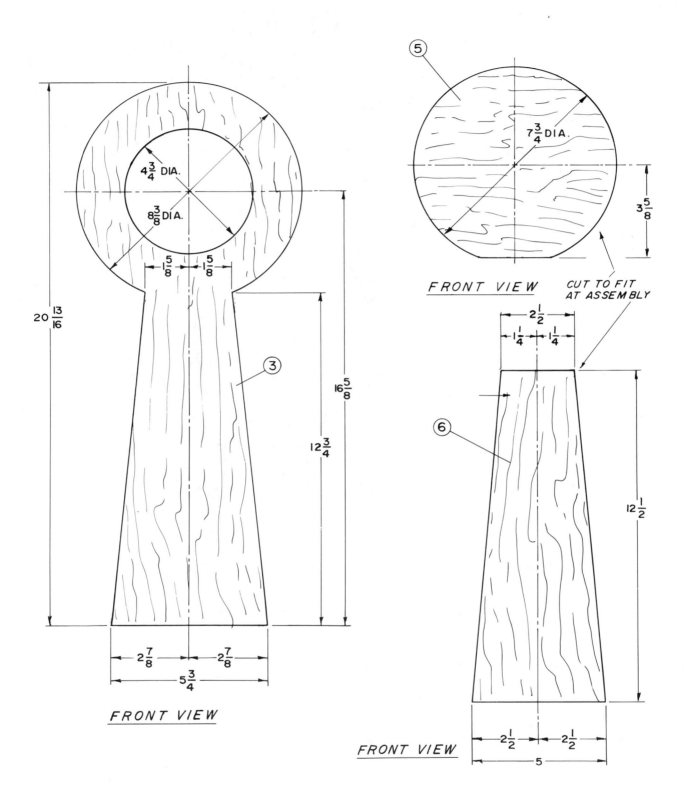

$4\frac{3}{4}$ DIA.

$8\frac{3}{8}$ DIA.

$1\frac{5}{8}$ $1\frac{5}{8}$

$20\frac{13}{16}$

③

$16\frac{5}{8}$

$12\frac{3}{4}$

$2\frac{7}{8}$ $2\frac{7}{8}$

$5\frac{3}{4}$

FRONT VIEW

⑤

$7\frac{3}{4}$ DIA.

$3\frac{5}{8}$

FRONT VIEW

CUT TO FIT
AT ASSEMBLY

$2\frac{1}{2}$

$1\frac{1}{4}$ $1\frac{1}{4}$

⑥

$12\frac{1}{2}$

$2\frac{1}{2}$ $2\frac{1}{2}$

5

FRONT VIEW

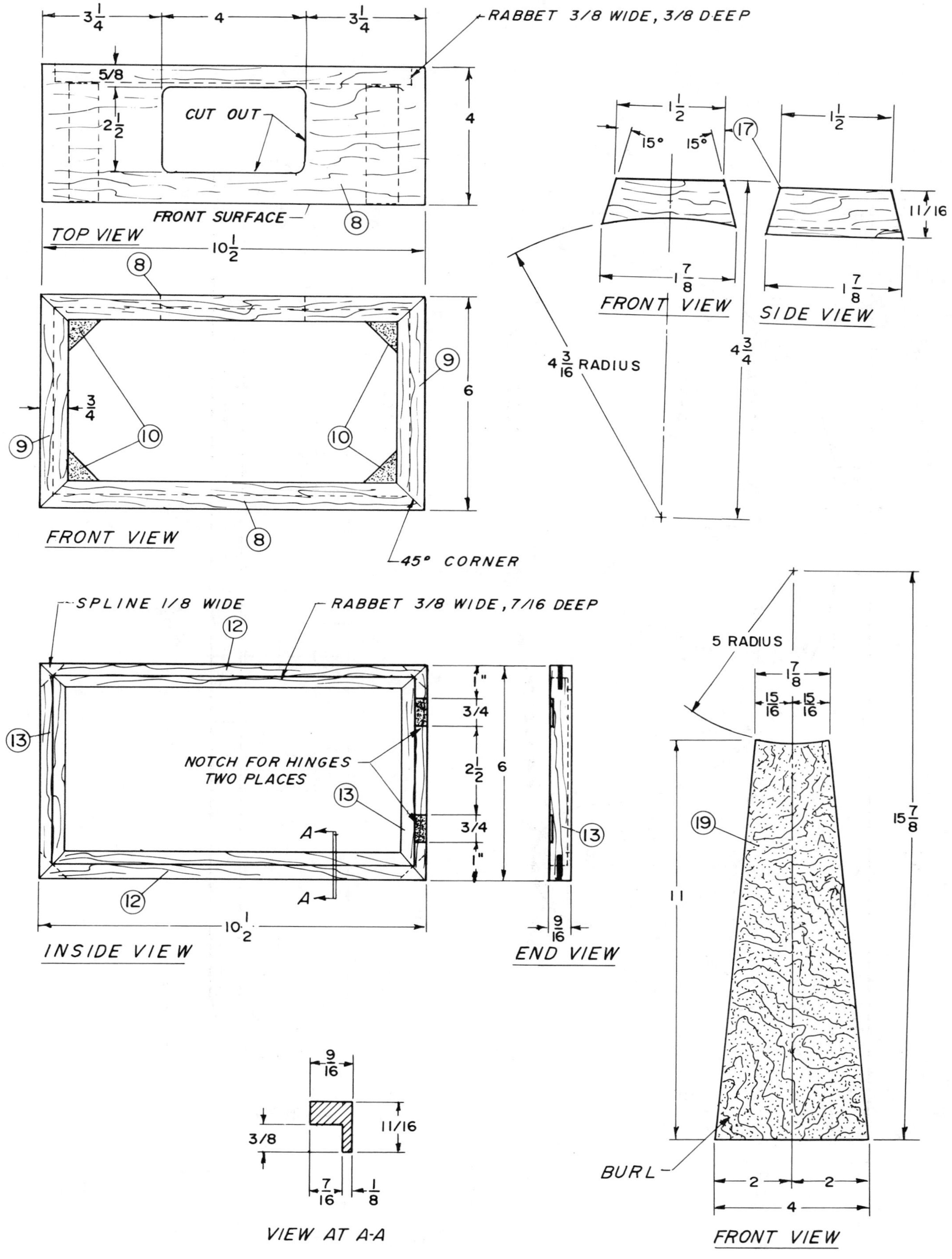
RABBET 3/8 WIDE, 3/8 DEEP
3 1/4
4
3 1/4
5/8
2 1/2
CUT OUT
4
FRONT SURFACE
8
TOP VIEW
10 1/2
8
9
3/4
9
10
10
6
8
FRONT VIEW
45° CORNER
1 1/2
15°
15°
17
1 1/2
11/16
1 7/8
1 7/8
FRONT VIEW
SIDE VIEW
4 3/16 RADIUS
4 3/4
SPLINE 1/8 WIDE
RABBET 3/8 WIDE, 7/16 DEEP
12
13
1"
3/4
NOTCH FOR HINGES
TWO PLACES
2 1/2
6
13
3/4
A
1"
13
A
12
10 1/2
9/16
INSIDE VIEW
END VIEW
9/16
11/16
3/8
7/16
1/8
VIEW AT A-A
5 RADIUS
1 7/8
15/16
15/16
19
11
15 7/8
BURL
2
2
4
FRONT VIEW

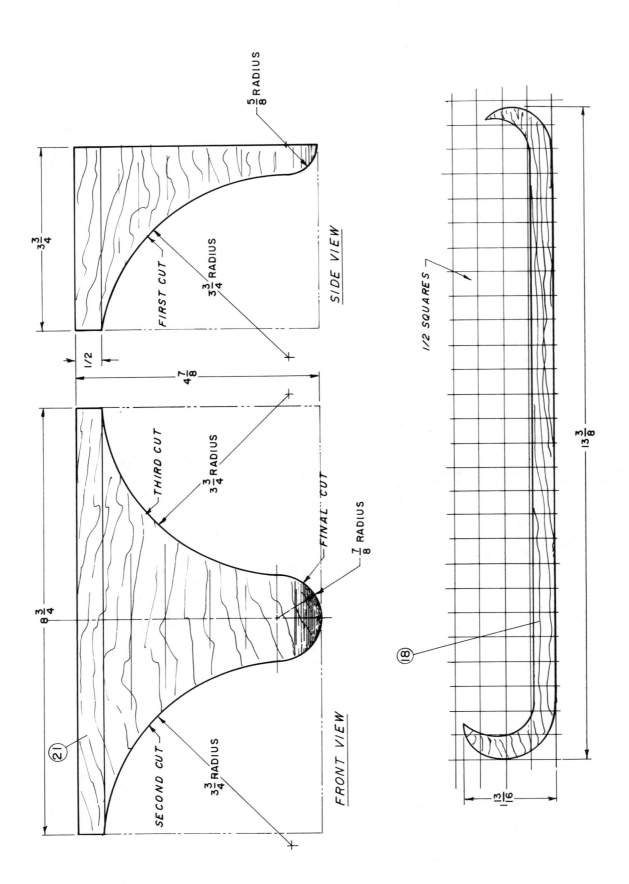

5/8 RADIUS

3 3/4

1/2

FIRST CUT

3 3/4 RADIUS

SIDE VIEW

4 7/8

THIRD CUT

3 3/4 RADIUS

8 3/4

FINAL CUT

7/8 RADIUS

21

SECOND CUT

3 3/4 RADIUS

FRONT VIEW

1/2 SQUARES

13 3/8

18

13/16

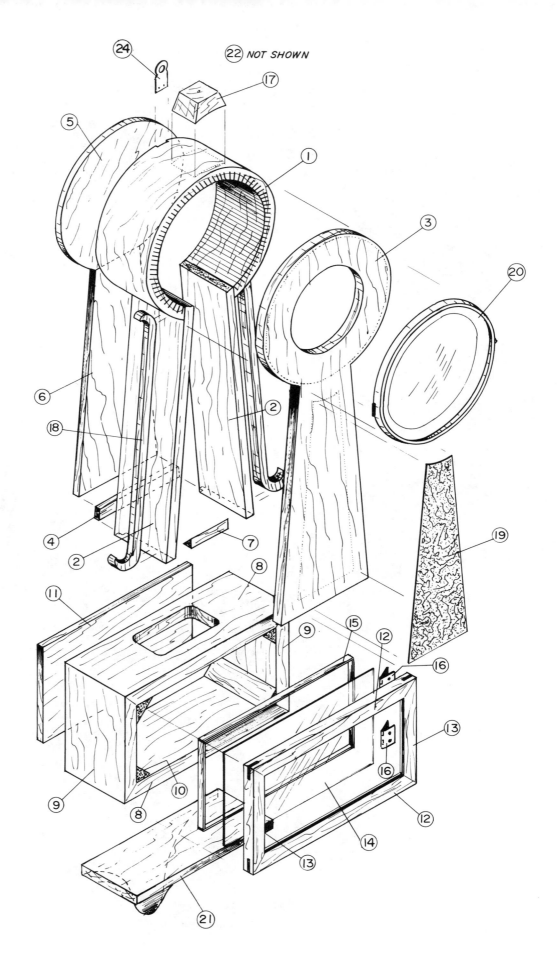

15

Schoolhouse Clock

FOR MANY MANY YEARS OF EARLY AMERICA, YOUNG AND EAGER EYES GAZED impatiently at schoolhouse clocks hung on the wall next to Gilbert Stuart's framed painting of George Washington. I hate to date myself, but I can vividly remember those days myself. Almost every school throughout the country had one of these clocks on their wall thus the name, schoolhouse clock (Fig. 15-1). Sad to say, but those wonderful old clocks have been replaced by high-tech automatic electronic clocks of today.

Ansonia Clock Company started business at Derby, Connecticut in 1850. Four years later the company burned to the ground, it was moved to Ansonia, Connecticut and renamed Ansonia Brass and Copper Company.

By 1875, they changed their name back to Ansonia Clock Company, and during that time, they developed a very popular model: their Model-A Long Drop Octagon Clock—a forerunner of the schoolhouse clock. This model became popular very quickly and was sold throughout the entire world. Most models of the schoolhouse clock were sold from 1875 to 1910; the clocks were made in all sizes by almost all major clock companies. Countries such as China and Korea made schoolhouse clocks in great quantities. Today many of the so-called antique schoolhouse clocks you see are actually Korean, not American. The foreign models have very cheap movements and do not last as long as the American models.

Ansonia Clock Company made many wonderful clocks and excellent high-quality movements, but due to the Great Depression, they went out of business in 1929. They moved what was left of it to Russia, but never really got going again, as the Russian Government took over most of their machinery.

Seth Thomas

The model shown was made by Seth Thomas around 1900 (Fig. 15-2). It has a time-only (no strike), brass, spring driven movement, (For more on Seth Thomas, see next project.)

Fig. 15-1. Opposite: Schoolhouse clock, circa 1900.

Fig. 15-2. Eight-day, time-only movement.

Instructions / Schoolhouse Clock

Be sure to purchase the dial pan and dial, parts 15 through 20, and the movement, part 24, before starting the clock. The dial and bezel parts can be purchased as *one* complete assembly, if you wish. This will save time and make an excellent assembly.

Study all drawings before starting. Always purchase the movement before starting this clock. If you use a quartz movement, you should have no problems but be sure it has a pendulum.

This is a rather easy clock to make. The only tricky part is gluing the eight sectors (part 8) together so you end up with no gaps between the eight joints. Each segment must be 6 5/8 inches long and cut at *exactly* 22 1/2 degrees. I usually glue-up two assemblies of four sectors each and let the glue set thoroughly. Then I dry-fit the two assemblies (halves) together. If they do not fit tightly, trim the edges until they do fit tightly.

STEP 1.

A spline was not used on the original clock. Instead, the sectors were held together by an unusual method. The original clock had eight, 2 1/4-inch-diameter, 1/4-inch-thick splines set in and glued between each joint as shown. If you use this method, simply glue the eight segments together, and when the glue sets, drill eight 2 1/4-inch-diameter holes, 1/4-inch deep at each joint of the segments. The original clock has held together for over 90 years now so this joint must be a good joint.

STEP 2.

Carefully lay out and cut all other pieces as shown.

STEP 3.

After cutting the parts to size, assemble the case per the illustrated front and side views; it should go together without any problem. Be sure to dry-fit all parts before gluing.

STEP 4.

See Section III for finishing instructions.

STEP 5.

Add the oval decal to the glass and paint all the area from the rear with black paint, leaving only the center open so the pendulum can be seen.

────────────────────────── PARTS LIST ──────────────────────────

No.	Name	Size	Req'd.
1	Side	¾ × 3⅜ — 19⅛ Long	2
2	Top	¾ × 3⅛ — 8½ Long	1
3	Bottom	¾ × 3⅜ — 3¹³⁄₁₆ Long	3
4	Back	¼ × 8½ — 21½ Long	1
5	Face-Top	½ × 1½ — 7¾ Long	1
6	Face-Side	½ × ¹⁵⁄₁₆ — 4¹¹⁄₁₆ Long	2
7	Face-Bottom	½ × ¹⁵⁄₁₆ — 3¼ Long	3
8	Sector	¾ × 3 — 6⅝ Long	8
9	Spline	⅜ × 2¼ Diameter	8
10	Door-Top	⅝ × ¹¹⁄₁₆ — 6¼ Long	1
11	Door-Side	⅝ × ¹¹⁄₁₆ — 3⁹⁄₁₆ Long	2
12	Door-Bottom	⅝ × ¹¹⁄₁₆ — 2½ Long	3
13	Trim-Side	¼ × ¹³⁄₁₆ — 6⅜ Long	2
14	Trim-Bottom	¼ × ¹³⁄₁₆ — 3¹³⁄₁₆ Long	3
15	Pan 12½ Dia.	Turncraft 712213	1
16	Bezel w/Glass	Turncraft 712213	1
17	Hinge	Turncraft 712213	1
18	Dial Face (Roman)	Turncraft 712213	1
19	Hands 5½ Size	Turncraft 591809	1 pr.
20	Lock (Brass)	Included w/No 15	1
21	Latch	⅜ × ½ — 1½ Long	1
22	Hinge-Brass	Turncraft 131043	2
23	Block For Hinge	³⁄₁₆ × ⁷⁄₁₆ — ¾ Long	2
24	Movement	See Below	1
25	Glass Door	³⁄₃₂ × 4⁵⁄₁₆ — 5⅛ Long	1
26	Insert	⅛ × ¼ — 20 Long	1
27	Hanger	Turncraft 272200	1
28	Decal 3¼ × 4	Turncraft 310159	1
29	Turnlatch	Turncraft 101029	1
30	Filler	⅛ × 1⅜ — 8½ Long	2

Movement: Brass, LaRose 084052
      Quartz, Turncraft 532065
        w/Hands 591809

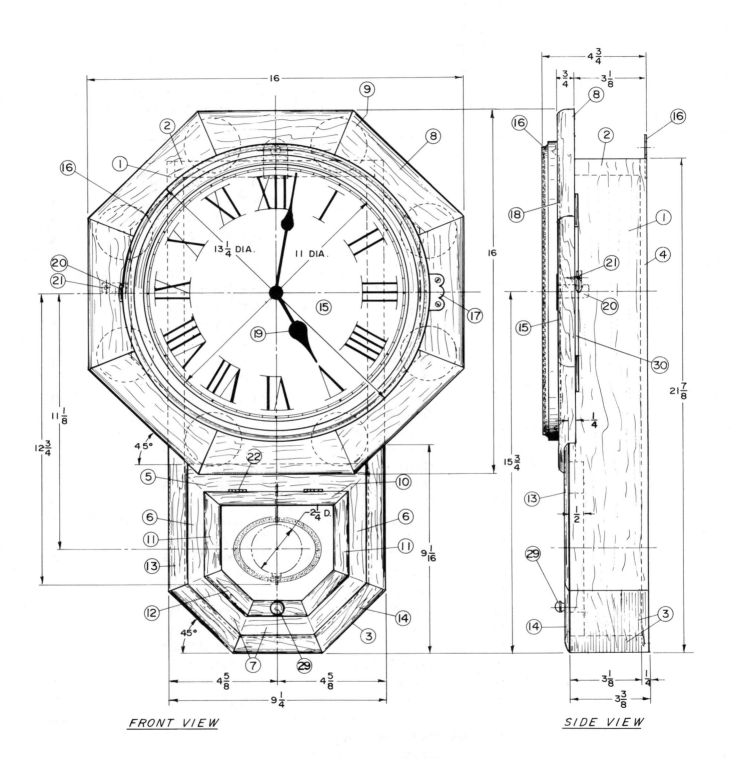

16

13¼ DIA.   11 DIA.

2¼ D.

45°

11⅛

12¾

45°

4⅝   4⅝

9¼

FRONT VIEW

4¾

¾   3⅛

16

16

15¾

9 1/16

21⅞

¼

½

3⅛   ¼

3⅜

SIDE VIEW

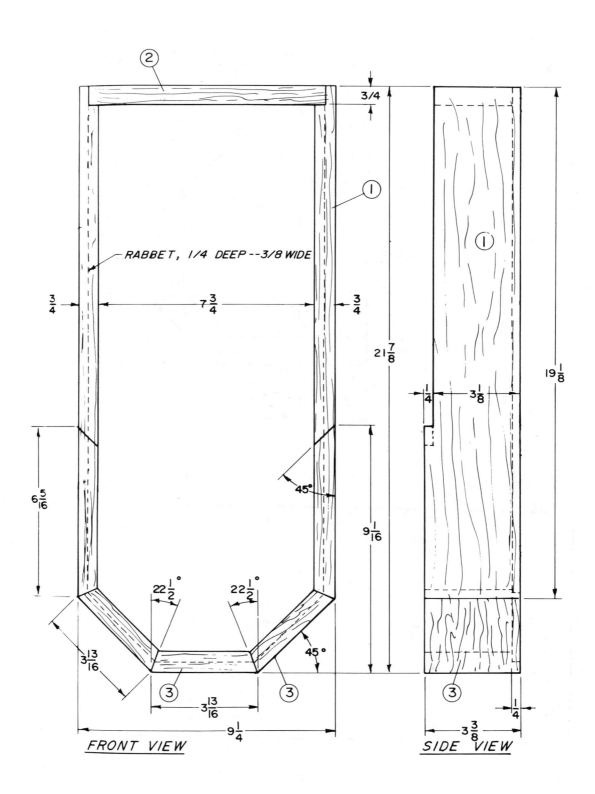

RABBET, 1/4 DEEP -- 3/8 WIDE

FRONT VIEW

SIDE VIEW

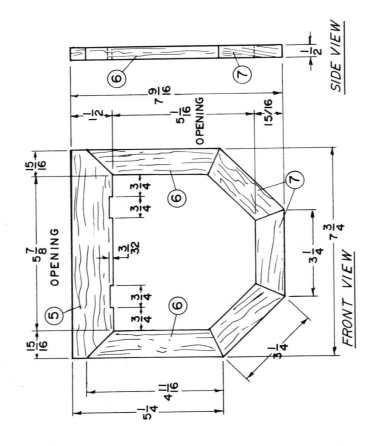

SIDE VIEW

⑥ 7 9/16 ⑦ 1/2

5 5/16 OPENING

15/16

15/16

⑥ 3 3/4

3 3/4

⑥ 3/32

5 7/8 OPENING

⑤ 3 3/4

3 3/4

⑥ 3 1/4

⑥ 3 1/4

15/16

7 3/4

4 11/16

5 1/4

FRONT VIEW

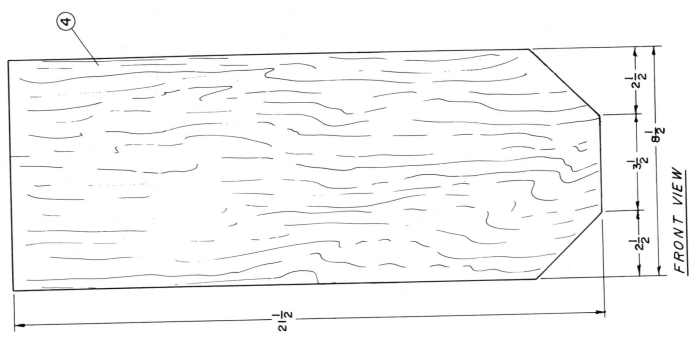

④

2 1/2

3 1/2

8 1/2

2 1/2

2 1/2

21 1/2

FRONT VIEW

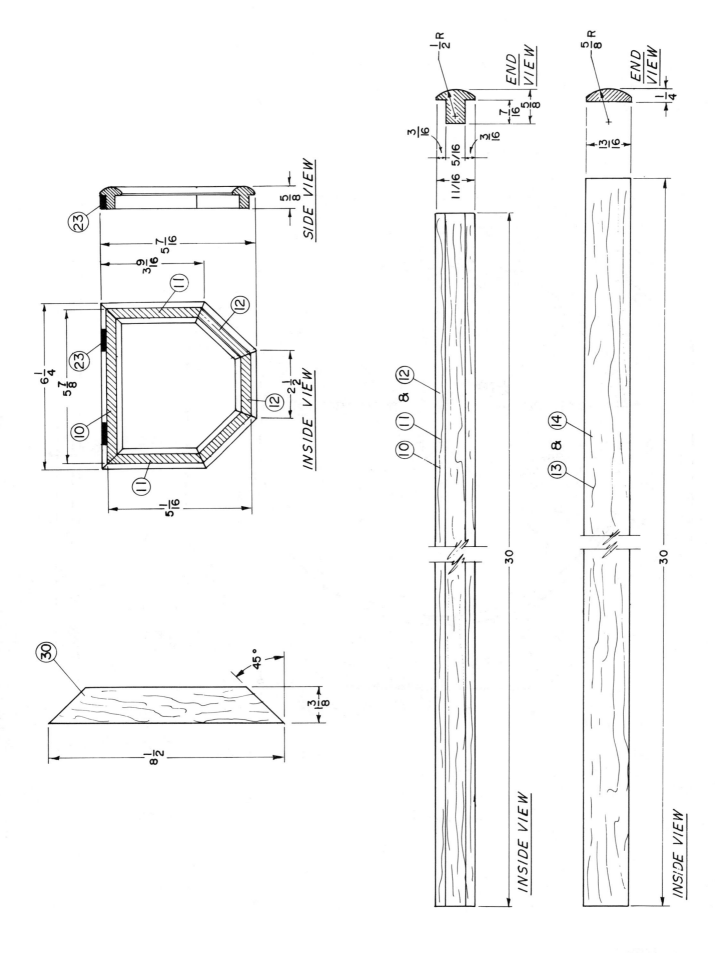

SIDE VIEW

INSIDE VIEW

END VIEW

END VIEW

INSIDE VIEW

INSIDE VIEW

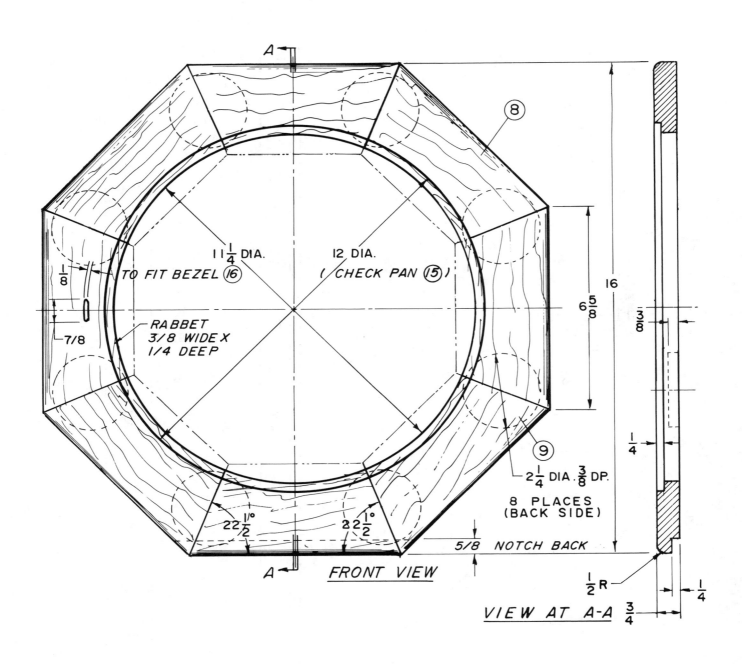

11¼ DIA.
TO FIT BEZEL ⑯

12 DIA.
(CHECK PAN ⑮)

⅛

7/8

RABBET
3/8 WIDE X
1/4 DEEP

22½°

22½°

A

A

FRONT VIEW

⑧

6⅝

16

⑨

2¼ DIA. ⅜ DP.

8 PLACES
(BACK SIDE)

5/8 NOTCH BACK

½ R

¾

VIEW AT A-A

⅜

¼

¼

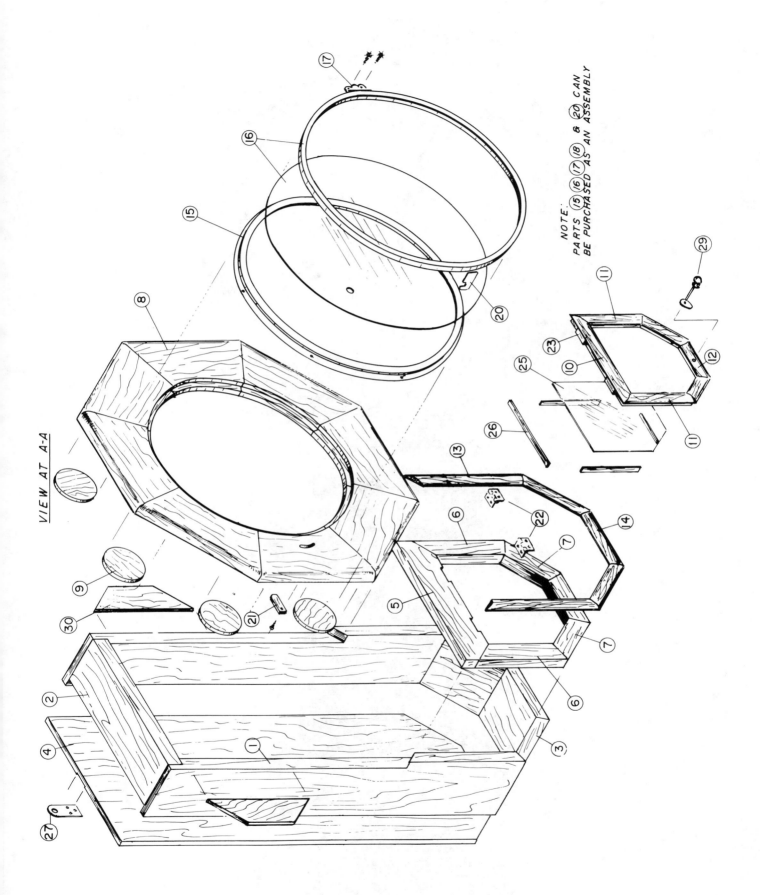

VIEW AT A-A

NOTE:
PARTS (15) (16) (7) (18) & (20) CAN
BE PURCHASED AS AN ASSEMBLY

Regulator Clock

THIS MODEL IS A LATE-MODEL REGULATOR NO. 2 MADE OF OAK, WITH A SINGLE 8-day, high-quality, weight-driven movement (Fig. 16-1). The original movement is mounted on a cast-iron support, which is a little unusual for most American clocks. An exact copy of this movement with the cast-iron support can be purchased today.

The term "regulator" generally refers to a very precise, plain-cased clock with a long pendulum and no strike. Seth Thomas' original and famous, regulator no. 2 wall clock was very popular in America from 1870 to 1920. Almost every office, church or bank of any size at all had a Regulator no. 2 hanging on the wall. They were usually made of oak or walnut and the design changed very little through the years (Fig. 16-2).

Seth Thomas

Seth Thomas was born in 1785 and died at the age of 74 in 1859. After working for Eli Terry, Seth Thomas purchased a small shop in Plymouth, Connecticut in 1813. He produced tall-case clocks and shelf clocks. Seth Thomas was not an innovator himself; he was a businessman. Most of his early clocks were very similar in design to those of Eli Terry—in fact, he produced Eli's popular pillar and scroll model. Seth Thomas was a shrewd businessman and had a knack for marketing clocks; his business thrived while others failed.

In honor of Seth Thomas, the name of Plymouth Hollow, Connecticut was changed to Thomston. Still in business today, Seth Thomas's company is part of Tally Industries, Seth Thomas Division.

Instructions / Regulator Clock

Be sure to purchase the latch, retaining ring, door latch, hinge and dial (parts 17, 20, 21, 22, and 28) and the movement (part 25) before starting the clock. The brass movement is an exact copy of the original movement. It will make your clock run and sound just like the original. You should use oak, as most originals were made of oak.

Fig. 16-1. Opposite: Regulator no. 2 (oak wood), circa 1900.

Fig. 16-2. A replacement movement can be purchased today that is exactly the same as the one on the original regulator, with a cast-iron support.

Study all drawings before starting. Always purchase the movement before starting this clock. If you use a quartz movement, you should have no problems, but be sure it has a pendulum and a fake weight.

This clock looks more difficult than it is—it is actually rather easy. The only tricky part is making the two eight-sided, glued-up assemblies (parts 7 and 12).

STEP 1.

To make these two subassemblies, glue-up two assemblies of four sectors each and let the glue set thoroughly. Then dry-fit the two assemblies (holes) together. If they do not fit tightly, trim the edges until they do. You can add a spline between segments of part 7 if you wish. The other assembly (part 12) must be turned to shape, so you cannot use splines on this assembly.

STEP 2.

Be sure the segments are thoroughly set before turning on the lathe. Also be sure to check the size of your retaining ring (part 20) before turning the segment dial (part 12). The 12^1/$_8$-inch inside diameter (see part 12) must be adjusted to fit your retaining ring (part 20). The retaining ring must fit and be held into the *inside*, ^{5}/$_{16}$-inch rabbet cut of the segment dial (part 12). It is snugly held in place by a thin ^{1}/$_{16}$- × -^{1}/$_8$-inch strip of wood (not shown), glued to the segment dial. This is why it is so important that you check the *outside* diameter of the retaining ring and turn the segment dial (bezel) for a snug fit. I have built two or three of these clocks and found the retaining rings vary slightly in size—even from the same supplier.

STEP 3.

Once the segment dial (part 12), door assembly (part 14), and segment case (part 7) are made, the rest of the clock is rather easy.

STEP 4.

After cutting all the other parts to size, assemble the case per the illustrated front and side views; it should go together without any problem. Be sure to dry-fit all parts before gluing.

STEP 5.

See Section III for finishing instructions.

No.	Name	Size	Req'd.
1	Side Panel	$5/8 \times 4\frac{1}{4} - 31\frac{1}{8}$ Long	1
2	Back	$3/8 \times 8\frac{7}{8} - 31\frac{5}{8}$ Long	1
3	Bottom	$\frac{1}{2} \times 5\frac{1}{8} - 10\frac{3}{8}$ Long	1
4	Top	$\frac{1}{2} \times 3\frac{1}{8} - 8\frac{7}{8}$ Long	1
5	Front Board	$\frac{1}{2} \times 2\frac{1}{2} - 9\frac{1}{2}$ Long	1
6	Front Trim	$\frac{1}{4} \times 13/16 - 10\frac{1}{8}$ Long	1
7	Segment-Case	$3/4 \times 3\frac{1}{4} - 6^{7}/_{16}$ Long	8
8	Center Block	$2 \times 4\frac{1}{4} - 6$ Long	1
9	Bottom Block	$1^{3}/_{16} \times 1\frac{3}{4} - 4\frac{1}{4}$ Long	2
10	Trim-Side	$5/8 \times 2\frac{1}{8} - 4^{7}/_{16}$ Long	2
11	Trim-Center	$5/8 \times 3\frac{1}{8} - 2^{15}/_{16}$ Long	1
12	Segment Dial	$1^{1}/_{16} \times 2 - 6^{7}/_{16}$ Long	8
13	Stop-Dial	Cut from Part 7	1
14	Door Molding	$\frac{1}{2} \times 1\frac{1}{2} - 60$ Long	1
15	Glass	$3/32 \times 7\frac{3}{8} - 14^{1}/_{16}$ Long	1
16	Glass Support	$3/16 \times 3/16 - 50$ Long	1
17	Latch-Brass	$1/16 \times 3/4 - 1\frac{5}{8}$ Long	1
18	Locking Pin	$5/16 \times 3/8 - 1\frac{1}{2}$ Long	1
19	Glass	$3/32 \times 12^{11}/_{16}$ Diameter	1
20	Retaining Ring	Merritt No. P-205	1
21	Door Latch	Merritt No. P-187	1
22	Hinge	Merritt No. P-93	2
23	Hanger	Merritt No. P-354	1
24	Hands	Merritt No. P-89	1 pr.
25	Movement	See Below	1
26	Pend. Indicator	Merritt No. P-66	1
27	Hinge Brass	$1\frac{1}{2} \times 1\frac{1}{2}$	2
28	Metal Dial (11")	Merritt No. P-710-4	1

Movement: Brass, (Weight Power) Merritt No. P-933
This is an exact copy of original movement
Brass, (Spring Power) Turncraft No. FM
Quartz, Klockit No. 11059-A (Hands-No. 66925-A)
Note, false weight (Merritt No. P-79-S) is req'd with spring or quartz movement for 'effect'

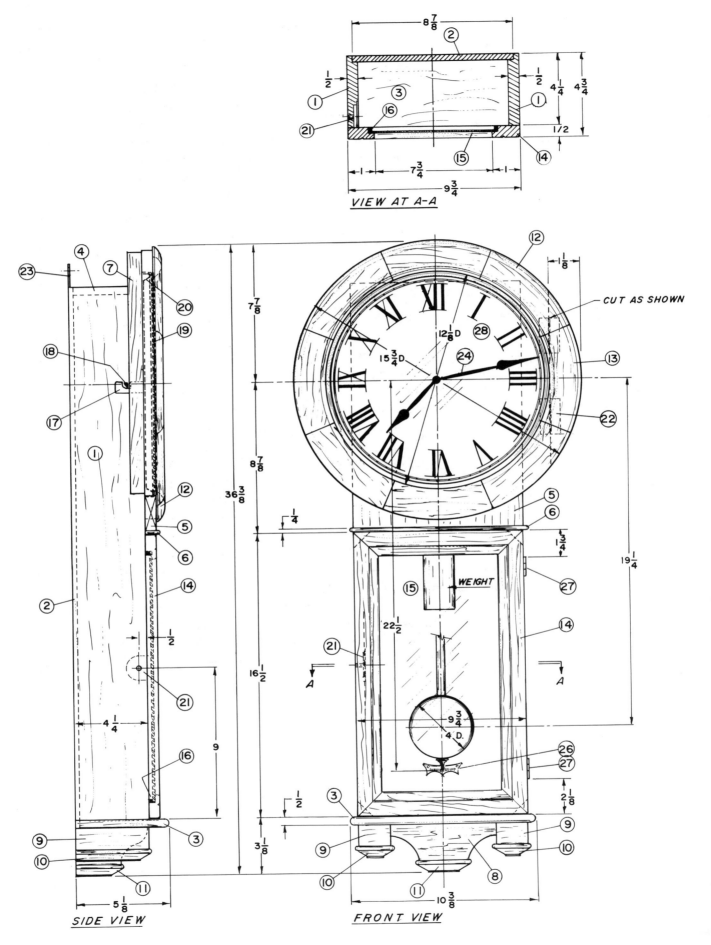

VIEW AT A-A

CUT AS SHOWN

WEIGHT

SIDE VIEW

FRONT VIEW

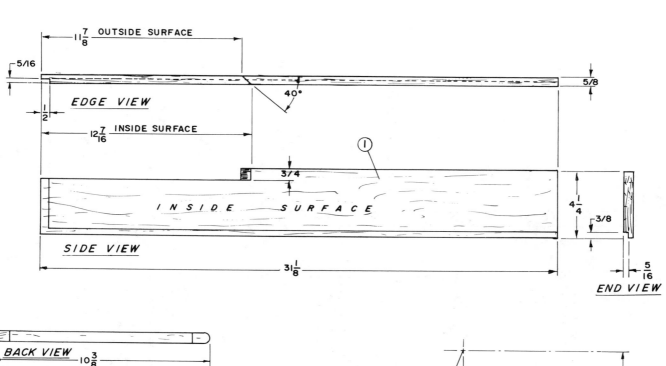

11 7/8 OUTSIDE SURFACE

5/16

EDGE VIEW

1/2

40°

5/8

12 7/16 INSIDE SURFACE

①

3/4

I N S I D E   S U R F A C E

4 1/4

3/8

SIDE VIEW

31 1/8

5/16

END VIEW

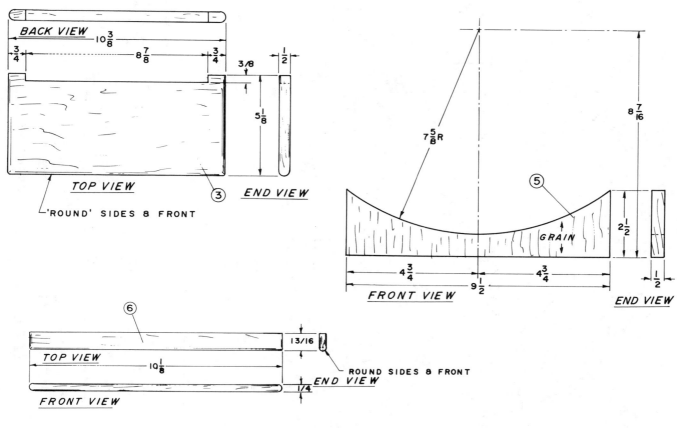

BACK VIEW 10 3/8

3/4

8 7/8

3/4

3/8

1/2

5 1/8

TOP VIEW

③

END VIEW

'ROUND' SIDES & FRONT

7 5/8 R

8 7/16

⑤

GRAIN

2 1/2

4 3/4

4 3/4

1/2

9 1/2

FRONT VIEW

END VIEW

⑥

TOP VIEW

13/16

10 1/8

1/4

FRONT VIEW

ROUND SIDES & FRONT

END VIEW

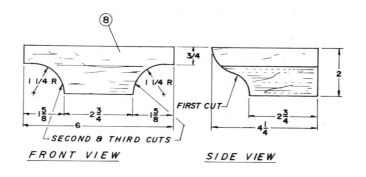

⑧

3/4

1 1/4 R

1 1/4 R

2

1 5/8

2 3/4

1 5/8

FIRST CUT

6

2 3/4

SECOND & THIRD CUTS

4 1/4

FRONT VIEW

SIDE VIEW

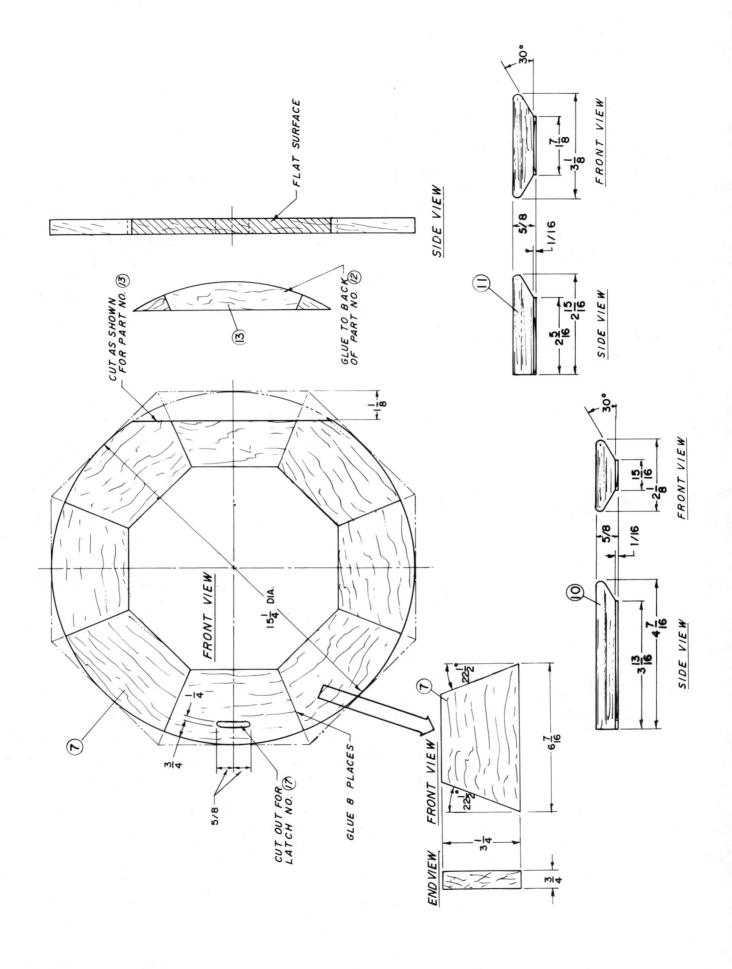

FLAT SURFACE

SIDE VIEW

CUT AS SHOWN
FOR PART NO. 13

13

GLUE TO BACK
OF PART NO. 12

30°

FRONT VIEW

1 7/8
3 1/8

5/8

1/16

SIDE VIEW

11

2 5/16
2 15/16

30°

FRONT VIEW

15/16
2 1/8

5/8

1/16

SIDE VIEW

10

3 13/16
4 7/16

15 1/4 DIA.

FRONT VIEW

1 1/8

— 1/4

3/4

5/8

CUT OUT FOR
LATCH NO. 17

GLUE 8 PLACES

7

17

22 1/2°

FRONT VIEW

6 7/16

22 1/2°

END VIEW

3 1/4

3/4

7

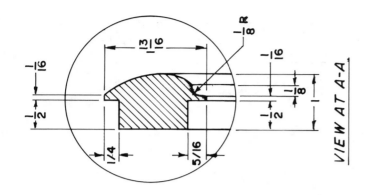

VIEW AT A-A

$\frac{13}{16}$

$\frac{1}{8}$ R

$\frac{1}{16}$

$\frac{1}{8}$

$\frac{1}{2}$

$\frac{1}{16}$

$\frac{1}{2}$

1/4

5/16

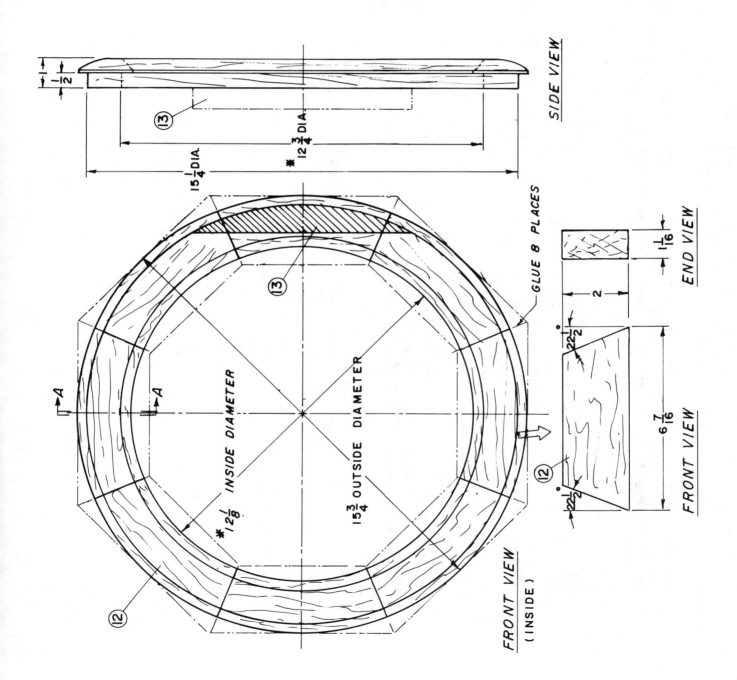

SIDE VIEW

$\frac{1}{2}$

13

$15\frac{1}{4}$ DIA.

✱ $12\frac{3}{4}$ DIA.

FRONT VIEW
(INSIDE)

13

✱ $12\frac{1}{8}$ INSIDE DIAMETER

$15\frac{3}{4}$ OUTSIDE DIAMETER

12

GLUE 8 PLACES

12

END VIEW

$1\frac{1}{16}$

2

$22\frac{1}{2}°$

$6\frac{7}{16}$

$22\frac{1}{2}°$

12

FRONT VIEW

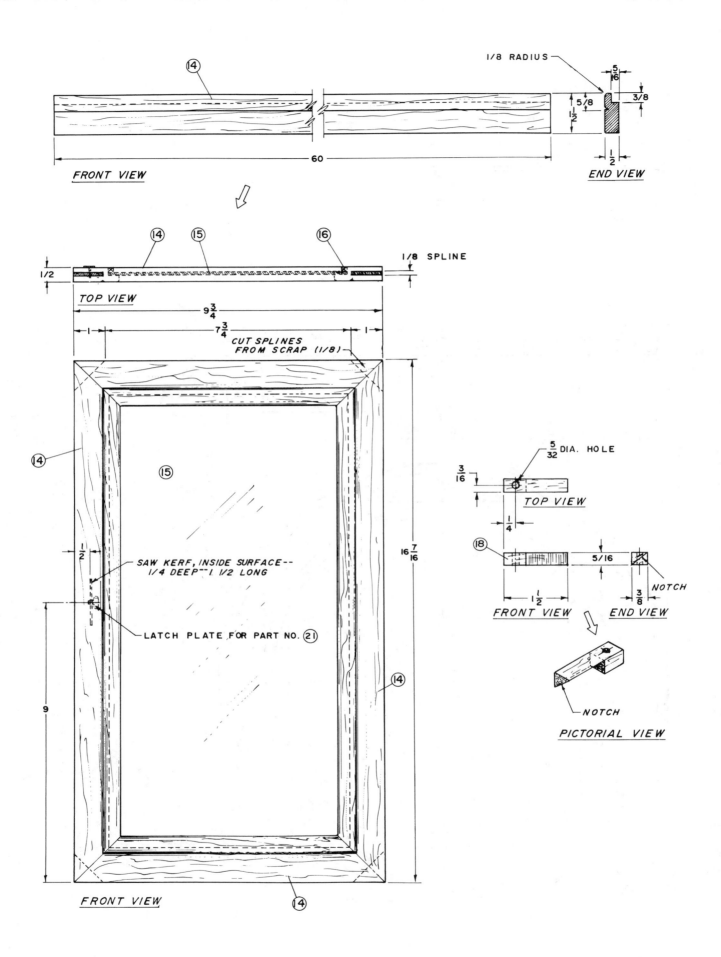

1/8 RADIUS

FRONT VIEW

END VIEW

1/8 SPLINE

TOP VIEW

CUT SPLINES
FROM SCRAP (1/8)

SAW KERF, INSIDE SURFACE--
1/4 DEEP--1 1/2 LONG

LATCH PLATE FOR PART NO. 21

FRONT VIEW

$\frac{5}{32}$ DIA. HOLE

TOP VIEW

NOTCH

FRONT VIEW   END VIEW

NOTCH

PICTORIAL VIEW

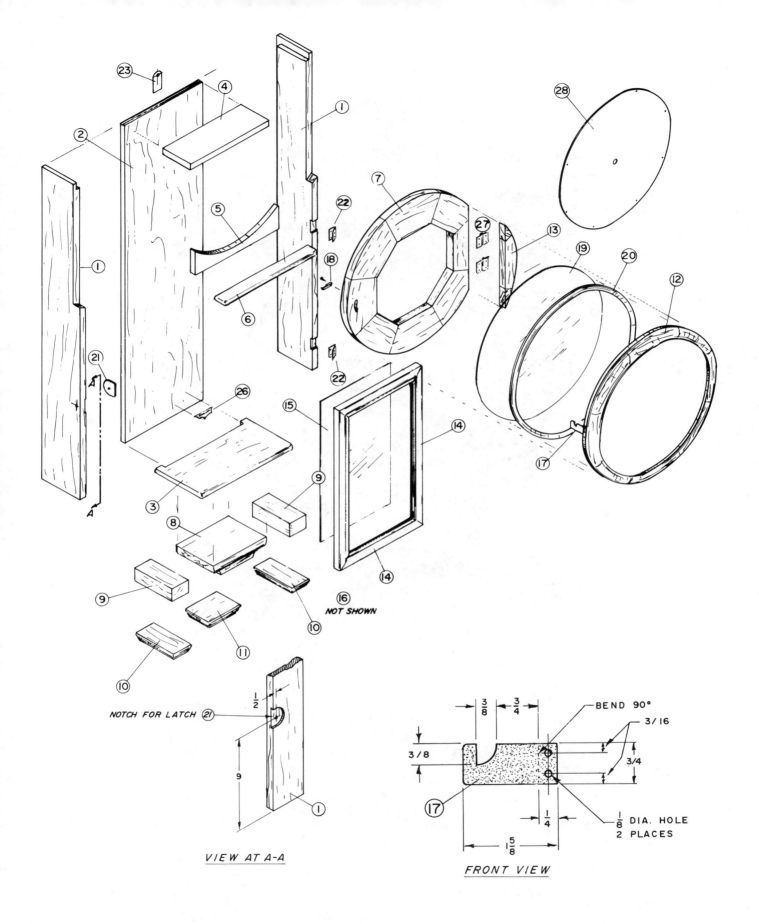

VIEW AT A-A

NOTCH FOR LATCH ㉑

$\frac{1}{2}$

9

NOT SHOWN

FRONT VIEW

BEND 90°

3/16

3/4

$\frac{3}{8}$

$\frac{3}{4}$

3/8

$\frac{1}{4}$

$1\frac{5}{8}$

$\frac{1}{8}$ DIA. HOLE
2 PLACES

17

Gingerbread Clock

B Y FAR THE MOST COMMON AND, UNTIL RECENTLY, THE *LEAST LIKED* CLOCK from the Victorian age is the gingerbread clock (Fig. 17-1). When first introduced, it was called the "kitchen clock." In their day, gingerbread clocks were very popular in the Victorian homes of the middle and lower classes. They reached their height of popularity by 1880 and were in vogue until 1900. Later models used pressed-molded wings and tops, literally stamped out of wood by the tens of thousands. Gingerbread clocks were made all shapes and sizes— although I have no idea why some of them even sold at all. Most of these clocks were made of oak or walnut. Today original gingerbread clocks are gaining in popularity again and their cost is very high.

Originals had striking movements for the hour and single strikes on a bell on the half hour (Fig. 17-2). Some even had loud, obnoxious alarms that would get you out of bed very quickly.

Personally, I feel the only pretty gingerbread clock made was the Patti Parlor Walnut model. It was manufactured by G.N. Welch Manufacturing Company in 1887, and today is sought after by many clock collectors.

The Waterbury Clock Company

The Waterbury Clock Company was a major maker of clocks in the United States from 1857 to 1944. The company started as the Benedict and Burnham Brass Manufacturing Company and in 1850, became part of Jerome Company. With only 60,000 dollars, the Waterbury Clock Company was formed in Waterbury, Connecticut in 1857.

Unfortunately the company went into receivership during the Great Depression in 1933. In 1944 it was sold to United States Time Corporation.

This is a model made by the Waterbury Clock Company. It is made of walnut, has an 8-day brass movement with strike on the hour and a bell on the half hour, and an original built-in alarm. The clock is one of the later models and was made around 1898.

Fig. 17-1. Opposite: Gingerbread clock (walnut wood), circa 1890.

Fig. 17-2. Alarm at lower left side of case.

Instructions / Gingerbread Clock

This is a rather simple clock to build. It is a little unusual but should be a fun clock to make. It surely will be a conversation piece.

Study all drawings before starting. As always purchase the movement before starting this clock. If you use a quartz movement, you should have no problems with dimensions, but it should have a pendulum.

The only difficult part of this clock is the door assembly and carving the simple design into the front parts. The case itself is very simple. Try to make all parts so that they have a thin, graceful appearance. You might want to keep the parts slightly thinner than the given dimensions.

STEP 1.

Carefully lay out and cut each piece as shown. For the rounded part of the case, make a series of 31 saw kerfs, 3/8 inch deep and 3/8 inch apart before bending (see detail of part 2). Then bend the body of the case (part 2) into a U shape as illustrated, keeping a 6½-inch *inside* dimension. The back (part 1) is made to fit into a rabbet in the back of the case.

STEP 2.

Make up the front and side moldings per the given dimensions and cut miter corners as shown at 26 degrees. Use the bottom blocks (part 11) to ensure a tight joint.

STEP 3.

The clock case goes together like a simple box. Keep everything square as you assemble the case. Make and add the door using the hinges, (part 24). Again be sure to keep everything square and fitted to the case.

STEP 4.

The trim (parts 7, 9, and 10) must be carefully laid out and cut to size. The simple designs can be carved into the parts or you could use a Moto-Tool—a hand-held carver made by Dremel. This tool is a natural for jobs like this.

STEP 5.

Screw the dial pan (part 25) to the top trim (part 7). Check that the door closed correctly.

STEP 6.

See Section III for instructions on finishing the clock case.

STEP 7.

You can attach a gold or silver decal to the glass; however, for a much more authentic look, purchase a glass that has a silkscreened design printed on it. This is what would have been used on an original clock. Refer to the list of suppliers in Appendix A for addresses.

PARTS LIST

No.	Name	Size	Req'd.
1	Back	¼ × 7⅛ — 14½ Long	1
2	Case	½ × 2⅞ — 34¾ Long	1
3	Base	⅜ × 3⅝ — 13½ Long	1
4	Screw-Flat Head	No. 6 1″ Long	4
5	Molding-Front	7/16 × 2⅞ — 15½ Long	1
6	Molding-Side	7/16 × 2⅞ — 4½ Long	2
7	Top Trim	⅜ × 7 11/16 — 12 7/16 Long	1
8	Top Brace	5/16 × 1 3/16 — 3⅛ Long	1
9	Center Trim	⅝ × 1⅝ — 3 Long	2
10	Bottom Trim	⅜ × 2¾ — 6⅝	2
11	Bottom Brace	5/16 × 1 — 2¼ Long	2
12	Rosette	¼ × 1½ Diameter	1
13	Latch	Merritt No. P-120	1
14	Center Design	⅞ Half Round	1
15	Side Design	⅞ Half Round	2
16	Block	½ × ⅜ — 1⅛ Lg.	2
17	End Design	¼ × 1½ — 2¼ Long	2
18	Tip Design	¼ × ⅝ — ⅝ Long	2
19	Door Side	¾ × ¾ — 12 9/16 Long	2
20	Door Bottom	¾ × ¾ — 7 9/16 Long	1
21	Door Top	¾ × ¾ — 3⅛ Long	3
22	Glass	Merritt No. KG-5	1
23	Glass Insert	⅛ × ¼ — 11½ Long	2
24	Hinge Brass	Merritt No. P435	2
25	Dial Pan 6⅜ D.	Merritt No. P-391	1
26	Dial Face 5 D.	Merritt No. R-500	1
27	Movement	See Below	1
28	Hands 2½ Size	Merritt No. P-89	1 pr.
29	Decal*	T.E.C. No. Style C-C	1
30	Optional Alarm	Merritt No. P378	1

*If Plain Glass (22) is used.

Movement: Brass w/Pendulum, Merritt No. P-386 (Gong P-547) or LaRose No. 084015 (w/081028)

Quartz, Klockit No. 11908-A (Hands 66936-A)

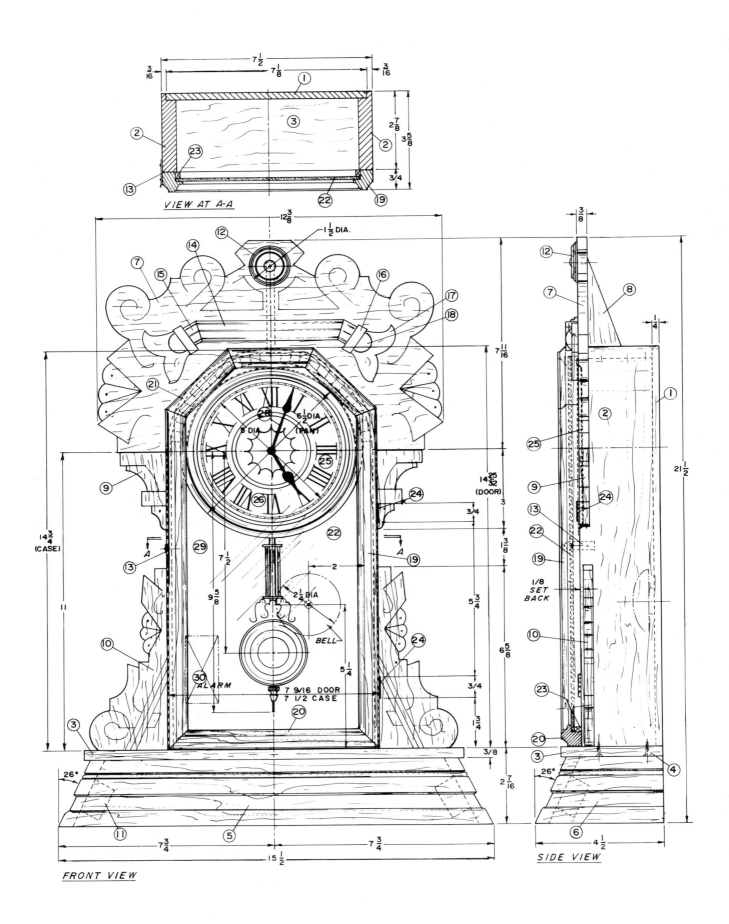

VIEW AT A-A

FRONT VIEW

SIDE VIEW

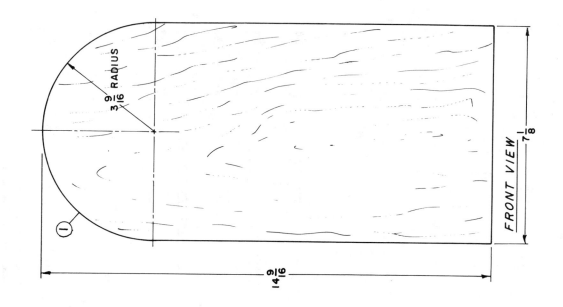

$\frac{9}{16}$ RADIUS

$3\frac{9}{16}$

①

$14\frac{9}{16}$

$7\frac{1}{8}$

FRONT VIEW

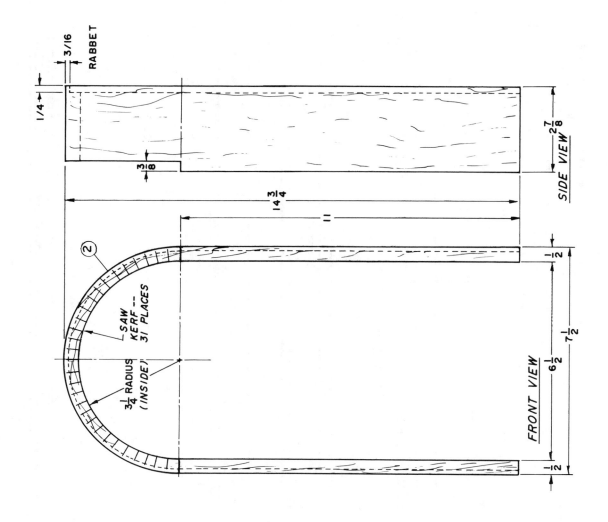

3/16

RABBET

1/4

$3\frac{1}{8}$

$2\frac{7}{8}$

SIDE VIEW

$14\frac{3}{4}$

②

SAW KERF --
31 PLACES

$3\frac{1}{4}$ RADIUS
(INSIDE)

$\frac{1}{2}$

$\frac{1}{2}$

$7\frac{1}{2}$

$6\frac{1}{2}$

FRONT VIEW

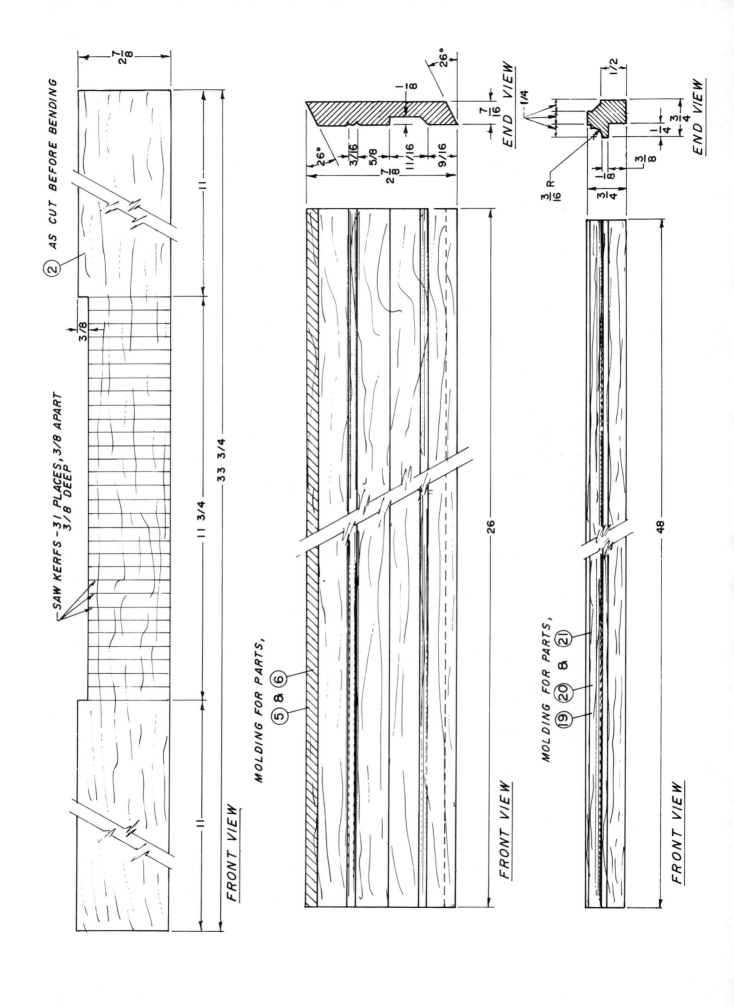

$2\frac{7}{8}$

AS CUT BEFORE BENDING

②

$\frac{3}{8}$

SAW KERFS - 31 PLACES, 3/8 APART
3/8 DEEP

11

11 3/4

33 3/4

11

FRONT VIEW

26°

$-\frac{1}{8}$

26°

$\frac{3}{16}$

$\frac{5}{8}$

$2\frac{7}{8}$

$\frac{11}{16}$

$\frac{9}{16}$

$\frac{7}{16}$

END VIEW

MOLDING FOR PARTS,

⑤ & ⑥

26

FRONT VIEW

$\frac{1}{2}$

$-\frac{1}{4}$

$\frac{3}{4}$

$-\frac{1}{4}$

$\frac{3}{16}$ R

$-\frac{1}{8}$

$\frac{3}{8}$

$\frac{3}{4}$

END VIEW

MOLDING FOR PARTS,

⑲ ⑳ & ㉑

48

FRONT VIEW

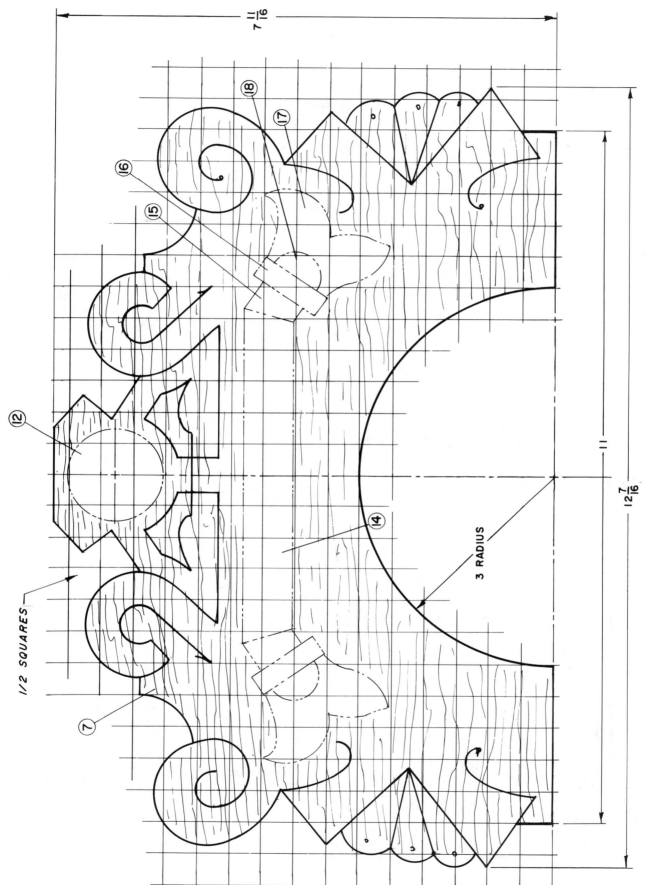

1/2 SQUARES

7 11/16

11

12 7/16

3 RADIUS

FRONT VIEW

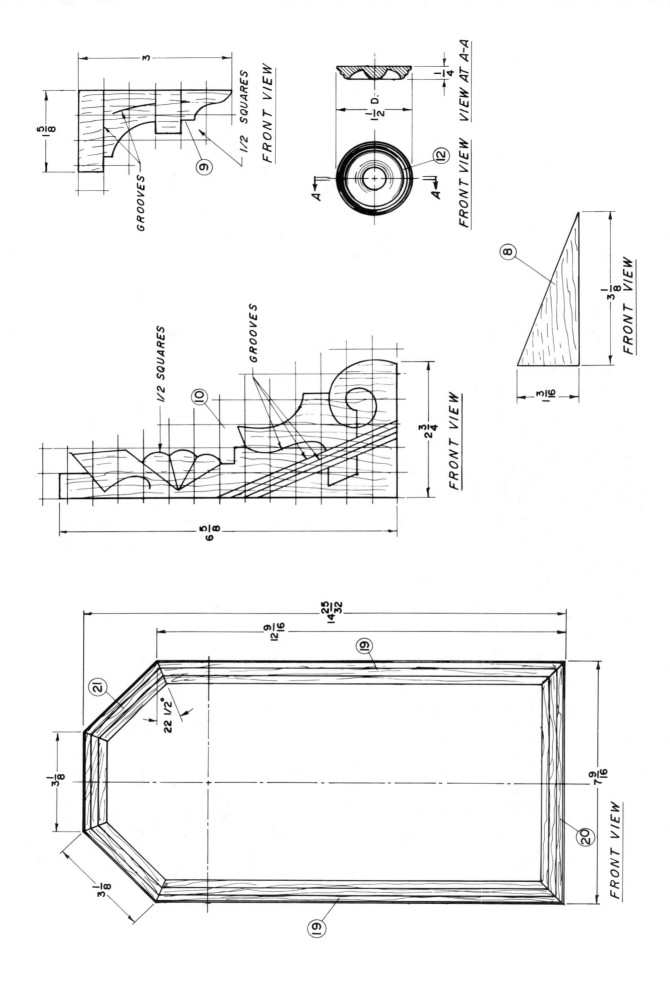

3

1 5/8

GROOVES

9

1/2 SQUARES

FRONT VIEW

1 1/4

1 1/2 D.

12

A

A

FRONT VIEW   VIEW AT A-A

8

3 1/8

1 3/16

FRONT VIEW

1/2 SQUARES

GROOVES

10

2 3/4

6 5/8

FRONT VIEW

14 25/32

12 9/16

19

21

22 1/2°

3 1/8

7 9/16

3 1/8

20

19

FRONT VIEW

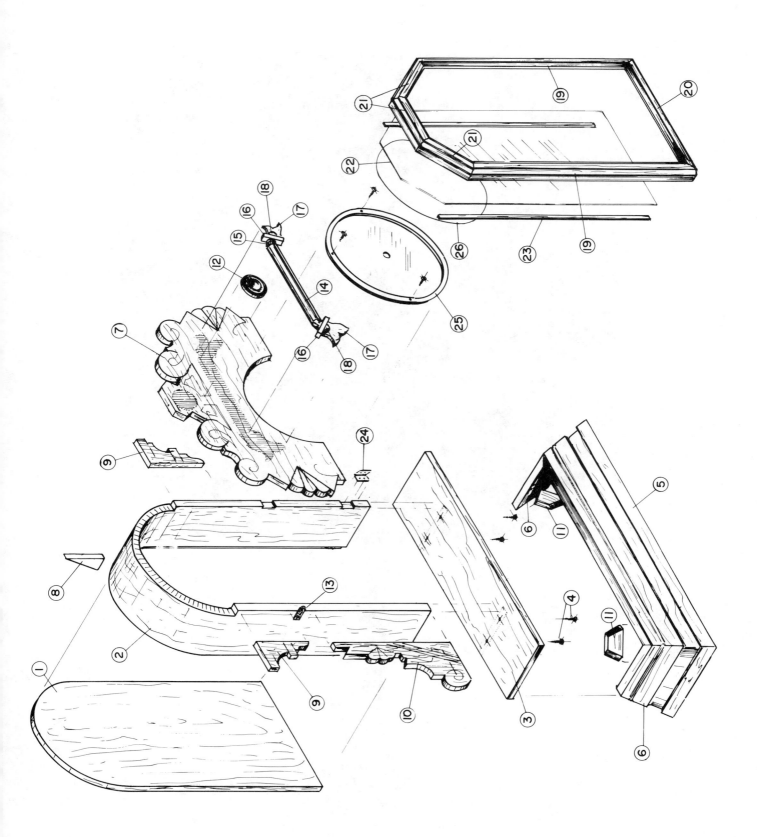

18

Mission Wall Clock

T HE MISSION WALL CLOCK WAS DEVELOPED AT THE END OF THE VICTORIAN era and replaced the gingerbread clock models. They were an effort to return to a simple and honest design. Mission clocks were usually made of oak, as was most mission furniture of the time. This model shows the functionalist designer's sense of moral commitment or "mission" to create a simple and pure design. They were popular from 1900 to 1930 or so. Mission clocks were made as tall-case clocks, wall clocks, and mantel clocks.

The wall mission clock is a very simple, box-like structure made of oak, with Arabic numbers on the dial face (Fig. 18-1). It features an 8-day movement and a large pendulum. It strikes on the hour and was made around 1925. I would say this model was made and sold in very large quantities; it can be seen in many antique shops throughout New England. This particular model was made by the Sessions Clock Company of Bristol-Forestville, Connecticut (Fig. 18-2).

Sessions Clock Company

The Sessions Clock Company was formed in 1903 by William E. Sessions of the Sessions Foundry Company in Bristol, Connecticut. He produced many of the older Welch Clock Company's line of clocks, especially the black mantel and kitchen clocks. In 1936 the company discontinued making spring-wound clocks and concentrated on manufacturing the "new" electric clocks. The Consolidated Electric Industries Corporation of New York purchased the company in 1958 and continued making clocks in Forestville, Connecticut until 1968. In 1968, the Metal Goods Company of Brooklyn, New York purchased the company and moved it to Brooklyn.

Instructions / Mission Wall Clock

This is the easiest clock in the book to make. If you are just getting started in woodworking, you should not have any trouble making this interesting and original wall clock.

Fig. 18-1. Opposite: Mission wall clock, circa 1930.

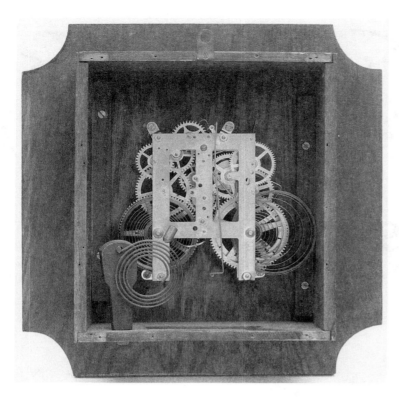

Fig. 18-2. Simple, box-like construction and front-mounted movement.

Study all drawings before starting. As always, be sure to purchase the movement before starting this clock. If you use a quartz movement you should have no problems with the dimensions, but make sure the movement has a pendulum.

The only step in making this clock that might be considered tricky is cutting the ⅛-inch radius on the edges of part 1. The case itself is hidden behind the front board and is very simple to make.

STEP 1.

Carefully lay out and cut each piece as shown. The ⅛-inch radius, concaved edge of the face board (part 1) is achieved with a router that has an ⅛-inch bit and ball bearing follower.

STEP 2.

The case itself is simply an open box made up of parts 2, 3, 4, and 6. Be sure to check that all parts are square before the glue sets.

STEP 3.

Using a compass with a soft lead, draw a light 11-inch-diameter minute circle. Using the dial layout illustrations in Chapter 23 (Figs. 23-1 through 23-4), locate each of the numbers within the 11-inch diameter. *Lightly* draw each number in place. Erase or sand off the 11-inch diameter line so it will not be seen.

STEP 4.

See Section III for instructions on finishing the clock case.

STEP 5.

After finishing the clock, tack or glue the brass numbers in place, keeping all letters in a vertical position as shown.

No.	Name	Size	Req'd.
1	Face Board	5/8 × 12½ — 12½ Long	1
2	Side-Case	3/8 × 3½ — 9¾ Long	2
3	Top/Bottom-Case	5/16 × 3½ — 8⅛ Long	2
4	Adapter	½ × 5/8 — 8 Long	2
5	Screw-Fl. Hd.	No. 8, 1" Long	4
6	Hanger-Brass	½ × 1¼	1
7	Numbers 1½" H.	Klockit No. 60051-A	Set
8	Movement (11")	See Below	1
9	Hands-Black	5½ Size	—

Suggested Movement: Brass, Klock No. 13019-A w/Bell-12½" Pendulum Mason
& Sullivan No. 3370-X 14½" Pen.
Quartz, Klockit w/67912 Hands

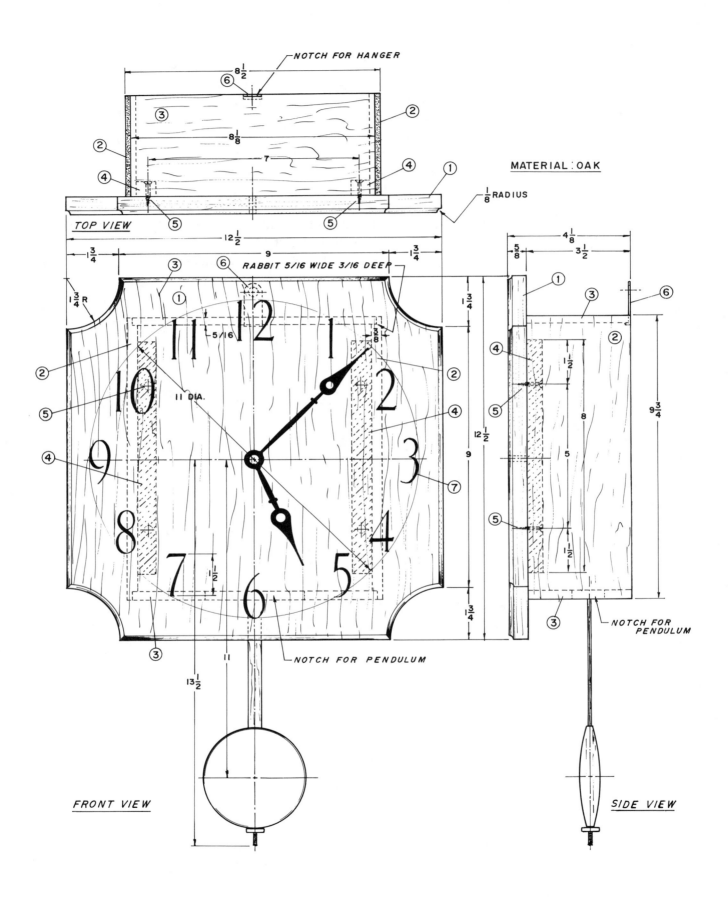

NOTCH FOR HANGER

8 1/2

8 1/8

7

MATERIAL : OAK

1/8 RADIUS

TOP VIEW

12 1/2

9

RABBIT 5/16 WIDE 3/16 DEEP

1 3/4

1 3/4

1 3/4 R

5/16

11 DIA.

1 1/2

11

13 1/2

NOTCH FOR PENDULUM

FRONT VIEW

4 1/8

5/8

3 1/2

1 3/4

12 1/2

9

9 3/4

1 1/2

8

5

1 1/2

NOTCH FOR PENDULUM

SIDE VIEW

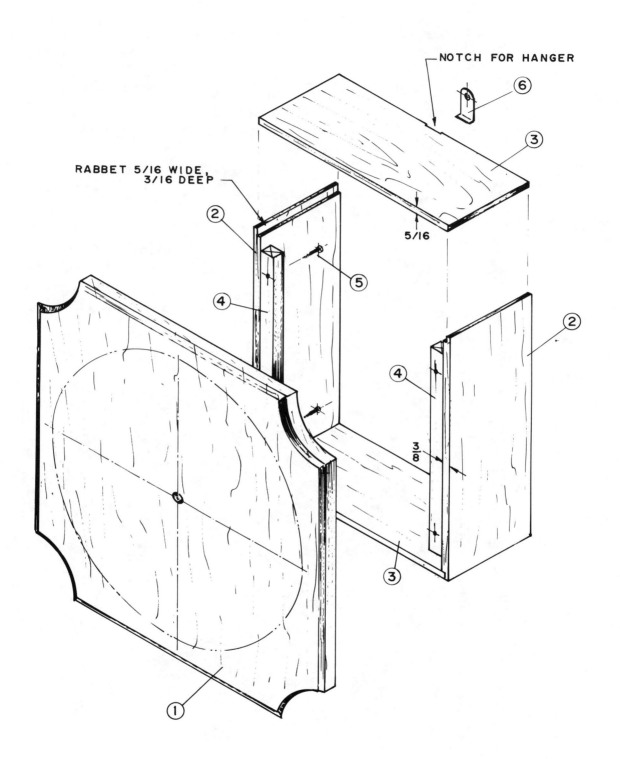

NOTCH FOR HANGER

RABBET 5/16 WIDE
3/16 DEEP

5/16

3/8

19

Mission Shelf Clock

LIKE THE MISSION WALL CLOCK, THE MISSION SHELF CLOCK WAS ALSO MADE BY THE Sessions Clock Company between 1910 and 1920 (Fig. 19-1). It has a dark stained, tower-like case and an 8-day, brass, spring-powered movement, with Arabic numbers on the dial face (Fig. 19-2).

The shelf mission clock actually was a gift given by movie theaters to encourage people to go to the movies on a regular basis. My wife's grandmother received this clock in the early 20s from a theater in Providence, Rhode Island. Each time she went to the movies, she received a coupon. After accumulating a certain number of coupons, she cashed them in for this clock.

Instructions / Mission Shelf Clock

This is one of the easiest clocks in the book to make. If you are just getting started in woodworking, you should not have any trouble making this clock.

Study all drawings before starting. Always obtain the movement before beginning construction. If you use a quartz movement, you should have no problems with dimensions, but be sure the movement has a pendulum.

This clock is made up of a lot of simple rectangular pieces; there are no difficult steps whatsoever. After building the box-like case, you simply add legs or rails to the box and the clock is completed.

STEP 1.

Carefully lay out and cut each piece to size as shown. Sand each piece, keeping all edges sharp and square. Rabbet the ends of the sides (part 2).

STEP 2.

Assemble the case using parts 1 through 5. (See Assembly A on p. 169). Nail the subassembly together, using square-cut nails. Again, sand all over keeping all edges sharp and square. Be sure to locate and drill the 3/8-inch diameter hold through parts 1 and 4. Figure out where the opening for the pendulum should be and cut it out of the bottom board.

Fig. 19-1. Opposite: Mission shelf clock, circa 1915.

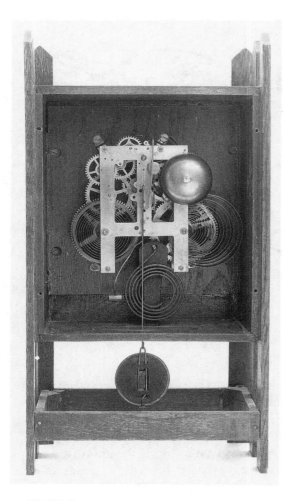

Fig. 19-2. Rear view of box-like case with legs attached.

STEP 3.

Glue together parts 7, 9, and 10, keeping the back surface flat. Sand all over, keeping all edges sharp and square. Referring to Assembly B on p. 169, glue this subassembly to the case and add the rails and corner braces (parts 8, 11, 12, and 13). Take care not to get any glue on the case. Sand all over.

STEP 4.

Draw a light 5³/₄-inch-diameter minute circle using a compass with soft lead. Then locate each of the numbers within the 5³/₄-inch diameter, referring to the dial layout illustration. *Lightly* draw each number in place. Erase or sand off the 5³/₄-inch-diameter line.

STEP 5.

See Section III for finishing instructions.

STEP 6.

After finishing the clock, tack or glue the brass numbers in place, keeping all letters in a vertical position as shown.

PARTS LIST

No.	Name	Size	Req'd.
1	Front Board	$5/16 \times 8 - 9^{5}/8$ Long	1
2	Side	$5/16 \times 4^{7}/16 - 10^{1}/4$ Long	2
3	Top/Bottom	$5/16 \times 4^{7}/16 - 8^{5}/16$ Long	2
4	Support Movement	$5/8 (1/4) \times 8 - 8^{1}/2$ Long	1
5	Back	$5/16 \times 8^{5}/8 - 10^{1}/4$ Long	1
6	Screw Fl. Hd.	No. 4, $5/8$ Long	4
7	Stile-Large	$3/4 \times 1^{1}/8 - 17^{3}/8$ Long	2
8	Stile-Small	$5/16 \times 1^{1}/16 - 17^{3}/8$ Long	4
9	Rail-Center	$5/16 \times 2 - 7^{3}/8$ Long	1
10	Rail-Top/Bottom	$5/16 \times 1^{1}/8 - 7^{3}/8$ Long	2
11	Rail-Inner	$5/16 \times 1^{1}/8 - 4^{7}/8$ Long	2
12	Rail-Inner	$5/16 \times 1^{1}/8 - 8^{5}/8$ Long	1
13	Corner-Brace	$5/8 \times 5/8 - 1^{1}/8$ Long	4
14	Number $3/4$ H.	Klockit No. 60097-A	1
15	Hour Dot	Brass Tack-$1/8$ D.	12
16	Minute Dot	Brass Tack-$1/16$ D.	48
17	Movement (7" Lg.)	See Below	—
18	Hands 2½" Size	See Below	1

Suggested Movement: Brass, Mason and Sullivan No. 3390 $\times$ 7" Pendulum
Quartz, Klockit No. 11907-A — Hands No. 66936

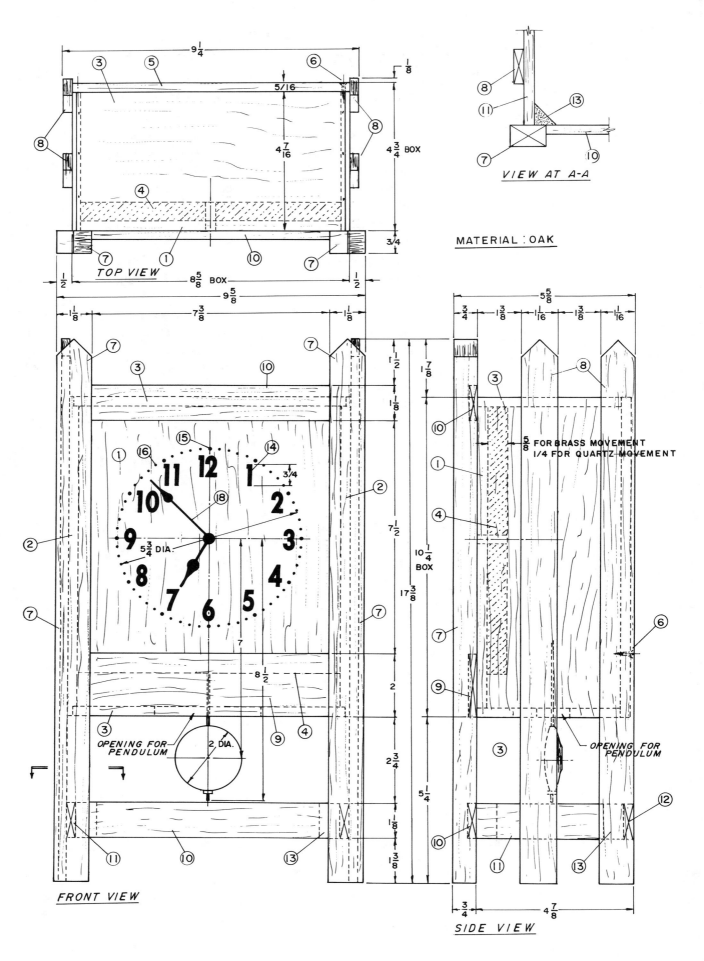

$9\frac{1}{4}$

$\frac{1}{8}$

③ ⑤ ⑥

5/16

$4\frac{7}{16}$

$4\frac{3}{4}$ BOX

⑧ ⑧

⑧

④

⑦ ① ⑩ ⑦

$\frac{3}{4}$

$\frac{1}{2}$ $8\frac{5}{8}$ BOX $\frac{1}{2}$

TOP VIEW

⑧
⑪ ⑬
⑦ ⑩

VIEW AT A-A

MATERIAL : OAK

$9\frac{5}{8}$

$\frac{1}{8}$ $7\frac{3}{8}$ $\frac{1}{8}$

$5\frac{5}{8}$

$\frac{3}{4}$ $1\frac{3}{8}$ $1\frac{1}{16}$ $1\frac{3}{8}$ $1\frac{1}{16}$

⑦ ⑦

③ ⑩

$1\frac{1}{2}$

$1\frac{7}{8}$

$1\frac{1}{8}$

⑩ ③ ⑧

$\frac{5}{8}$ FOR BRASS MOVEMENT
1/4 FOR QUARTZ MOVEMENT

① ⑯ ⑮ ⑭

11 12 1

10 2

⑱ ② ①

$\frac{3}{4}$

9 5¾ DIA. 3

④

8 4

7 6 5

$7\frac{1}{2}$

$10\frac{1}{4}$ BOX

②

⑦

⑥

⑦ ⑦

⑨

$8\frac{1}{2}$

③ ④ 2

$17\frac{3}{8}$

⑨

OPENING FOR PENDULUM

③

2 DIA.

⑨ ④

OPENING FOR PENDULUM

$2\frac{3}{4}$

③

⑩ ⑫

$5\frac{1}{4}$

⑪ ⑩ ⑬

$1\frac{1}{8}$

$1\frac{3}{8}$

⑩ ⑪ ⑬

FRONT VIEW

$\frac{3}{4}$ $4\frac{7}{8}$

SIDE VIEW

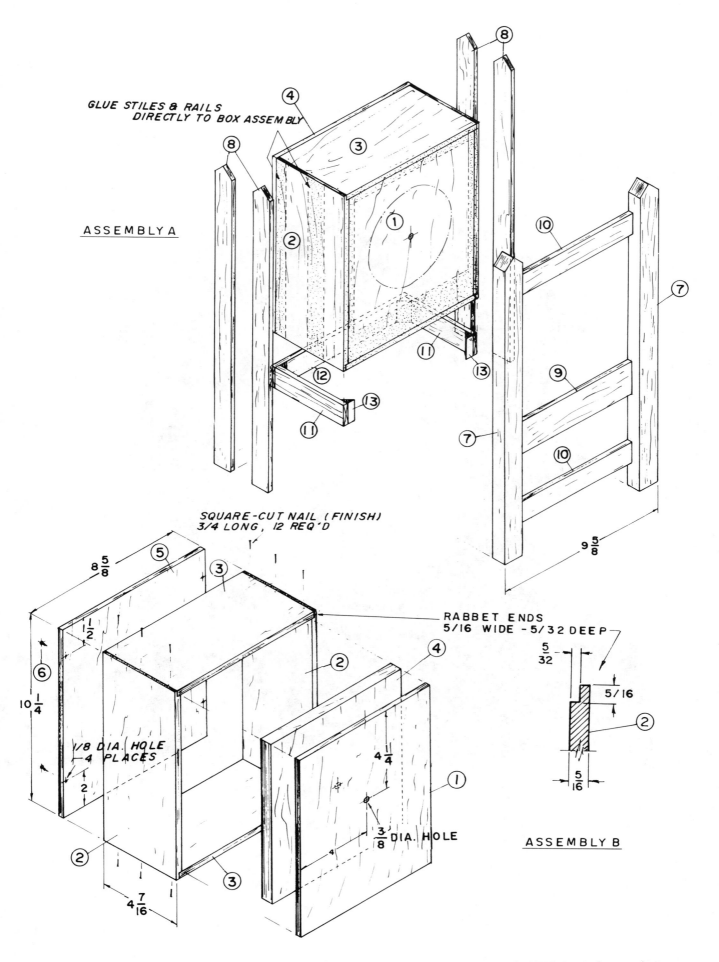

GLUE STILES & RAILS
DIRECTLY TO BOX ASSEMBLY

ASSEMBLY A

SQUARE-CUT NAIL (FINISH)
3/4 LONG, 12 REQ'D

RABBET ENDS
5/16 WIDE - 5/32 DEEP

1/8 DIA. HOLE
4 PLACES

3/8 DIA. HOLE

ASSEMBLY B

20

Black Mantel Clock

A ROUND 1870, AMERICAN CLOCK COMPANIES DEVELOPED A TOTALLY NEW AND innovative small black mantel clock (Fig. 20-1). These clocks were inexpensive and well made; they were manufactured using the latest clock technology and had all the popular features of the day.

Actually these clocks are nothing more than a rectangular black box with either Doric or Ionic columns. Many of these clocks have lion heads mounted on the sides, and brass, claw-like feet. In the late 1800s, they were referred to as "blacks."

During the height of the Victorian era, real marble was used in the design and construction of these clocks. Most clockmakers, however, used a painted, marble veneer, called adamantine over wood. These clocks were popular for over 40 years, from 1880 to 1920, but were eventually replaced by the tambour clock.

Ansonia, Seth Thomas, William Gilbert, Welch, along with other clock manufacturing companies of the day, made these clocks in very large quantities. They were made in all kinds of shapes with all kinds of column combinations and decorations. Even today you can still find many of these clocks in antique shops throughout the country.

Up until recently these clocks had not been very popular, but they are currently gaining in popularity and are still reasonably priced. Their movements are of the highest quality, keep excellent time, and will run for another 100 years or more. These black clocks are the "sleepers" of the antique world. Within a few years they will be in demand and their prices will increase dramatically. This particular model is unusual because it is almost square.

The model in this chapter is an Ingraham clock made around 1900 (Fig. 20-2). It is painted black and has a column on either side of the dial face, the usual lion heads on the sides and of course, cast claw-feet. The clock has an 8-day brass movement with the usual gong strike counting the hour and a single gong strike on the half hour.

Fig. 20-1. Opposite: Black mantel clock, circa 1900.

Fig. 20-2. Back view showing construction.

Elias Ingraham

Elias was born in 1805 at Marlborough, Connecticut. After completing a five-year apprenticeship in cabinetmaking in 1825, he worked as a journeyman for Daniel Dewey of Hartford, Connecticut. By 1828 he was designing and building clock cases. As noted in Chapter 10, he is credited with designing the popular steeple clock in 1845.

The Ingraham Clock Company was purchased by McGraw-Edison Company in 1967 and is still producing clocks in North Carolina.

Instructions / Black Mantel Clock

This is a clock that looks more difficult to make than it actually is. If you are just getting started in woodworking, you should not have any trouble making this interesting and unique shelf clock. For the most part, it has only rectangular parts.

Study all drawings before starting. Remember to purchase the movement and the various purchased parts before beginning construction. If you use a quartz movement, you should have no problems with the dimensions.

STEP 1.
Carefully lay out and cut each piece to size as shown. Sand each piece very smooth, using fine sandpaper and keeping all edges sharp and square.

STEP 2.
If you do not have a lathe you may want to have the turnings custom-made. (See Appendix B for address of River Bend Turnings.) You will have to send a copy of the page illustrating the turning (part 9).

STEP 3.
Make the molding (part A) and cut it to make parts 1 and 2, (see Assembly A on p. 176 for details). Add parts 3 and 4 as shown. Be sure to make a 45-degree cut so the angles will be exactly 90 degrees.

STEP 4.
Make the matching pair (left-hand and right-hand) of part 5, taking care to drill all holes as illustrated. Sand all over with fine sandpaper.

STEP 5.

Make up part B and cut at 45 degrees as shown in Assembly B on p. 177. Be sure to make a left-hand and right-hand pair as above. Sand all over using fine paper.

STEP 6.

Cut part 6 as shown in the front, side, and top views. Be sure to locate and drill all holes as illustrated. Sand all outer surfaces with fine paper.

STEP 7.

Make up part 12 per given dimensions and add it to part 13, as shown in Assembly C on p. 178. Sand all over.

STEP 8.

Cut to size parts 10, 11, 14, 15, and 16 per the given dimensions. Sand all over, using fine sandpaper.

STEP 9.

Except for the above subassemblies, this clock is screwed together with flathead screws throughout. Temporarily, assemble the clock case using the appropriate size screws (see Assembly D on p. 180). Keep everything square as you go. Add the legs (part 19) using screws; add the lion heads (part 18) and the dial pan and face (part 20). Line up and add the movement, carefully locating and drilling the winding holes in the dial pan and dial assembly. Drill whatever other holes are required to secure the movement and chime or gong. Check that the pendulum swings correctly. Check that the clock is complete and ready for finishing. Refer to the drawings of the front and side views.

STEP 10.

Disassemble the entire clock, except the few subassemblies that were glued together—keep track of which flathead screws were where. Resand all over using very fine sandpaper—refer to the instructions for finishing the case and marbleizing the columns.

STEP 11.

After the parts are primed, painted black, rubbed down with 0000 steel wool, and waxed, reassemble the clock case.

Finishing the Case

The black finish must be smooth and jet-black. There should be no sign of wood grain whatsoever on the finish. To achieve this, you must start with a very smooth finish, sanding up to at least a 400-grit sandpaper. Assemble the clock with screws only, do not use any glue. This is the way most clocks were originally made.

After the clock is fully assembled, including the movement, hardware, glass, and bezel, take the clock completely apart. Paint the individual parts while the clock is apart. Apply two or three coats of primer and sand between coats. Apply three or four coats of high gloss black enamel paint to each part and sand between each coat. When the surfaces are perfectly smooth and no grain can be seen, apply a top coat of black paint. Allow each part to dry for at least 60 hours. With 0000 steel wool, carefully rub each part, taking care not to rub through the edges. The rubbing will have a tendency to dull the finish somewhat, but do not worry about that at this time. Apply a coat of paste wax and buff all over after it is dry. This should give you a beautiful, smooth, black finish. Reassemble the clock and add the hardware, movement, and bezel.

Marbleizing

To get a marble effect for the columns and top, you will have to experiment a little. Experiment on a few pieces of scrap wood before painting on your parts. To get a marble effect, finish the surfaces as noted above for the case. The surfaces must be very smooth, free of any grain. Apply two coats of primer and sand between coats with 400-grit paper. For the columns, paint them with two coats of bright red enamel paint, sanding between coats. Apply two coats of varnish and allow to dry for 24 hours or more. Using a wad of newspaper, a sponge or whatever, dab white paint here and there. After the white paint dries, do the same thing with black paint. Allow the original red base coat color to show through here and there. Apply three or four coats of varnish all over. Using 0000 steel wool, rub between the last two or three coats. Apply a coat of paste wax, and you should have a finish very similar to the original. If you are not satisfied with your marble effect, you might want to look over a book or two on other methods of marbleizing.

PARTS LIST

No.	Name	Size	Req'd.
Ⓐ	Base Material	$1\frac{3}{4} \times 2\frac{11}{16} - 30$ Long	1
1	Base-Front	$1\frac{3}{4} \times 2\frac{11}{16} - 13\frac{5}{16}$ Long	1 Ⓐ
2	Base-Side	$1\frac{3}{4} \times 2\frac{11}{16} - 6\frac{13}{16}$ Long	2 Ⓐ
3	Brace	$\frac{3}{8} \times 1\frac{3}{8} - 4\frac{1}{2}$ Long	2
4	Support	$\frac{1}{2} \times \frac{1}{2} - 1\frac{13}{16}$ Long	2
5	Side Wall	$1\frac{5}{8} \times 4\frac{5}{16} - 5\frac{1}{16}$ Long	2
6	Front	$1\frac{3}{4} \times 6\frac{7}{16} - 6\frac{9}{16}$ Long	1
Ⓑ	Trim	$\frac{3}{4} \times 1\frac{11}{16} - 32$ Long	1
7	Trim-Side	$\frac{3}{4} \times 1\frac{11}{16} - 5\frac{1}{2}$ Long	4 Ⓑ
8	Trim-Front	$\frac{3}{4} \times 1\frac{11}{16} - 2\frac{1}{8}$ Long	4 Ⓑ
9	Column	$\frac{3}{4}$ Diameter $- 5\frac{1}{16}$ Long	2
10	Back Board (Top)	$\frac{1}{4} \times 6\frac{9}{16} - 8\frac{1}{2}$ Long	1
11	Divider	$\frac{5}{16} \times 6\frac{1}{8} - 11\frac{1}{8}$ Long	1
12	Ends-Top	$1\frac{1}{2} \times 2\frac{1}{4} - 5\frac{5}{8}$ Long	2
13	Center-Top	$1\frac{1}{2} \times 6\frac{1}{8} - 5\frac{7}{8}$ Long	1
14	Top Board	$\frac{5}{8} \times 6\frac{1}{16} - 7$ Long	1
15	Bottom Board	$\frac{5}{16} \times 5\frac{9}{16} - 10\frac{3}{4}$ Long	1
16	Back Bd. (Bottom)	$\frac{5}{16} \times 2\frac{1}{8} - 10\frac{1}{8}$ Long	1
17	Case Back	Merritt P-443	1
18	Lion Head	Merritt P-115	2
19	Feet Set	Merritt P-116	4
20	Dial and Bezel	LaRose FL-13-8113	1
21	Movement	(See Below)	1
22	Flat Gong w/Base	LaRose FL-26-8302	1
23	Key for Movement	To suit	1
24	Flat Head Screw	To suit	14

Movement: Brass, Front-Mount/8-day LaRose 084023
　　　　　Quartz, LaRose 812056

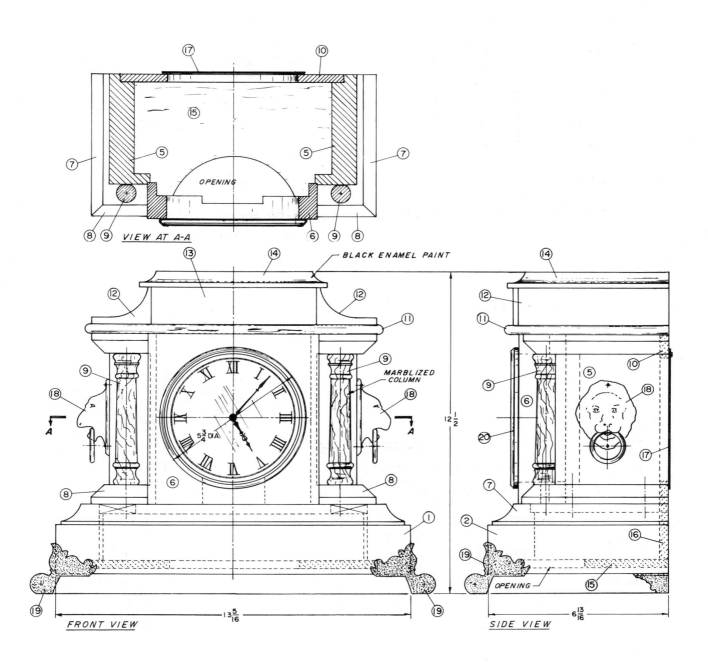

VIEW AT A-A

BLACK ENAMEL PAINT

MARBLIZED COLUMN

$5\frac{3}{4}$ DIA

OPENING

$12\frac{1}{2}$

$13\frac{5}{16}$

FRONT VIEW

$6\frac{13}{16}$

SIDE VIEW

OPENING

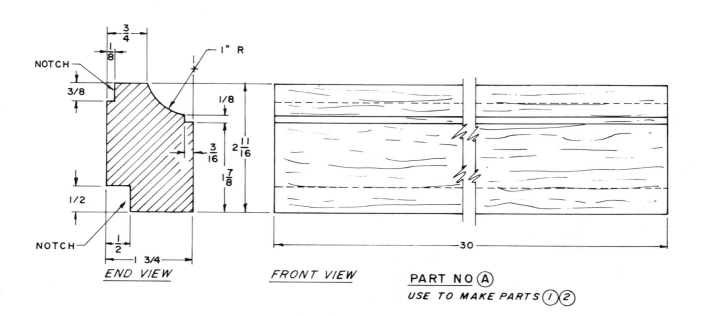

NOTCH

NOTCH

1" R

3/4
1/8
3/8
1/2
1/2
1 3/4

1/8
3/16
2 11/16
1 7/8

30

END VIEW

FRONT VIEW

PART NO (A)
USE TO MAKE PARTS (1) (2)

ASSEMBLY A

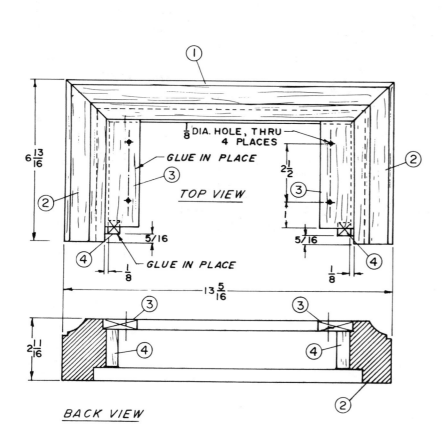

⅛ DIA. HOLE, THRU
4 PLACES

GLUE IN PLACE

TOP VIEW

GLUE IN PLACE

6 13/16

2 1/2

5/16

1/8

5/16

1/8

13 5/16

2 11/16

BACK VIEW

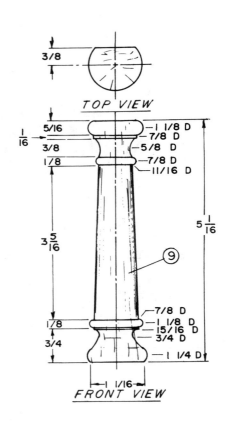

3/8

TOP VIEW

5/16
1/16
3/8
1/8

1 1/8 D
7/8 D
5/8 D
7/8 D
11/16 D

3 5/16

5 1/16

1/8
3/4

7/8 D
1 1/8 D
15/16 D
3/4 D
1 1/4 D

1 1/16

FRONT VIEW

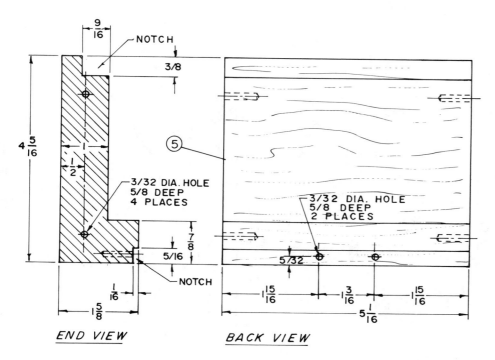

END VIEW

BACK VIEW

ASSEMBLY B

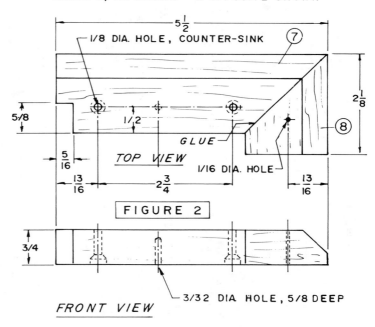

MAKE 2, AS SHOWN -- 2 OPPOSITE SHOWN

TOP VIEW

FIGURE 2

FRONT VIEW

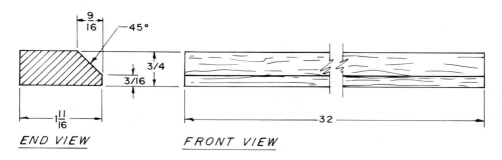

END VIEW   FRONT VIEW

PART NO (B)

USE TO MAKE PARTS (7) (8)

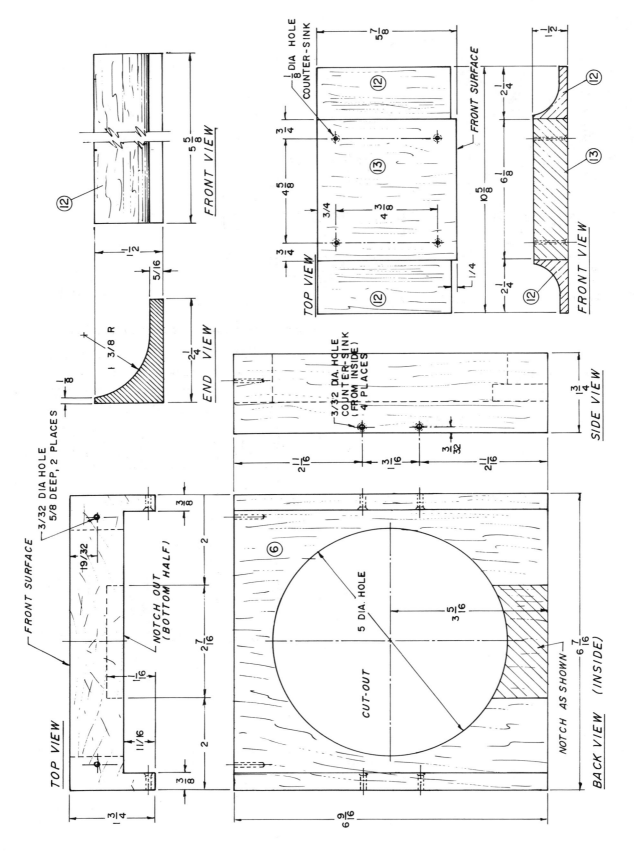

FRONT VIEW

⑫

END VIEW

1/2
5/16
1 3/8 R
1/8
2 1/4

3/32 DIA HOLE
5/8 DEEP, 2 PLACES

FRONT SURFACE

19/32

NOTCH OUT
(BOTTOM HALF)

TOP VIEW

3/8
2
2 7/16
1 1/16
11/16
2
3/8
3/4

1/8 DIA HOLE
COUNTER-SINK

⑫

⑬

TOP VIEW

3/4
3/4
3/4
4 3/8
4 5/8
5 7/8

FRONT SURFACE

2 1/4
6 1/8
10 5/8
2 1/4
1/4

FRONT VIEW

⑫

⑬

⑫

1/2

3/32 DIA. HOLE
COUNTER-SINK
(FROM INSIDE)
4 PLACES

SIDE VIEW

3/4

2 1/16
1 3/16
2 1/16
3/32

5 DIA. HOLE
CUT-OUT

3 5/16

6

NOTCH AS SHOWN

BACK VIEW (INSIDE)

6 7/16
6 9/16

ASSEMBLY C

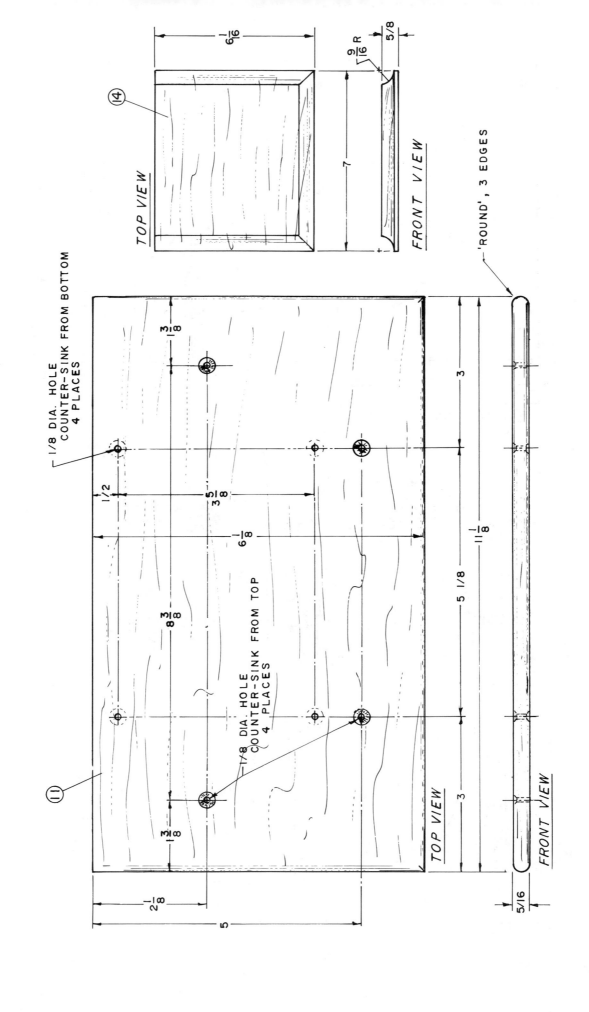

TOP VIEW

(14)

FRONT VIEW

9/16 R

5/8

6 1/16

7

'ROUND', 3 EDGES

1/8 DIA. HOLE
COUNTER-SINK FROM BOTTOM
4 PLACES

3/8

1/2

3 5/8

6 1/8

8 3/8

1/8 DIA. HOLE
COUNTER-SINK FROM TOP
4 PLACES

(11)

3/8

2 1/8

5

3

11 1/8

5 1/8

3

TOP VIEW

5/16

FRONT VIEW

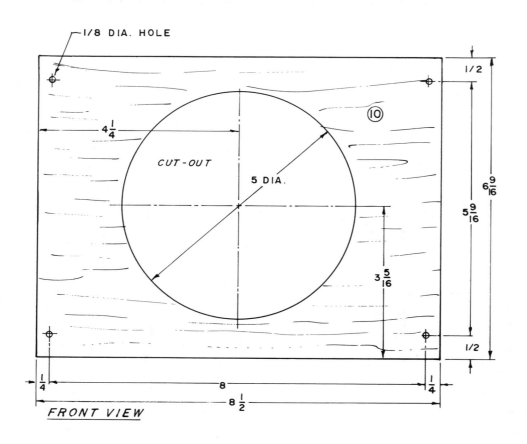

1/8 DIA. HOLE

CUT-OUT

5 DIA.

10

4 1/4

1/2

6 9/16

5 9/16

3 5/16

1/2

1/4

8

8 1/2

1/4

FRONT VIEW

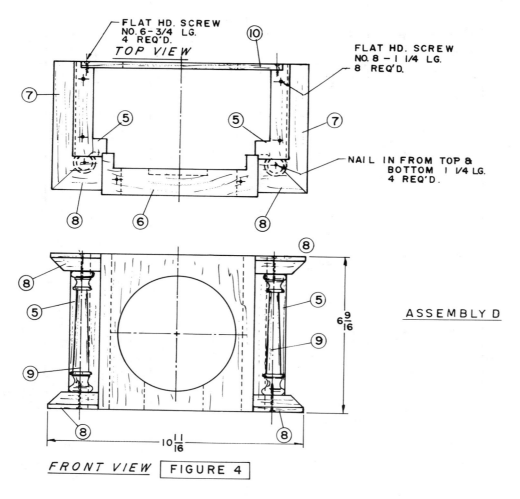

FLAT HD. SCREW
NO. 6-3/4 LG.
4 REQ'D.

TOP VIEW

10

FLAT HD. SCREW
NO. 8 - 1 1/4 LG.
8 REQ'D.

7

5

5

7

NAIL IN FROM TOP &
BOTTOM 1 1/4 LG.
4 REQ'D.

8

6

8

8

8

8

5

5

6 9/16

ASSEMBLY D

9

9

8

8

10 11/16

FRONT VIEW   FIGURE 4

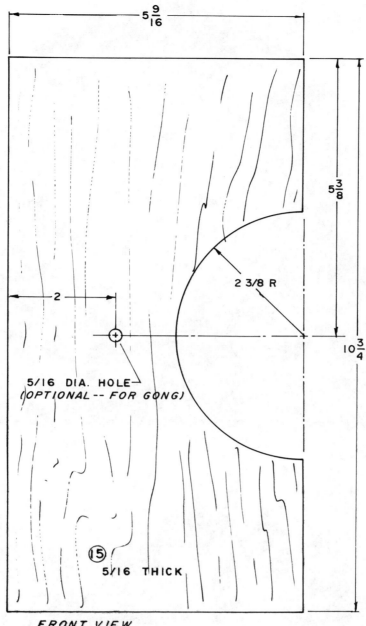

$5\frac{9}{16}$

$5\frac{3}{8}$

$10\frac{3}{4}$

2 3/8 R

2

5/16 DIA. HOLE
(OPTIONAL -- FOR GONG)

⑮ 5/16 THICK

FRONT VIEW

1/8 DIA. HOLE, COUNTER-SINK
FRONT VIEW

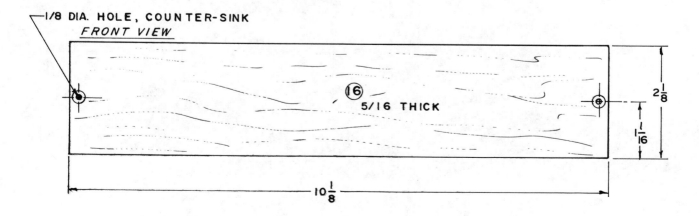

⑯ 5/16 THICK

$2\frac{1}{8}$

$1\frac{1}{16}$

$10\frac{1}{8}$

21

Tambour Clock

THE TAMBOUR CLOCK GREW IN POPULARITY AROUND 1908 AND THE BLACK CLOCKS were forced off the market (Fig. 21-1). Sometimes they were referred to as "humpback" clocks. They had their heyday from 1920 to 1930 and were popular right up to 1950 or so. The name "tambour" came about because the clock is shaped like a tambourine drum. Today these clocks are not considered an antique, as most of them are not over 50 years old. After the year 2008 they will be listed as antiques.

Experts estimate that over a million of these clocks have been made. Most contain either an 8-day or 30-day movement. Today they are referred to simply as mantel clocks and are still being made.

Although this clock is not a true antique this book would not be complete without it, since the tambour clock is the last link of the long list of clocks developed here in United States. It is really the last vastly popular American model to be developed. No other clock model has since been produced to take its place. Most tambour clocks manufactured today incorporate the new quartz movement; I know of no company in America making tambour clocks with spring-powered movements.

Seth Thomas

The model shown is another clock made by Seth Thomas. For information about Seth Thomas, refer to Chapter 16 on the regulator clock.

Instructions / Shelf Tambour Clock

The construction of this clock is a little different from all the other clocks in this book, perhaps because it is the newest clock and requires the latest construction methods.

Study all drawings before starting. As always, purchase the movement before starting this clock. You should not have any problems if you use a quartz movement, but make sure it has a pendulum.

Fig. 21-1. Opposite: Tambour clock, circa 1920. Also shown: Rear view with bottom piece removed, showing construction. Note the front-mounted movement.

This clock should be rather easy to make. Except for the unusual laminated top arch (part 6) and arched molding (part 9), there are no difficult parts to make.

STEP 1.
Glue up the four, 1/16-inch-thick parts for the top arch, (part 6). For exact details, refer to the drawing. Note that the two pieces do *not* go all the way around, rather they end 3½ inches up from the sides. Keep the sides parallel as shown.

STEP 2.
Make the molding (parts 9 and 10) per the given dimensions.

STEP 3.
Carefully lay out and cut the other pieces to size as shown. Sand each piece, keeping all edges sharp and square.

STEP 4.
Assemble the case using parts 1 through 10, along with part 15.) Refer to the rear view with door and part 5 removed.

STEP 5.
Fit the door (part 12) with hinges (part 13). Add the dial pan, (part 11) and fit the movement and hands. Check that the pendulum swings freely.

STEP 6.
Remove the door, dial pan, and movement, and then finish the case.

STEP 7.
See Section III for instructions on finishing the clock case.

─────────────────── **PARTS LIST** ───────────────────

No.	Name	Size	Req'd.
1	Base-Front	1 × 1¼ — 13⅜ Long	1
2	Base-Side	1 × 1¼ — 4⅝ Long	2
3	Block	¾ × 2⅜ — 3⅜ Long	2
4	Bottom	¼ × 3¾ — 12⅛ Long	1
5	Back	¼ × 1¼ — 12⅛ Long	1
6	Top Arch	1/16 × 4³/16 — 20 Long	4
7	Front	½ × 6⅞ — 6¹⁵/16 Long	1
8	Side Trim	2½ × 4¹/16 — 3½ Long	2
9	Molding Front	5/16 × 3¹¹/16 — 18 Long	1
10	Molding Side	5/16 × ⅜ — 4½ Long	2
11	Dial Pan & Bezel	LaRose No. FL-13-8113	1
12	Door	7/16 × 7⅛ — 7⁷/16	1
13	Hinge-Brass	¾ Size	2
15	Knob-brass	¼ Diameter	1
15	Foot-Brass	¾ Diameter — ⅛ Thick	4
16	Movement W/Hands	See Below	1

Movement: Brass, LaRose No. 084023/Hands, No. 816015
Quartz, LaRose No. 81-4003 (w/Dial Pan)

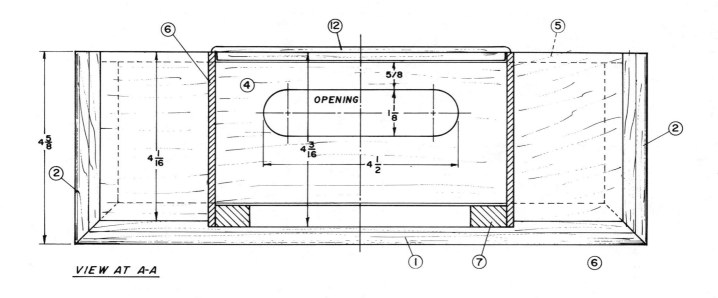

VIEW AT A-A

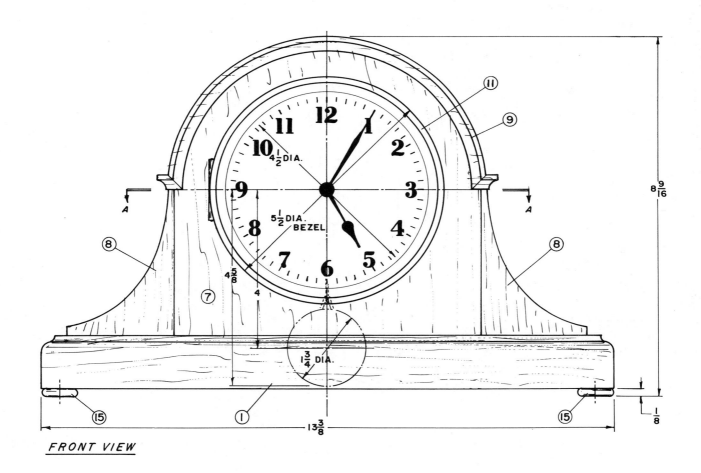

FRONT VIEW

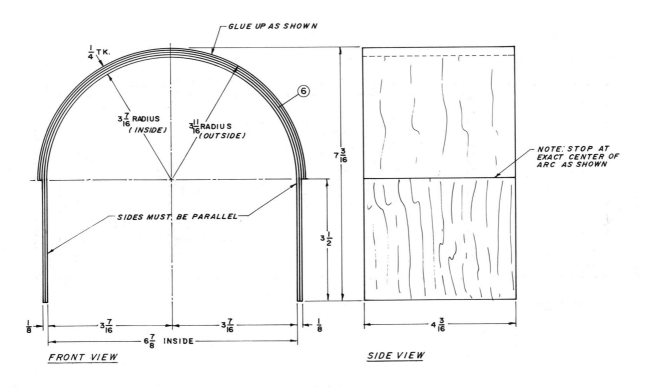

GLUE UP AS SHOWN

¼ TK.

3 7/16 RADIUS (INSIDE)

3 11/16 RADIUS (OUTSIDE)

⑥

SIDES MUST BE PARALLEL

7 3/16

3 ½

NOTE: STOP AT EXACT CENTER OF ARC AS SHOWN

⅛

3 7/16

3 7/16

⅛

6 7/8 INSIDE

4 3/16

FRONT VIEW

SIDE VIEW

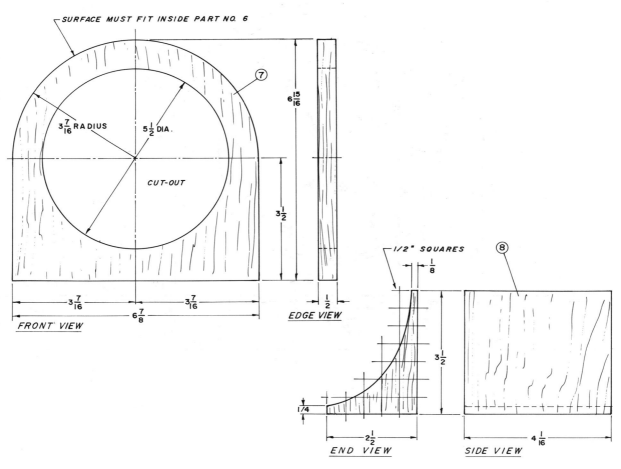

SURFACE MUST FIT INSIDE PART NO. 6

3 7/16 RADIUS

5 ½ DIA.

⑦

CUT-OUT

6 15/16

3 ½

3 7/16

3 7/16

6 7/8

FRONT VIEW

½

EDGE VIEW

1/2" SQUARES

⅛

⑧

3 ½

¼

2 ½

END VIEW

4 1/16

SIDE VIEW

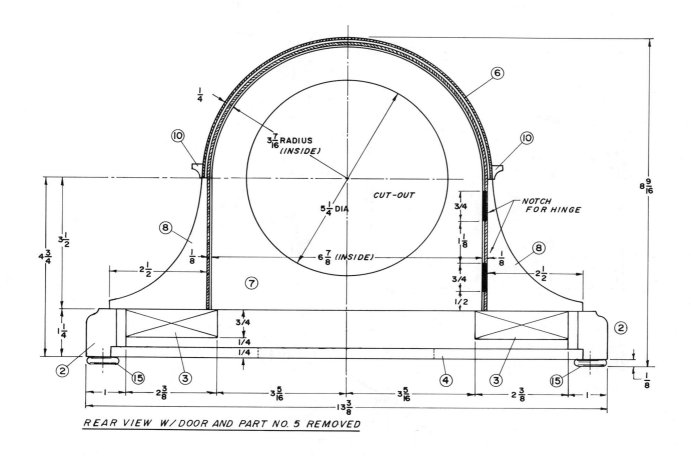

$3\frac{7}{16}$ RADIUS (INSIDE)

$5\frac{1}{4}$ DIA

CUT-OUT

$6\frac{7}{8}$ (INSIDE)

NOTCH FOR HINGE

$\frac{1}{4}$

$8\frac{9}{16}$

$\frac{3}{4}$

$1\frac{1}{8}$

$\frac{1}{8}$

$\frac{3}{4}$

$\frac{1}{2}$

$3\frac{1}{2}$

$4\frac{3}{4}$

$2\frac{1}{2}$

$\frac{1}{8}$

$2\frac{1}{2}$

$1\frac{1}{4}$

$\frac{3}{4}$

$\frac{1}{4}$

$\frac{1}{4}$

$\frac{1}{8}$

1

$2\frac{3}{8}$

$3\frac{5}{16}$

$3\frac{5}{16}$

$2\frac{3}{8}$

1

$13\frac{3}{8}$

REAR VIEW W/ DOOR AND PART NO. 5 REMOVED

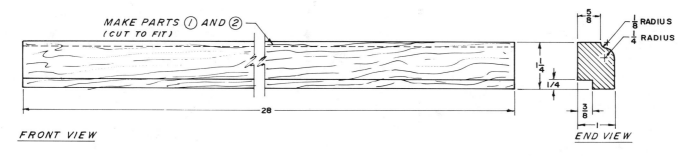

MAKE PARTS ① AND ② (CUT TO FIT)

28

$1\frac{1}{4}$

$\frac{1}{4}$

$\frac{5}{8}$

$\frac{1}{8}$ RADIUS

$\frac{1}{4}$ RADIUS

$\frac{3}{8}$

1

FRONT VIEW

END VIEW

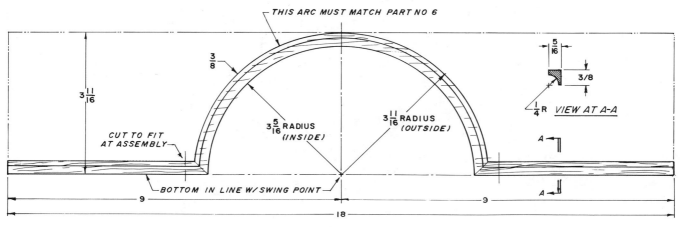

THIS ARC MUST MATCH PART NO 6

$\frac{3}{8}$

$3\frac{11}{16}$

$3\frac{5}{16}$ RADIUS (INSIDE)

$3\frac{11}{16}$ RADIUS (OUTSIDE)

CUT TO FIT AT ASSEMBLY

BOTTOM IN LINE W/ SWING POINT

9

9

18

$\frac{5}{16}$

$\frac{3}{8}$

$\frac{1}{4}$ R   *VIEW AT A-A*

A

A

FRONT VIEW

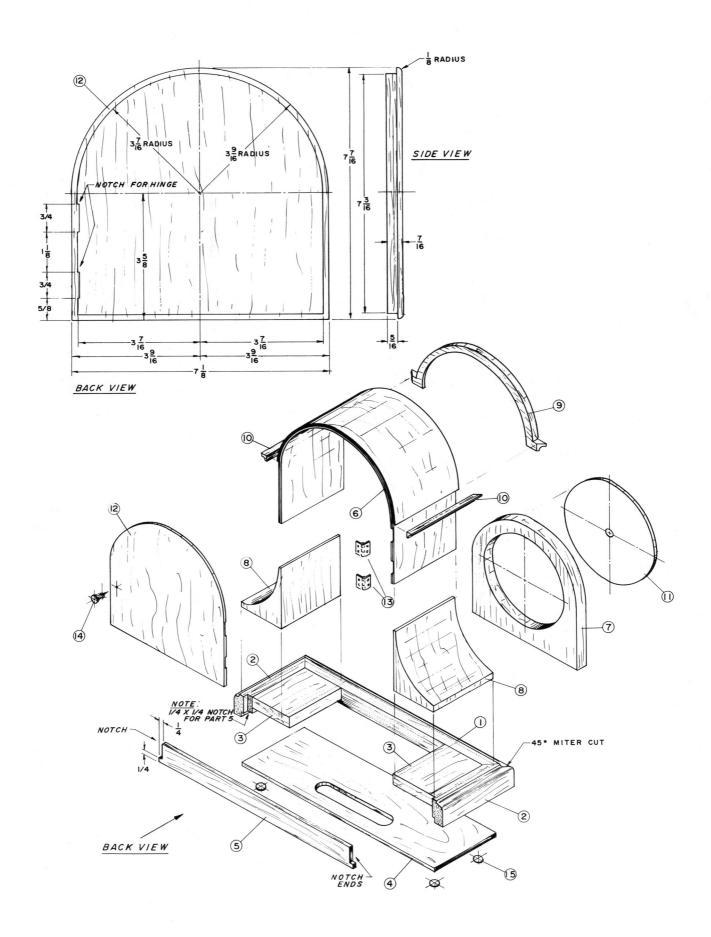

Section III

FINISHING & FINAL DETAILS

Finishing Instructions

AFTER COMPLETING YOUR CLOCK, YOU ARE NOW READY TO FINISH IT. THIS IS THE important part and should not be rushed. Remember, this is the part that will be seen for years to come. No matter how good the wood and hardware you use, or how good the joints are, a poor finish will ruin your project.

Preparing

Before applying any stain, you must first prepare the wood. The following preliminaries are imperative to a quality finish.

STEP 1.

All joints should be checked for tight fits. If necessary, apply water putty to all joints, allowing ample time for drying. For your clock, it will not be necessary to set and fill nail heads, as most were left showing on the original clock. If, however, you do not want the nail heads exposed, set and water putty nail heads, also.

STEP 2.

Sand the clock all over in the direction of the wood grain. If you are sanding by hand, use a sanding block and keep all corners sharp at this time. Sand all over using an 80-grit paper. Resand all over using a 120-grit paper, and, if necessary, resand all over using a 180-grit paper. Take care not to round edges at this time.

STEP 3.

If you want any of the edges rounded, use the 120-grit paper and later the 180-grit paper.

STEP 4.

These are *old* clocks and your reproduction should *look* old. A copy of an antique that looks new seems a direct contradiction. Distressing can be done many ways. One method is to roll a piece of coral stone about 3 inches in diameter, or a similar object, across the various surfaces. Don't' be afraid to add a few random scratches here and there, especially on the bottoms or backs where an object would have been worn the most through the years. Carefully study the clock and try to imagine how it would have been used through the years. Using a rasp judiciously, round the edges where you think wear would have occurred. Resand the entire project and the new "worn" edges with 180-grit paper.

STEP 5.
Carefully check that all surfaces are smooth, dry, and dust free, especially if you used soft wood.

Staining

There are two major kinds of stain: water stain and oil stain. Water stains are purchased in powder form and mixed as needed by dissolving the powder in hot water. Water stain has a tendency to raise the grain of the wood. If you use a water stain after it dries, you should sand lightly with fine paper. Oil stains are stains from pigments ground in linseed oil and do not raise the grain.

Fillers

Use a paste filler for porous wood such as oak or mahogany. Purchase paste filler slightly darker than the color of your wood because the new wood you use will turn darker with age. Before using paste filler, thin with turpentine so it can be brushed on. Use a stiff brush and brush with the grain in order to fill the pores. After 15 or 20 minutes wipe off with a piece of burlap across the grain, taking care to leave filler in the pores. Apply a second coat if necessary. Let the filler dry for 24 hours.

STEP 1.
Test-stain on a scrap piece of the same kind of lumber to make certain it will be the color you wish.

STEP 2.
Wipe or brush on the stain as quickly and as evenly as possible to avoid overlapping streaks. If you want a darker finish, apply more than one coat of stain. Try not to apply too much stain on the end grain. Allow to dry in a dust-free area for at least 24 hours.

Finishes

Shellac is a hard finish that is easy to apply and dries in a few hours. For best results, thin slightly with alcohol and apply an extra coat or two. Several coats of thin shellac are much better than one or two thick coats. Sand lightly with extra-fine paper between coats, rubbing the entire surface with a dampened cloth. Strive for a smooth satin finish—not a high glossy finish coat—for that antique effect.

Varnish is easy to brush on and dries to a smooth, hard finish within 24 hours. It makes an excellent finish that is transparent and will give a deep-finish look to your project. Be sure to apply varnish in a completely dust-free area. Apply one or two coats directly from the can with long even strokes. Rub between each coat. After the last coat, rub with 0000 steel wool. As with shellac, do not leave a glossy finish—an antique would not have a high-gloss finish after 100 or so years.

Oil finishes are especially easy to use for these projects. It is easy to apply, long lasting, never needs sanding, and actually improves wood permanently. Apply a heavy wet coat uniformly to all surfaces and let set for 20 or 30 minutes. Wipe completely dry until you have a nice satin finish.

Wash Coat

Your clock probably still looks new—even with the distressing marks and scratches. To give your project that century-old look, simply wipe on a coat of oil-base black paint directly from the can with a cloth. Take care to get the black paint in all distress marks and scratches. Wipe off all paint immediately before it dries, but leave the black paint in all the corners, joints, scratches, and distress marks. Experiment. If you goof or don't like your results, simply wipe it off using a cloth with turpentine. This wash coat should make your project look like the original clock.

Painted-Grain Cases

Many early clocks had a painted-grain effect. This is an art in itself. If you wish to give your clock a painted grain, go to a local library and check out a book on the subject. I have done a little grain painting and have good results with no training at all, but do not feel qualified enough to explain in detail all the tricks associated with this skill.

Where any case has a painted finish, I have given basic instructions in order that your clock be finished as the original was.

23

Painting
the Dial Face

THE DIAL IS THE MOST NOTICEABLE PART OF THE CLOCK. IT SHOULD LOOK ATTRAC-
tive and authentic, so as not to detract from the clock's appearance. Painted
dials came into use on clock faces around 1800. They are simple to do and within
the ability of most woodworkers.

After the dial face blank has been primed, painted, and lightly sanded, it is
ready for the numbers and painted designs. The numbers and dial ring are put in
using a draftsman's ink pen and an inking compass. The painted designs are put
on with simple tole painting or stenciling techniques.

Commercial dials can be purchased from one of the many clock suppliers
listed in Appendix B, but you will have more satisfaction if you do the entire
clock yourself—*including* the dial face. The face is not difficult, and with a little
practice, can be done by most anyone. If you study some original clock dial faces,
you can see they were all done by hand and are not completely perfect. Try it. If it
does not work out, you can always purchase a commercial face. It is especially
important to make the dial face for the tall-case clock, as this model uses a spe-
cial-sized wooden dial, and it is impossible to match the original face with a commercial dial face.

Commercial faces come in all sizes and styles and are very nice but all look
new and usually do not have as much character as hand-painted faces. However,
if you decide to order a commercial dial face, make sure you order it by the dial
ring diameter. Also the style of the dial face should complement the style of the
clock you are making.

All layout lines are drawn with a soft H-grade pencil lead and all inking is
done with a No. 0 or No. 1 draftsman's inking pen. Before starting, be sure to
study an original clock dial face. You will get a feel for how to paint and finish the
dial face on your clock.

Using the Divider

Figure 23-1 is a divider to help you lay out the 60 equal spaces on the dial. Make a
copy of the drawing and locate the center of the divider over the center of the dial

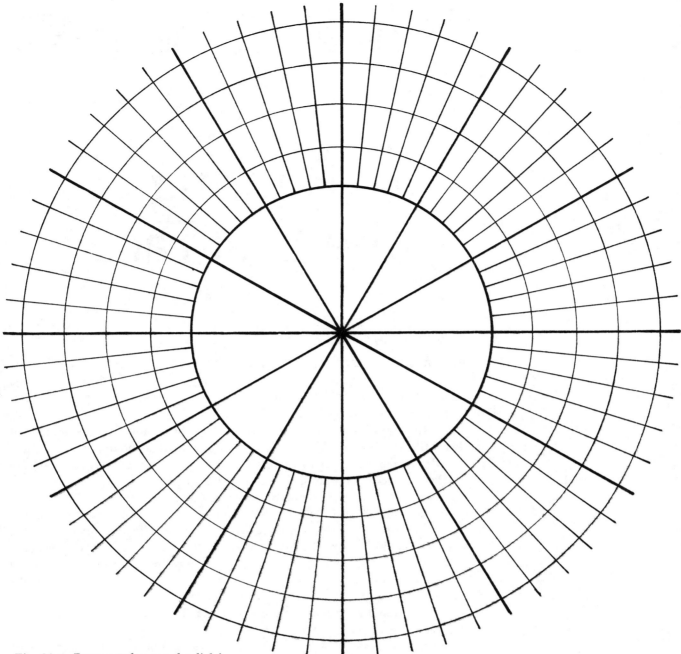

Fig. 23-1. *Pattern to lay out the dial face.*

you are laying out. Lightly extend the lines out to your minute circle noted in Steps 2 and 3 below.

STEP 1.
Using a compass, lightly lay out the dial ring diameter from the center of the dial (see Fig. 23-2).

STEP 2.
Lightly divide this circle into 12 equal hour spaces (30 degrees apart), referring to the drawing.

STEP 3.
Lightly divide the 12 parts into 5 equal minute spaces (6 degrees apart), again, referring to Fig. 23-2.

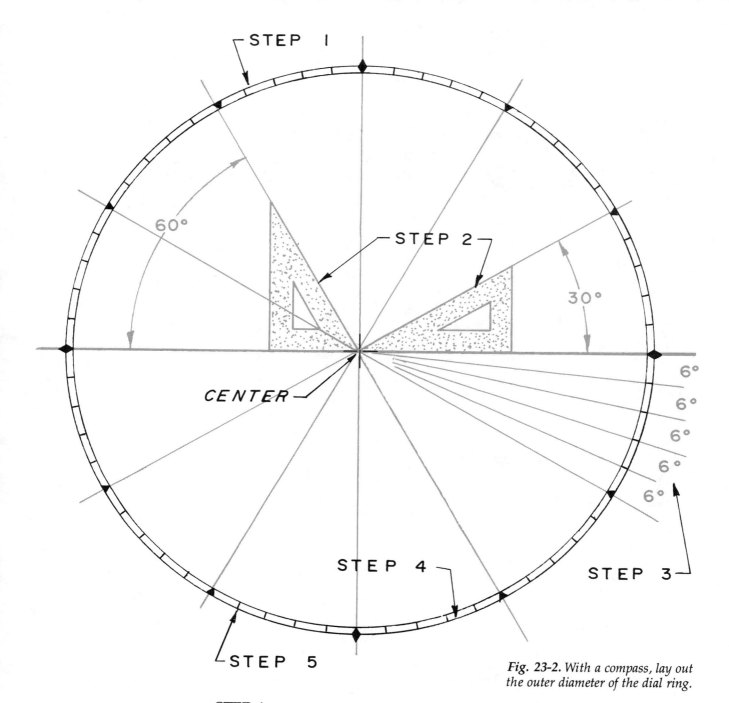

Fig. 23-2. *With a compass, lay out the outer diameter of the dial ring.*

STEP 4.

Ink in the diameter ring (s) using a No. 0 or No. 1 drafting ink pen and ink compass.

STEP 5.

Using an inking pen, put a short dash or ¹/₁₆-inch diameter dot at each of the places found in Step 3. This is the hour ring. There should be 60 dashes or dots.

STEP 6.

Lightly lay out a diameter as a guideline for the *top* of the hour numbers (see Fig. 23-3).

STEP 7.

Again referring to Fig. 23-3, lightly lay out a diameter as a guide for the *bottom* of the hour numbers.

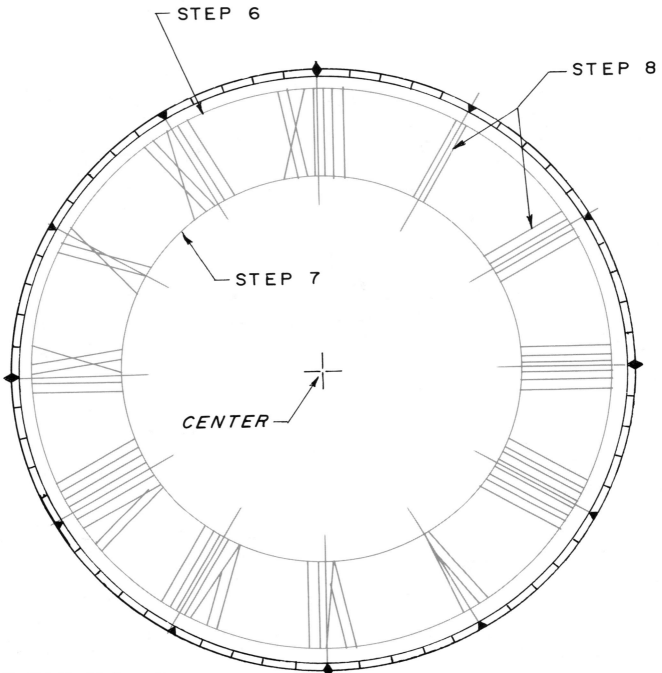

Fig. 23-3. Use this diagram to
lay out the top and bottom of the hour ring.

STEP 8.

Using a straightedge, lightly lay out the hour numbers as shown. Note how the
number 4 is made.

STEP 9.

Darken in all numbers with an inking pen, using a straightedge plastic triangle
for all hour numbers as shown. The minute numbers are inked in by hand. Your
numbers should look similar to the illustrated dial in Fig. 23-4.

STEP 9 —

Fig. 23-4. This is how your hour ring should look after completion. Note how the number four is drawn.

Painting the Design (if required)

STEP 10.

Draw the pattern you are going to use on a sheet of thin paper, using a 1/2-inch grid. Locate and transfer the patterns to the dial face. Using simple tole painting strokes, paint them to suit in whatever colors you desire. If you wish to stencil the pattern instead, you will have to cut out a stencil pattern. Refer to a good stencil book for instructions. The original clock faces were very bright. Don't be afraid to use vivid colors.

STEP 11.

Allow the paint to dry for 48 hours and paint the dial face with a light coat of satin-finish water varnish, taking care not to smudge the inking.

Drilling for the Center Shaft and Winding Holes

STEP 12.

Make a paper pattern of the center hole and the two winding holes. Be sure to double-check for accuracy. If correct, transfer the locations of the holes to the dial face and drill the holes large enough to accept the center shaft and winding key.

STEP 13.

You may wish to antique your clock face slightly. With a small cloth, apply a little brown paint around the edges of the dial to give it that aged look. From the edges of the dial, carefully feather the paint onto the dial face in about 1 inch or so. Again, this does not have to be perfect. Be sure to do this *after* Step 11. In the event you don't like it, you can simply wipe it off.

STEP 14.

The dial is now ready for the clock case.

Installing the
Clock Movement

THE MOVEMENT IS VERY DELICATE, SO EXERCISE EXTREME CARE WHEN HANDLING it. Keep the movement out of the workshop area so as not to get any dirt or dust in it.

Quartz movements are rather simple to install and instructions are usually included with them. The mechanical brass movements usually *do not* include instructions, so you should have a basic knowledge of how to adjust and set up these movements.

Whether purchasing a quartz or mechanical movement, you must consider the following:

+ Price. (It is best not to purchase the least expensive.)
+ Length of center shaft. Quartz movements are usually attached to the dial face through the center hole. Be sure to double-check this length. Refer to Fig. 24-1.
  Note: Because the quartz movement is attached through the dial face, you must purchase a movement with the correct center shaft length. Refer to Fig. 24-2. A thin dial requires a short center shaft (see Fig. 24-2A). A thick dial requires a long center shaft (see Fig. 24-2B). Allow enough length for the nut and washer.
+ Pendulum length, if required. The pendulum does not make the quartz movement run; they are for appearance only.
+ Chimes, if required or desired
+ Size if space is tight

Considerations when purchasing a mechanical brass movement:

+ Price. Purchase the best movement you can afford.
+ Style. Try to purchase one exactly like the original.
+ Length of running time. 30-hour, 8-day, 30-day.

Refer to Fig. 24-3 for the following:

+ Overall size of plates (be sure it will fit in the case)

- ◆ Length of pendulum (some measure from the center of the dial to the bottom of the pendulum, others measure from the center of the dial to the center of the pendulum bob)
- ◆ Depth of movement (from back plate to tip of center shaft)
- ◆ Hour gong or bell (again, try to match the original)
- ◆ Chimes, if specified
- ◆ Pendulum style (it should match the style of clock)

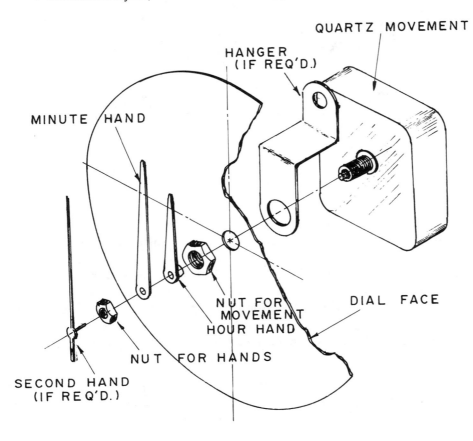

Fig. 24-1. Installing a quartz movement.

Listed for each clock is a suggested movement (brass or quartz). These are only *suggested* movements. Most are not exact copies of the original, therefore you may have to adapt the movement to case. If, on a rear-mounted movement, the center shaft is not long enough, you will have to add blocks behind the legs to bring it out. If the center shaft is too long, you must remove the legs or widen the case. This is why it is so important that you have the movement before starting.

With weight-driven or spring-driven movements, the pendulum length cannot be changed whatsoever. A quartz pendulum is only for appearance, so you can cut it to any length you wish.

The biggest problem with a mechanical brass clock movement is getting it into "beat"—in other words, making it tick-tock evenly. This is a very easy adjustment to make and accounts for 60 percent of the problems with old clocks. After the movement has been installed in the clock, level the clock perfectly using a level. Hang the pendulum and either add the weights, if it is a weight-powered movement, or wind the clock. Gently start the pendulum swinging and listen to the ticktock. It must be regular. If it is *not* regular: tick—tock-tick—tock-tick—tock or tick-tock—tick—tick-tock, for instance, it is *out of beat* and must be adjusted. (Some newer movements have a built-in self-regulating system that do not need adjusting.)

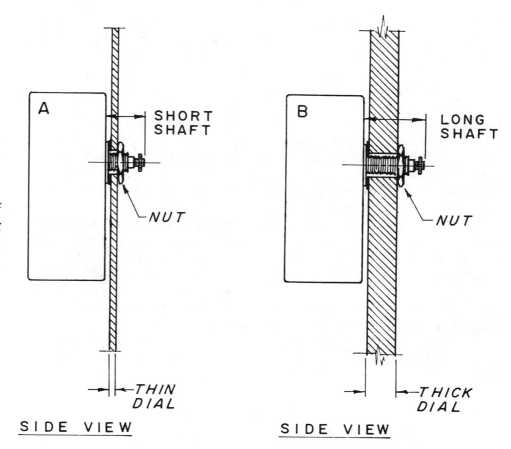

Fig. 24-2. Adjust the length of the center shaft (bolt) according to the thickness of the dial.

A SHORT SHAFT

NUT

THIN DIAL

SIDE VIEW

B LONG SHAFT

NUT

THICK DIAL

SIDE VIEW

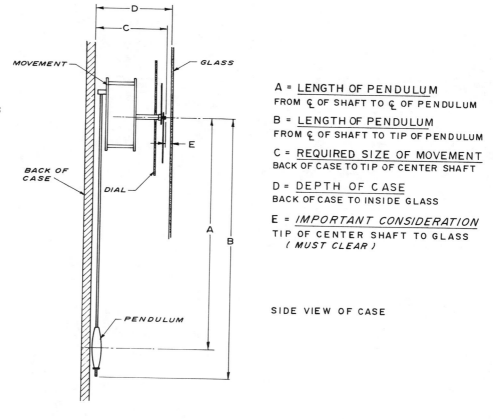

Fig. 24-3. Important considerations when selecting a clock movement.

MOVEMENT

GLASS

BACK OF CASE

DIAL

PENDULUM

A = <u>LENGTH OF PENDULUM</u>
FROM ℄ OF SHAFT TO ℄ OF PENDULUM

B = <u>LENGTH OF PENDULUM</u>
FROM ℄ OF SHAFT TO TIP OF PENDULUM

C = <u>REQUIRED SIZE OF MOVEMENT</u>
BACK OF CASE TO TIP OF CENTER SHAFT

D = <u>DEPTH OF CASE</u>
BACK OF CASE TO INSIDE GLASS

E = <u>*IMPORTANT CONSIDERATION*</u>
TIP OF CENTER SHAFT TO GLASS
(*MUST CLEAR*)

SIDE VIEW OF CASE

To adjust the clock, carefully bend the crutch to one side until you feel it give slightly. Start the clock and again listen to the beat. It if has been improved, continue until the clock beats perfectly. If you made it worse, bend the crutch in the opposite direction.

Once the beat is correct, add the hour hand. This is usually a tight slip-fit. Add the minute hand, which usually fits into a square or rectangular shaft and is held in place with a washer and nut. If your movement has a bell or gong strike, temporarily attach the minute hand and turn it clockwise until it strikes and count the strikes. Set the hour hand to the time struck by sliding the hour hand to the correct hour. Set the minute hand to 12 o'clock and attach the washer and nut or pin. Slowly turn the minute hand clockwise around to the next hour to recheck for correct striking on the hour.

Once the clock is in beat and the hands are on, set the correct time and let it run for 24 hours without touching it. If it is running too fast, lower the pendulum bob by turning the round nut below the pendulum bob a turn or two. If it is running too slow, raise the pendulum bob, again, by turning the nut below the bob. Remember: *up* for speed up, *down* for slow down. Reset and let the clock run for 24 more hours and note if it has gained or lost time. Readjust the bob accordingly. Keep doing this until the clock keeps perfect time.

Oil the movement very sparingly every 3 or 4 years at the pivot points only, not on the gears themselves. With care, the movement should last for another 100 years.

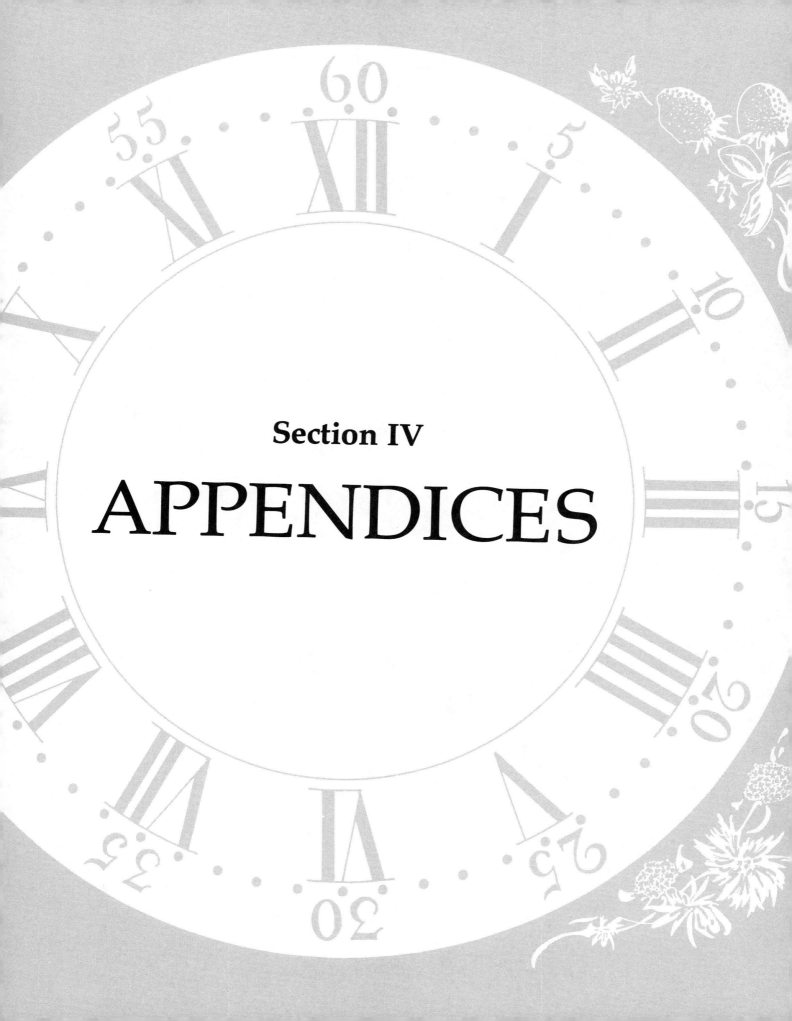

Section IV
APPENDICES

Antique Hardware Suppliers

THE EXTRA SPENT ON HARDWARE OF HIGH QUALITY VERSUS LOW-COST HARDWARE is very little in the overall cost of your project. This is the part of your project that is most noticed, so the extra spent in cost will be well worth the difference for many years to come.

Listed below are quality vendors that sell authentic, high-quality hardware. If possible, use the same hardware as listed to ensure a correct fit. For those antique copies, a good place to find hardware is a flea market. An old hinge or door lock, although rusty and worn, will add a lot of authenticity to your project and will really make it look original.

Beveled Glass

Beveled Glass Works
611 North Tillamook
Portland, OR 97227

Paint

Cohassett Colonials
Cohassett, MA 02025

Stulb Paint and Chemical Co. Inc.
P.O. Box 297
Norristown, PA 19404

Stains / Tung Oil

Cohassett Colonials
Cohasset, MA 02025

Deft Inc.
17451 Von Darman Avenue
Irvine, CA 92713-9507

Formby's Inc.
825 Crossover Lane, Suite 240
Memphis, TN 38117

Stulb Paint and Chemical Co. Inc.
P.O. Box 297
Morristown, PA 19404

Watco-Dennis Corp.
Michigan Avenue & 22nd Street
Santa Monica, CA 90404

Old-Fashioned Nails / Brass Screws

Equality Screw Co. Inc.
P.O. Box 1645
El Cajon, CA 92022

Horton Brasses
P.O. Box 120-K
Nooks Hill Road
Cromwell, CT 06416

Tremont Nail Co.
P.O. Box 111
21 Elm Street
Wareham, MA 02571

Brasses

Anglo-American Brass Co.
P.O. Box 9792
4146 Mitzi Drive
San Jose, CA 95157-0792

Ball and Ball
463 West Lincoln Highway
Exton, PA 19341

The Brass Tree
308 North Main Street
Charles, MO 63301

Garrett Wade Co. Inc.
161 Avenue of the Americas
New York, NY 10013

Heirloom Antiques Brass Co.
P.O. Box 146
Dundass, MN 55019

Horton Brasses
P.O. Box 120-K
Nooks Hill Road
Cromwell, CT 06416

Imported European Hardware
4295 South Arville
Las Vegas, NV 89103

19th Century Co. Hardware Supply Co.
P.O. Box 599
Rough and Ready, CA 95975

The Renovator's Supply
Millers Falls, MA 01349

The Shop, Inc.
P.O. Box 3711, R.D. 3
Reading, PA 19606

Ritter and Son Hardware
Dept. WJ
Gualala, CA 95445

Veneering

Bob Morgan Woodworking Supplies
1123 Bardstown Road
Louisville, KY 40204

General Catalogs

Brookstone Co.
Vose Farm Road
Peterborough, NH 03458

Constantine
2050 Eastchester Road
Bronx, NY 10461

Cryder Creek Wood Shoppe, Inc.
P.O. Box 19
Whitesville, NY 14897

The Fine Tool Shops
P.O. Box 1262
20 Backus Avenue
Danbury, CT 06810

Leichtung Inc.
4944 Commerce Parkway
Cleveland, OH 44128

Silvo Hardware Co.
2205 Richmond Street
Philadelphia, PA 19125

Trendlines
375 Beacham Street
Chelsea, MA 02150

Woodcraft
P.O. Box 4000
41 Atlantic Avenue
Woburn, MA 01888

The Woodworker's Store
21801 Industrial Boulevard
Rogers, MN 55374

Woodworkers Supply of New Mexico
5604 Alameda, N.E.
Albuquerque, NM 87113

Movements and Clock-Related Items

THERE IS A SLIGHT CHARGE FOR SOME OF THE FOLLOWING CATALOGS. IF THERE is a charge, most will refund it on the first order. Those of you who do a lot of woodworking will want many of these catalogs, as the vendors carry a very nice line of accessories that can be used on other woodworking projects.

Movements

Armor Products
P.O. Box 445
East Northport, NY 11731

Barap Specialties
835 Bellows Avenue
Frankfort, MI 49635

Craft Products Co.
2200 Dean Street
St. Charles, IL 60176

Craftsman Wood Service Company
1735 West Cortland Court
Addison, IL 60101

Emperor Clock Company
Emperor Industrial Park
Fairhope, AL 36532

International Clock Craft Ltd.
52 Isabel Street
Winnipeg, Manitoba, Canada

Kidder Klock Company
39-3 Glen Cameron Road #3
Thornhill, Ontario, Canada

Klockit
P.O. Box 542
N3211 Highway H North
Lake Geneva, WI 53147-9961

Kuempel Chime Clockworks and Studio, Inc.
21195 Minnetonka Boulevard
Excelsior, MN 55331

Mason and Sullivan (now Woodcraft Supply Corp.)
7845 Emerson Avenue
Parkersburg, WV 26102

Merritt Antiques Inc.
P.O. Box 277
Douglassville, PA 19518

M.L. Shipley and Co.
Rt. 2, Box 161
Cassville, MO 65625

Murray Clock Craft Limited
510 McNicoll Avenue
Willowdale, Ontario, Canada

National Artcraft Company
23456 Mercantile Road
Beachwood, OH 44122

Newport Enterprises, Inc.
2313 West Burbank Boulevard
Burbank, CA 91506

Pacific Time Company
138 West 7th Street
Eureka, CA 95501

Precision Movements
P.O. Box 689
2024 Chestnut Street
Emmaus, PA 18049

Selva Borel
347 13th Street
Oakland, CA 94604

S. LaRose Inc.
234 Commerce Place
Greensboro, NC 27420

Southwest Clock Supply Inc.
2442 Walnut Ridge
Dallas, TX 75229

T.E.C. Specialties
P.O. Box 909
Smyrna, GA 30081

Viking Clock Co.
Foley Industrial Park
P.O. Box 490
Foley, AL 36536

Westwood Clock 'N Kits
2850-B East 29th Street
Long Beach, CA 90806

Wooden Finials

Boland V Tapp Imports
13525 Alondra Boulevard
Santa Fe Springs, CA 90670

Reverse Glass and Dial Painting

Astrid C. Donnellan
21 Mast Hill Road
Hingham, MA 02043

Marianne Picazio
P.O. Box 1523
Buzzard's Bay, MA 02532

Linda Rivard
27 Spur Lane,
Newington, CT 06111

Linda Abrams
26 Chestnut Avenue
Burlington, MA 01803

Judith W. Akey
173 Penn Harb Road
Pennington, NJ 08534

The Shipley Company
2075 South University Boulevard #199
Denver, CO 80210

Clock Books

Adam Brown Co.
26 North Main Street
P.O. Box 357
Crandbury, NJ 08512

Ken Roberts Publishing Co.
P.O. Box 151
Fitzwilliam, NH 03447

Nathan Torry Clockworks
P.O. Box 123
Hanover, MA 02339

Special Custom Wood Turnings

River Bend Turnings
Box 364
RD 1
Wellsville, NY 14689

Wooden Needle
Box 908
Kamloops, B.C., Canada

Further Study

I**N THE EVENT YOU REALLY GET THE "CLOCK-BUG" YOU MIGHT WANT TO JOIN THE** National Association of Watch and Clock Collectors, Inc. (NAWCC). They are located at 514 Popular Street, Columbia, PA 17512. This is a national organization devoted solely to horology—the art of clock- and watchmaking. It has a national network of local clock clubs throughout the country that hold meetings and help each other with clock problems, study history of clocks, buy and sell clocks of all kinds to each other, and teach each other various aspects of clock repair and making. It is a great organization to belong to if you are interested in clocks.

Another aspect of clocks is clock repair. Years ago I took a clock repair home study course from the School of Clock Repair (6313 Come About Way, P.O. Box 315, Awendaw, SC 29429). It was by far the best course I have ever taken and it really got me going on clock repair. If interested, you might want to write them for details and a brochure of the course outline and costs.

Museums

THIS LIST OF MUSEUMS INCLUDES MUSEUMS THAT HAVE A SUBSTANTIAL COLLECtion of clocks, watches, or both.

To fully enjoy and study original clocks you should visit one or more of the following museums. Many will have exact original models of the eighteen clocks presented in this book. In seeing original clocks, you will have a feel as to how they should be finished so they look very much like the originals do.

American Clock and Watch Museum
100 Maple Street
Bristol, CT
(203) 583-6070

Henry Francis DuPont
Winterthur Museum[1]
Winterthur, DE 19735
(302) 656-8591
or 1-800-448-3883

Smithsonian Institute
National Museum of American History
Washington, D.C.
(202) 357-1300

Time Museum
7801 E. State Street
Rockford, IL
(815) 398-6000

The Bily Clock Exhibit Horology Museum
Spillville, IA
(319) 562-3569

---

[1] Winterthur conducts guided tours with full information about each of their 80 clocks. Their clocks are the best examples found anywhere.

Old Sturbridge Village
Sturbridge, MA
(617) 347-3362

Willard House
Grafton, MA
(617) 839-3500

Henry Ford Museum/
Greenfield Village
Dearborne, MI
(313) 271-1620

Metropolitan Museum of Art
5th Avenue and 82nd Street
Manhattan, NY
(212) 535-7710

Hoffman Foundation
Newark Public Library
Newark, NY
(315) 331-4370

Old Salem, Inc.
614 Main Street
Winston-Salem, NC
(919) 723-3688

Museum of the American
Watchmakers Institute
3700 Harrison Avenue
Cincinnati, OH
(513) 661-3838

National Museum of Clocks and Watches
514 Poplar Street
Columbia, PA
(717) 684-8261

Old Clock Museum
929 East Preston
Pharr, TX
(512) 787-1923

Glossary

arbor—A steel shaft on which wheels and pinions are affixed.

boss—An attachment to a dial, usually round, on which the clockmaker's name and town is shown.

bushing—An insert of hard material in a clock plate at the point of arbor pivot to allow for additional wear.

chapter—The ring on the dial plate on which are painted or engraved the hour numerals and minute graduations.

collet—A brass collar that holds a wheel on the arbor.

cock—A bracket from which the pendulum suspends.

count wheel—A wheel with spaced slots that indexes the correct number of blows the hammer makes on the bell when the clock is striking.

crutch wire—A wire that carries the impulse from the escapement to the pendulum.

dial arch—The arched portion at the top of many dials; it may contain a boss, a moon dial, or decoration. If the dial is square, this is omitted.

dial foot—A pillar on the back of a dial for attaching the dial to a false plate or movement.

dial plate—A plate, usually brass, iron, or wood, on which the dial is engraved or painted.

escapement—A device by which the pendulum controls the rate of timekeeping. It consists of an anchor and an escape wheel.

escape wheel—A wheel at the end of the wheel train that is engaged by the anchor to regulate the clock's running.

false plate—An intermediate plate between the movement and dial on some clocks to aid fitting the dial to the movement.

fly—A wind-resistant fan that regulates the speed of striking.

gear—See *wheel*.

great gear—The first wheel in a train to which is usually attached the winding arbor and drum; the weight is attached to this wheel.

moon dial—A dial, often found in the arch portion of a clock dial, that indicates the cycle of the moon.

motion train—A series of wheels that regulates the rotation of the hour and minute hands.

pendulum—A swinging device attached to the escapement by means of the crutch that controls the rate of timekeeping.

pillar—A turned post of metal or wood that connects to the front and back plates and establishes a fixed distance between them.

pinion—A small gear with twelve or less teeth, called *leaves*, that meshes with larger gears.

pivot—A round hole in a clock plate in which an arbor end rotates.

plates—Two parallel pieces of metal or wood between which the gears, pinions, and arbors are fitted.

rack and snail—An indexing system for striking that sets itself for correct striking shortly before striking begins.

seat board—A wooden board on which a clock movement sits when in a case.

sprandrels—Painted or cast-metal decoration for dials.

trains—A series of gears and pinions through which power is transmitted from the weights to the escapement.

verge—A device that regulates the speed of rotation of the escape wheel.

wheel—A circular piece of metal on the perimeter of which are cut teeth (also called a *gear*).

winding drum (barrel)—A cylinder onto which the cord holding the weight is wound.

Index

Other Stackpole Books by John A. Nelson

EARLY AMERICAN CLASSICS: 33 Projects for Wood-workers, with Complete Plans and Instructions

Plans for furniture and decorative accessories accompanied by easy-to-follow instructions.

FOLK ART WEATHER VANES

Detailed patterns and instructions for making 68 weather vanes modeled on American folk art masterpieces.

COUNTRY CLASSICS: Authentic Projects You Can Build in One Weekend

Plans for 64 projects that are exact reproductions of fine primitive, colonial, or Early American antiques.

COLONIAL CLASSICS YOU CAN BUILD TODAY

Drawings and plans for 80 shelf/counter, wall, and floor projects.

PATTERNS AND PROJECTS FOR THE SCROLL SAW

—Joyce C. Nelson and John A. Nelson

Detailed instructions on how to use a scroll saw plus 340 patterns.

HOLIDAY WOODWORKING PROJECTS: 90 Patterns for Festive Decorations

—Joyce and John Nelson

Instructions and patterns for handcrafted centerpieces, window decorations, candleholders, and ornaments.

TO ORDER, CALL 1-800-732-3669 / IN CANADA, CALL 613-237-5577